W9-BUB-980

Transcending the Talented Tenth

Transcending the Talented Tenth

Black Leaders and American Intellectuals

JOY JAMES

Routledge
New York   London

Published in 1997 by
Routledge
29 West 35th Street
New York, NY 10001

Published in Great Britain by
Routledge
11 New Fetter Lane
London EC4P 4EE

Library of Congress Cataloging-in-Publication Data
James, Joy
Transcending the talented tenth: black leaders and American intellectuals / by Joy James.
p. cm.
ISBN 0-415-91762-X (cloth). — ISBN 0-415-91763-8 (pbk.)
1. Afro-Americans—Intellectual life.
2. Afro-American leadership.
3. United States—Intellectual life—20th century.
I. Title.
E185.86.J36   1996   96-21488
305.896'073—dc20   CIP

Contents

The Present Future: Contemporary Crises and Black Intellectuals

Illustrations

It is not the kings and the generals that make history but the masses of the people.
—Nelson Mandela

Charlene Mitchell, Nelson Mandela, and Angela Davis at African National Congress Headquarters, South Africa, 1991.

Acknowledgments

Minnie James, Mattie Bailey, Rick, Tempii, Sally, and Madrina sustained me throughout this project. Angela Davis, Lewis Gordon, Geoffrey Jacques, Charlene Mitchell, Nell Painter, and Tracey Sharpley-Whiting offered valuable suggestions and editorial comments.

Support from the University of Massachusetts-Amherst's Institute for the Advanced Study of Humanities, the Rockefeller Humanities Program, the Ford Foundation, and the Aaron Diamond Foundation (through the Schomburg Center for Research in Black Culture) greatly assisted in the development of this manuscript.

The Department of Ethnic Studies at the University of Colorado-Boulder provided essential support for the completion of this book. Special thanks to Karen Moreira, Heather Davis, Michelle Foy, Veronica Martinez, Don Dudrey, and Candice Fletcher for their assistance.

Foreword

Lewis R. Gordon

An ongoing presumption in American politics is that African Americans are objects who, by virtue of their pariah status, have persistent need for translators and representatives. There are leaders, and then there are black leaders. Thus black leaders whatever their self-perception, have suffered the insult of the herd-ascriptions that have come to bear on the nation's misrepresentations of black communities. To be a black leader is regarded, for the most part, as a relegation to the status of sheep dog—to keep the flock in line until they are available for Master consumption. (National elections are times at which this analogy usually transcends the realm of metaphor.)

The most progressive, radical assessment of the leadership question, though, inevitably came from one of its most active voices: "Strong people," declared Ella Baker, "don't need strong leaders."

You hold before you more than a theoretical work on questions of leadership in Africana communities in the United States. You also hold a *testament* to a story whose telling has been impeded by many political obstacles. Joy James's *Transcending the Talented Tenth* is an activist scholar's intervention at a moment of full-scale historical revision of black political reality. Her task is significant and twofold: to issue a critical statement on how leadership has been articulated in and for black communities and to make sure that her testimony serves as a contradiction to contemporary ideological, counter-revolutionary predilections toward "selective memory." Her first goal is no mean task, indeed, for as James demonstrates so well in her inimical way, the Present Age is marked by admonitions against radical progressive thinking and the subjects of such thought. James's second goal comes to the fore through both the ancestral voices that she so carefully evokes—not as interesting relics from our past but as living ideas with which to grapple and from which to learn—and the contemporary voices who need to be challenged as they attempt to erase and misrepresent, so beguilingly, their past. Her task is formidable. For the context of her discussion has seeds in one century and consequences in another.

The first two decades of the twentieth century were marked by a classic prophecy in Africana thought and an epoch-making accomplishment in revolutionary praxis, both of which have their genesis in the nineteenth century: W. E. B. Du Bois's declaration of the infamous problem of the color line on the one hand, and the Bolshevik revolution on the other. These two moments were both classic diagnoses of and prescriptions against twentieth-century antisocial realities. As the twentieth century comes to its close, there is ironically the arrogant globalization of a counterrevolutionary reconstruction of material resources and an antirevolutionary *ethos*, as well as a continued resilience of the Du Boisian diagnosis, in the face of sustained denial to the contrary. Although the point may have been to change the world, inheritors of the challenge are now facing the quandary not only over what is to be done, but also whether they are willing to do anything at all.

The Du Boisian diagnosis is both literal and metaphorical. It pertains literally to the realities of racism that have wreaked havoc on the life forces, blood, and spiritual resistance of multitudes. It is metaphorical in that its recognition of misanthropy and evasion demands an understanding of its significance in all facets of human-evading projects.

An added dimension of the task set forth in *Transcending the Talented Tenth*, then, is to address the contemporary denial of two persistent realities in a world that has managed to dominate its environment sufficiently to become *the world*. In spite of great struggles, struggles that have thrown many individuals into the oblivion of denied significance and brought forth others into the chicanery and folly of "acceptable" representation, struggles with regard to which national memories are short and selective, the problem of the color line is now denied in the midst of its status of leitmotif in political affairs. The response has been to hate, with renewed vigor, the people who demand a change that moves forward. With counterrevolution also comes the appropriation of revolutionary language for the sake of moving backward. Progressive radical history is being rewritten into the obscenity of right-wing "revolution" and the occlusion of the very notion of institutional oppression. At the heart of this development are a number of ironies.

Race is big business, a major first-world knowledge-producing commodity. The struggle against racism, on the other hand, is not.

Gender and sexual orientation sell knowledge productions and make careers for ingratiated individuals. The struggle against sexism and fear of ambiguous sexual identity does not.

Class is a respected appeal to explain social evil. The struggle against class exploitation is not.

The proverbial conjunction of "theory and practice" has been severed. In practice, theory now explores only itself to the point, ironically, of no longer having a reference point from which to be either theoretical or practical. Another god has died, and we find our age coming to a close with an idealism so pervasive that it generally fails to see itself.

The effort to gain self-reflection, what is at times known as "consciousness," has been an arduous journey of a struggle between critical action and bad-faith reaction. It is the nature of the proverbial beast to sustain itself through denying alternatives. In the midst of this struggle are the entire human species in general and those among it whose vocation and commitment are supposed to be the critical dimension of this divide. Du Bois realized this when he adopted the American Baptist Home Missionary Society's strategy of developing a talented tenth, and he himself underwent some self-critical evaluations as he transformed his positions, dialectically, to an understanding of an elite *who needs to be led* by mass, working-class movements instead of an elite that leads. The very framework of both the intellectual and the political needed to be reconfigured.

Du Bois was not alone with this insight. It was the insight of Claudia Jones and Ella Baker. It was the insight of Frantz Fanon. It was the insight of Almicar Cabral. It was also the insight of forgotten voices of a century ago.

The occlusion of black radical voices is rooted in a complex history of narrowing the scope and understanding of political reality in the United States. Politics can be understood as activity whose objective is to have an impact on a specified community or the institutions by which conventional resources of power are administered. One type of activity is *consensus-building*. Its concerns are with matters of speech and agreement, and the heart of its values is a commitment to democracy. Another type is *instrumental*. Its concerns are primarily functional and administrative. In American politics, these two types of political activity have undergone a schism from which there seems to be no hope of building any bridges. What is lost by this circumstance is recognition of the obvious interdependence of the two, for activity geared toward building up institutions and responding to social problems can foster an environment conducive to building coalitions and consensus. Yet, we find quite often that political activities are usually governed by the model of consensus building. With consensus building as our objective, a peculiar model of both leadership and intellectuals emerges: the public intellectual.

We should differentiate a public intellectual from a *popular* intellectual. Toward the close of the twentieth century, the popular intellectual has become the primary model of the public intellectual in the United States. Although a popular intellectual is obviously a public figure, it does not follow that one will be popular by virtue of being public. There are many intellectuals who will never find themselves at the center of popular attention because of the unpopularity of their political beliefs. For these intellectuals, however, what marks them as public is the nature of their work, which addresses issues that have an impact on the communities in which they live and conditions these intellectuals' roles in such communities.

Given our two conceptions of political activity, we can see straightaway how, in the struggle against race, gender, and class oppression, this distinction emerges in the difference between the classical sociological model of the charismatic leader-intellectual and the leader-intellectual who is guided by a sense of vocation and public responsibility.

While W. E. B. Du Bois and Paul Robeson have become well-known as charismatic leaders and consensus builders, Ella Baker's and Claudia Jones's many hours of instrumental organizing and institution building have been rendered nearly invisible. Baker played substantial roles in the NAACP and the organizing of the Student Nonviolent Coordinating Committee (SNCC), and Jones was a major Harlem organizer in the Communist Party USA. Similarly, political activity and leadership in black churches tend to be sought among the male ministers, in spite of the fact that day-to-day administering and developing of those institutions stand in the rarely seen but essential boards and officers and key congregation members, members who are predominantly women.

The distinction between the charismatic leader and the instrumental question of facilitating responses to community needs comes to the fore on the question of a demonstrated track record. Cornel West, one of the most prominent contemporary public intellectuals, has complained about the general distrust that black communities seem to harbor toward black academics—a major focus of West's political concerns. We may wonder, however, why black communities should not be suspicious of such intellectuals. It is vital for all communities to test the political integrity and competence of their intellectuals, to see evidence of demonstrated performance. The consensus-building model requires a charitable relationship of presumed membership, whereas the instrumental model requires earning the community's trust and thereby earning membership.

The current, popular intellectual environment for Africana intellectuals is one of demonstrated hostility to models of earned membership. The divide is striking in *Transcending the Talented Tenth*, where James takes on the overdue and ironic task of undoing the erasure of praxis intellectuals in contemporary African-American political thought. The collapse of theorizing practice into *theory as practice* has provided some contemporary intellectuals with an imaginary access to political achievement. What more can be done beyond what they have said, when the world has become the transcendental reality of the written word?

We find, then, among the contemporary progressive public intellectual's many tasks—of subverting oppressive institutions and building liberating ones, of articulating possibilities for imprisoned souls and nurturing healthy, fighting ones, of speaking as truthfully as possible—the apocalyptic *Geist* War, the War of the Spirit, that has been waged on every front since the moment humanity discovered that it can speak across many generations. We have now gone from interrogating the souls of black folk to the struggle over and for those souls. In the midst of this struggle, the messages from the past are being scrambled, and they run the risk of being lost as we are now asked to forget about our past and dance to the rhythms of a deceptive tune. We need the decoding voices of integrity made manifest in testaments like James's now, proverbially, more than ever.

Lewis R. Gordon,
Providence, Rhode Island
Summer, 1996

Toni Morrison delivering a eulogy at the 1987 memorial service for James Baldwin, the Cathedral of St. John the Divine, New York City.

Preface

The American crisis, which is part of a global, historical crisis, [is not] likely to resolve itself soon. An old world is dying, and a new one, kicking in the belly of its mother, time, announces that it is ready to be born. This birth will not be easy, and many of us are doomed to discover that we are exceedingly clumsy midwives. No matter, so long as we accept that our responsibility is to the newborn: the acceptance of responsibility contains the key to the necessarily evolving skill.

—James Baldwin,
No Name in the Street

James Baldwin describes his attempts to write *No Name in the Street*[1] from 1967 to 1971—the years in which Martin Luther King Jr., was assassinated, Jonathan and George Jackson killed, and Angela Davis incarcerated as a political prisoner—noting in the book's epilogue that the work was "much delayed by trials, assassinations, funerals, and despair."[2] As a gay African-American writer deeply committed to social justice, Baldwin persevered in demanding and organizing for human rights. His 1987 memorial service at New York City's Cathedral of St. John the Divine—with its procession of African drummers, testimonials from Amiri Baraka, Maya Angelou, and Toni Morrison, and immense love filling the cavernous hall—was one of many tributes to a great American intellectual.

In the last decade, the crossing over of Baldwin and so many other progressive and gifted intellectuals—including Audre Lorde, Marlon Riggs, Toni Cade Bambara, Essex Hemphill, Haywood Burns—has had a sobering effect on those who remain on this side, facing the dehumanizing realities of a society undermined by racial-sexual violence and economic exploitation, as well as the disappointing performances of celebrated leaders who often seem to lack the necessary skills or commitments for transforming society.

What constitutes a black leadership capable of building on the legacy of historical radical intellectuals in order to promote a future free of economic and racial misery as well as sexual bigotry and violence is highly debated. *Transcending the Talented Tenth* examines the political thought of historical and contemporary black elites advocating social justice. It furthers contemporary debates by black intellectuals to argue that the erasure of black radical praxis from the continuum of American intellectualism allows contemporary elites and rhetoricians the *appearance* of radical progressivism. This appearance masks the elite acceptance of conventional theories of political leadership and activism that acquiesce to rather than challenge structural oppression.

Beginning with "Our Past: Historiography, Erasure, and Race Leadership," this book counters the elision of militant African Americans, particularly female leaders, in American thought. Chapter one reviews W. E. B. Du Bois's early advocacy and later repudiation of an elite, educated black vanguard that shepherds black masses toward racial uplift; Du Bois's gradual rejection of the Talented Tenth as race leaders has influenced contemporary black elites and academics such as Henry Louis Gates Jr., Cornel West, and Angela Davis. Chapter two raises questions about male-biased intellectualism and Du Bois's profeminist politics, focusing on his tendency to masculinize the black intellectual and erase the agency of his influential contemporaries Anna Julia Cooper and Ida B. Wells-Barnett. Black feminist narratives that reconstruct black women's antilynching radicalism, represented by Wells-Barnett, as gender-regressive also diminish the historical significance of radical female race leadership. Chapter three reviews representations of the antilynching crusader's sexual politics in writings by Alice Walker and Valerie Smith. Building on feminist scholarship that works as a corrective to male and elite biased historiography, chapter four discusses the "disappearance" of radical civil rights women in literature on the movement that minimizes the significance of leaders such as Ella Baker.

Since the end of the civil rights and black power movements of the previous decades, struggles for human rights have continuously mutated as have antiblack racism and antiradicalism. In, "The Present Future: Contemporary Crises and Black Intellectuals," chapter five addresses the persistence of racial violence in U.S. democracy. The search for a common program among black Americans, one that recognizes and synthesizes struggles to dismantle sexism, heterosexism, and elitism alongside the battles for racial and economic justice, is the quandary for American intellectuals and the subject of chapter six. How African-American intellectuals—as the postmodern Talented Tenth straddling the twentieth and twentieth-first centuries (much as their predecessors bridged the nineteenth and twentieth centuries)—will manifest or falter as effective black leadership is the focus of the remaining chapters. Chapter seven, on women, caretaking, and academic intellectualism, critiques the theorizing of bell hooks, Pat Hill Collins, Elsa Barkley Brown, and Bernice Johnson Reagon on intellectual leadership and community. Chapter eight critically examines male elite educators' constructions of political agency and "the heroic intellectual," citing the work of Cornel West, Jerry Gaio Watts, and Derrick Bell, while exploring the model of the heroic intellectual as a nonelite, nonacademic writer such as African-American activist Charlene Mitchell. *Transcending the Talented Tenth* concludes by reflecting on radicalism and black intellectual life.

Reading this work, some may consider its critical assessments regarding the liberalism or antiradicalism of black elites too harsh. Echoing throughout this critique of black elites and American intellectuals, however, is recognition of their contributions. Acknowledging the limitations of progressive black intellectualism (limitations that are often obscured by radical rhetoric) seems a necessary skill to develop given the apparent clumsiness of our political and intellectual midwifery; the acquisition of such skill though is a Pyrrhic victory if it is unaccompanied by the desire to shoulder and share responsibility for democratic praxes with nonelites and black radicals.

We need an "act of faith," writes Baldwin, such as the one that sustained the movement, demonstrations, and protests before King's assassination. Yet, our postmodern post-movement times seem to have little faith in radical praxis, particularly when the most progressive work to transcend antidemocratic policies often takes place beyond the range of television cameras and outside the ken of intellectual elites. Despite or because of our liabilities, committed thinkers do employ Baldwin's council to work for birthing a new world. A quarter of a century ago, Baldwin wrote:

> One could scarcely be deluded by Americans anymore, one scarcely dared expect anything from the great, vast, blank generality; and yet one was compelled to demand of Americans— and for their sakes, after all—a generosity, a clarity, and a nobility which they did not dream of demanding themselves.[3]

Today, we could ask no more or less of the contemporary Talented Tenth—or of ourselves as we evolve beyond the constrictions of elite race leadership.

Introduction

I may be able to speak the languages of men and even of angels, but if I have no love, my speech is no more than a noisy gong or a clanging bell.

—1 Corinthians 13:1

When our fears have all been serialized, our creativity censured, our ideas "marketplaced," our rights sold, our intelligence sloganized, our strength downsized, our privacy auctioned; when the theatricality, the entertainment value, the marketing of life is complete, we will find ourselves living not in a nation but in a consortium of industries, and wholly unintelligible to ourselves except for what we see as through a screen darkly.

—Toni Morrison

While on university leave in the fall of 1995, I worked at the New York Public Library's Schomburg Center for Research in Black Culture.[1] During my late-afternoon walks home from the library, I usually browsed through the book tables of Harlem street vendors. My route down Lenox Avenue (renamed Malcolm X Boulevard) also took me past Liberation Books on 131st Street. Seeking a copy of Frantz Fanon's *The Wretched of the Earth*, one day I entered the bookstore. Inside, several middle-aged African-American women stood or sat reading and talking among the stacks. I made my request noting that I was the only customer in the store. After searching for a few minutes, one woman found a copy of *The Wretched of the Earth*, which turned out to cost more money than I had with me. Liberation Books does not accept credit cards or checks. The nearest bank was blocks away. Explaining that I would have to return, I rummaged in my backpack to find one subway token (value $1.50) and change, which I added to my last dollar bill on the counter. The older black woman who held the book

1

refused my nickles, quarters, and token. "Now," she said, as she presented Fanon to me, "you can go to the head of your class."

Even in times rankling with grim observations about the failures of American intellectualism and the limits of black intellectuals, the generosity of progressive community educators reassures. The work of nonelite black intellectuals is largely unknown to those outside their communities, and many within them; yet, it promises pragmatic examples of progressivism and democratic politics that tend to be elusive for American elites. Activist intellectuals in Harlem and other working-class and poor communities continue to instill a passion for the liberation legacy and agency of historical race leaders.

Intellectuals in poorer communities face conditions unfamiliar to, ignored, or forgotten by most elites. As a reminder, a few select academic publications routinely call our attention to social devastation structured by racism. For instance, *The Journal of Blacks in Higher Education* features a regular column, "Vital Signs: Statistics that Measure Racial Inequality," that outlines social crises as well as academic intellectuals' responses. Vital signs survey not only the breadth of racial and economic inequality; they also suggest the standard for a critical black intellectual intervention in crises. In 1994, *The Journal of Blacks in Higher Education* cited a host of disturbing signs. It noted that the U.S. Bureau of the Census documented that while the ratio of whites infected with the HIV virus was 1:1,873, the ratio of blacks infected was 1:552. The journal also listed a *New York Newsday* report that, in the history of the New York Police Department, the number of black officers shot by fellow white members is eighteen, while the number of white police officers shot by black police is zero. According to "Vital Signs," the Centers for Disease Control document that for the year 1990, the number of white infants dying in their first year per 1,000 live births was 7.3; the number of black infants dying was 17.6. Also that year, the ratio of black infant mortality to white was 2.4:1, an increase from the 1980 ratio of two black infant deaths to every one white infant death. Another vital race demographic is taken from the House Judiciary Committee: although 75 percent of all federal drug prosecutions involved white defendants, the number of federal death penalty prosecutions of black defendants in drug cases approved by Attorney General Janet Reno in 1993 was ten; Reno approved no death penalty prosecutions against white defendants in drug cases for that year.[2]

At times, fortunately, elite and academic discourse highlights the vital signs of communities in crises. This form of literary agency coexists with, but is not a surrogate for, the intellectual activism found in neighborhood streets and legislative halls. In our anti-civil rights, conservative era, without Jim Crow or racial slurs, social policies work to reinforce racial and economic hierarchies. Often, as American intellectuals we face these crises with few substantive strategies and struggles to democratize the United States and diminish its abusive practices.

Since emancipation, black intellectuals have confronted lynching, Jim Crow, electoral and economic disenfranchisement, restrictions to higher education, racist violence, and police brutality. In times of crises, in the national tumult for identity and stability, our interventions expand democratic thought and practice. They shape America's national discourse, even while agitating for inclusion within it. Given its mission and longevity, black intellectualism has become the form of American intellectualism best adept and well versed in truth telling about democracy crippled by racism. Consequently, it is one of the least valued and most contested forms of intellectualism in a racialized society. Despite the cool reception given to its most radical formulations, the concerns of progressive black intellectuals continually push American intellectualism to consider and reconsider the place of racial and sexual justice in a democratic state.

Our intellectualism, like our persistent critiques of American democracy, raises questions about the possibilities of an expansive and expanding community in a racially and economically polarized United States. These questions about the struggles of black Americans pertain to the entire racialized nation.[3] Questions such as one posed by Toni Morrison illustrate the pointedness of our interrogation: "Is this country willing to sabotage its cities and school systems if they're occupied mostly by black people?"[4] Often black intellectuals' queries call out injustices while sustaining the vision of intergenerational community and responsibilities. For instance, during a February 1990 Black

History Month performance, Maya Angelou asked the audience in a packed auditorium at Miami University-Ohio: "If your ancestors were to appear today would they say, in looking at you, 'So this is what I struggled and died for?'" Her question elicits a variety of responses, each reflecting some bond or severed tie with community and its past, present, and future members. In that auditorium, it was unclear how many shrugs of indifference were the response to Angelou. Rather than shrugging off the question, we may reply by reconsidering our relationships to ancestral radicals such as W. E. B. Du Bois, Ida B. Wells-Barnett, or Ella Baker, all of whom worked and battled with black elites in emancipation struggles. Our relationship to the legacy of past race leaders infuses contemporary responses to racism and American intellectualism. At times, these current relationships of black intellectuals prove disconcerting and seem far removed from the struggles and gains of past antiracist radicals.

African-American intellectuals who posit obligations to "the black community" and community-centered worldviews are sometimes discredited by charges of essentialism for identifying as *black* thinkers who privilege community building and antiracism. (When generalized,the charge of essentialism can be used as a political club, much as the "p.c." or politically correct charge was used to dismiss the demands of progressives.) Obviously, some nationalism and Afrocentrism have engaged in romantic, racialized essentialist discourse; however, not all black writers who advocate or demand American and black responsibility toward a black people or Africana community can be uniformly dismissed as essentialist. There is no one "authentic" way of being black, or American, or intellectual. There are, however, ways of being political. And, while all blacks (even those with contempt for nonwhites and nonelites) are "authentic," their intellectual stances reflect a politics that will either challenge or accommodate oppression. At their best, our debates on the relevance and significance—what some consider to be the "authenticity"—of black and antiracist American intellectuals attest to our strong, desperate need for liberating thought. Today we find ourselves amid heated, contested claims for progressive black intellectualism precisely because the stakes seem so high and the vital signs so low.

Debating the African-American Intellectual

In the resurgence and rationalization of racism at the close of this century, conservative American intellectuals and propagandists make familiar arguments discrediting the very idea of black equality by disparaging black intellectual ability. In 1994, a series of books on the bell curve theory by white academics proselytized the "mental inferiority" of blacks. Promoted by influential press and publishers, curve devotees and their right-wing financiers, such as the Pioneer Fund, attempted to legitimize recycled racism as scientific, and thereby influence public legislation and social policies through academic literature that constructs *le negre* rather than institutional racism as the national problem to be censured, solved, or isolated. These works posed reactionary questions to nullify those questions raised by antiracists challenging racial inequality and the national ideals and pretensions of U.S. democracy. The well-publicized questions of reactionaries, "How well can Negroes think?" and "Can they be civilized—or only segregated or incarcerated?" took center stage.

Effectively marketed, the books preoccupied both those who accepted and those who rejected their assertions of innate black (intellectual) inferiority. Progressive intellectuals' critical publications offer bell curve counters: Morrison's *Playing in the Dark*, David Theo Goldberg's *Racist Culture*, and Lewis Gordon's *Bad Faith and Antiblack Racism* provide vital analyses of racism in American culture, ideology, and social consciousness.[5] Some intellectuals, seeing no need, and no way, to "prove" black humanity, concentrated on advocacy for social and government policies to redress inequality. A few intellectuals countered with satire. At a 1994 University of California-Berkeley meeting to discuss the *New York Times Book Review*'s promotion of scientific racism in IQ genetics discourse,[6] a prominent black woman professor ironically suggested calling a press conference complete with charts, pointers, and research statistics as equally impressive as those in the geneticist literature to announce a new scientific breakthrough: that we have isolated the gene for white racism.

In the postmodern eugenics campaigns, conservatives play to racial and elite fears about an allegedly declining, quantifiable American intelligence. These fears of diminishing test-score intelligence are linked to dark-skinned peoples rather than to cultural bias in testing and education, inequitable school funding, undernourished students, and unsafe, substandard schools. Immigrants, African Americans, Native Americans, Chicanos, and Latino Americans as subalterns all serve as a receptacle to contain American intellectual inferiority. Such a repository frees the larger society to cauterize mental deficiency as it contains blackness. These American phobias about demonstrable intellect remain black fears as well.

For instance, some black intellectuals seem preoccupied with disproving the bell curve by the quality of their competent prose or intellectual performances. For some, there seems to be an intense desire to prove themselves as American intellectuals to white elites by eloquent responses to the neoconservative "Can the Negro think?" and the liberal "What does the Negro think?" line of query. Black intellectuals have come under fire for playing the role of race sage to white elites and middle America. From the battles between Du Bois and Booker T. Washington at the turn of the century, through Harold Cruse's 1967 manifesto, *The Crisis of the Negro Intellectual*, to Cedric Robinson's 1983 scholarly text *Black Marxism*,[7] we have witnessed heated debates about the role of black intellectuals in a racist society. Part of these old, in-house debates focused on the historic mandate of the black intellectual to be a race leader advancing the conditions of the black masses. In the past, black elites progressing up the mythic American ladder, and "lifting as they climbed," were constructed as a Talented Tenth. That elite, which celebrated its 100th anniversary in 1996, had a conservative function as managerial race leaders; nevertheless, they saw themselves largely committed to leading black nonelites toward economic, social, and political equality. Talented Tenth intellectuals garnered respect for lifting not just themselves as they progressed up the proverbial ladder. Consequently, although resented for their class snobbery and pretensions, they were also valued among African Americans because they symbolized black equality and channeled resources into black communities. (Even Booker T. Washington, who proselytized black intellectual subservience to whites, produced jobs and institutions.) Unlike their predecessors, today's elite intellectuals may not seem very effective or overly ambitious in their political challenges and confrontations on behalf of nonelite blacks. In our more pessimistic and individualistic age, another spirit of race leadership prevails among elites.

African Americans now debate the commodification of the black intellectual as entertainer or public relations intermediary who interprets blackness for consensus politics. Yet this is not a new phenomenon in race relations. Increasingly, the black intellectual performer routinely applauded in academic halls and on talk show stages for his sagacity is later severely reprimanded by critical blacks for his—males dominate the profession of public intellectual—performance. Market incentives for experts on blackness encourage the reification of black intellectuals as cultural performers, predictably as financial or career considerations mute radical analyses of antidemocratic, racialist and sometimes violent state practices. In the commodification and alienation rampant in society, markets and fads debase American intellectualism in general; yet these trends seem especially pernicious for African-American intellectuals.

What some saw as the venality of oral and literary performances in black intellectual discourse sparked hostile reflections on the black public intellectual in 1995. In rapid succession, *The New Yorker, Atlantic Monthly, The New Republic,* and *The Village Voice,* published essays that put African-American intellectuals on display.[8] Black elites became the subject and spectacle of American intellectualism as upscale press promoted interest in contested black intellectualism.

When popular American magazines denounced black intellectuals for an alleged vacuity, those castigated were largely academics and popular authors who, with the exception of Henry Louis Gates Jr., defined themselves as "insurgents" or progressives. The most severely criticized in mainstream press were left-leaning liberals. White publications generally ignored black moderates and conservatives or heralded them through their conservative (white) writers as appropriate models of black intellectualism—which seemed consistent with the age of neoconservative contracts. Debating the worthiness of black intellectualism, the mainstream press reinscribed the historic roles of blacks as entertainment for whites.

Progressive black elites had themselves decried the decline of the "great black intellectual." For instance, Cornel West, the only intellectual mentioned in all of the 1995 essays, helped spark the flurry of articles on the crisis of the black public intellectual, the year following the bell curve spate of publications disparaging black intellectual ability. Criticizing West's position, a few countered that the (self-) marketing of black elites marked the so-called wane in black intellectualism. Any decline, it was argued, was a byproduct of black public intellectuals who performed as commodities for mostly white, privileged consumers. Adolph Reed takes this position in his *Village Voice* essay "What are the Drums Saying, Booker T?" Referring to popular intellectuals as cultural politicians, he contends that today's elite black public intellectual thrives on interrogation; engaging in a form of show-and-tell discourse that objectifies blacks, black elites seek steady employment as the interpreters of blackness for white audiences. Following Reed, in a later edition of the *Voice*, Michelle Wallace launched a disjointed diatribe against a prominent black feminist in order to denounce what she viewed as the superficiality and diminished scholarship of performing blackness.[9]

Unsurprisingly, these intellectual debates at times denigrate into ad hominem attacks. Disputes prove searing, partly because, personalized as a mark of individual character, black elite intellectuals' responsibilities to black nonelites is a sensitive topic. Traditionally, we have defined race men and race women as obligated to further emancipation projects. The quality of those interventions and the integrity of the race leaders were usually measured by political courage and efficacy in a nation wracked by racist ethos and violence. Our current contentious debates, and sometimes character assaults, are peculiar to today's black intellectual leadership in that the unprecedented assimilation of black elites has transformed the questions black intellectuals pose. Before this post-civil rights era of integration (disproportionately benefiting elites), black intellectuals debated not whether they were obligated to serve in the advancement of a besieged people, but how best to fulfill those obligations. Today, the disclaimers among black intellectuals, dismissals of the black community as an imaginary, and a preoccupation with "suvivor guilt" suggest other concerns as the post-movement age of migratory black intellectuals, hybridity, or service to white consumers (readers/students) strains connections with nonelite black communities. For black elites trained in white schools, and employed in white institutions, ties may be tenuous at best with the majority of black people. Furthering the divide, we see that what brings greater status to the black intellectual as an American intellectual paradoxically pushes her or him further away from the masses of black people. Alienation suggests the significant costs that some crossover intellectuals pay, and the abrasiveness of our self-criticisms reveals how little we hope for reconnection in community.

Supporting the contributions of black academics and writers to community, in the socialist journal *New Politics*, Manning Marable criticizes Reed's acerbic denunciation of black intellectual elites.[10] In his defense of bell hooks, Michael Eric Dyson, and Cornel West, Marable misses the incisiveness of Reed's analysis, although, he correctly notes that it is marred by ad hominem attacks. *New Politics* later provided a forum for black (male) intellectuals to respond to Marable's assessment of Reed as aligned with antiliberal politics. Peniel Joseph observed that Reed was accurate in highlighting the alienation of the black public intellectual in black nonelite communities. Arguing that Reed exempts himself from his own pointed analysis, Joseph emphasized the difficulty that progressive black intellectuals have in the American arena of performing and commodified intellectualism, an arena shaped by the tastes and interests of the dominant society. Our difficulties, though, badly serve as apologias for nonrigorous critiques of the conservative functions and radical pretensions of popularized intellectualism. For Joseph, elite black intellectuals share an "attempt to examine and analyze the reasons for continued African-American immiseration."[11] He adds that we also share an ability to undermine our own progressive intentions by profiteering from jargonistic writing irrelevant to the concerns of disenfranchised blacks. Regarding the black elites whom Marable defends, Joseph issues his own severe assessment: "The overtly political nature of their writing, since it is seemingly disconnected from organic vehicles of political organization and mobilization, smacks of opportunism and sloganeering."[12] Of course sloganeering and opportunism are heard within both the progressive and reactionary voices of American intellectuals.

To further develop and politicize progressive black intellectualism, some thinkers confront its contradictions as it ranges from the liberal through the radical to the revolutionary. Since their past and present contributions do not exempt the most privileged black voices from critiques, even harsh ones, the conservative, managerial roles of black elites, and their marketing of blackness, remain critical issues for debate in furthering democratic praxis. We have no control over whether our critiques of liberal blacks will be used by antidemocratic intellectuals, by racial conservatives and reactionaries who resist the idea and reality of black equality. Nor do we have the luxury of not developing piercing appraisals of what many American intellectuals consider to be their black intellectual vanguard, all the while ignoring how American intellectualism works to obscure the contributions of nonelite and radical race leaders.

Conclusion

Historically, progressive intellectuals dragged problems, racialized and denied, from the periphery to the center of American social consciousness and political debate. They continue these endeavors in a society whose authoritative voices assert the irrelevance of race and an impatience with speech critical of American racism and white privilege. Seemingly fatigued by antiracist discourse, reproducing the Africanist as marker for social pathology, American conservatives and neoliberals argue for new forms of social segregation and the dismantling of federal equity programs. In this context, African-American intellectuals pursue democratic projects. Sometimes we undermine our endeavors through commodification and performance. At times, our discursive elitism privileges the affluent over the poor, male over female, and liberal over radical agency to deradicalize black politics and political discourse as we reproduce and commercialize the construction of a Talented Tenth of elite race leaders. Promoting progressive agency without erasure or mythologizing black leadership, critical thinkers resist such constructions to further radical, inclusive democracy.

In an era of covert and coded antiblack racism, some focus

on the development of black intellectualism and leadership, seeking new ways of furthering American intellectualism and political agency unrestricted by racial, sexual, economic, or elite bias.

Although our democratic struggles continue to splinter on a mystified, marbleized racism in a nation that denies racial dominance and reconstructs institutional repression as a past phenomenon, by democratizing American intellectualism, we extend to all the opportunities to advance to the head of their class in social and political equality.

Our Past
Historiography, Erasure, and Race Leadership

Mbungi a kanda va kati kwa nsi ye yulu: The center (cavity) of the community is located between the above and below world. The reality of the cultural heritage of the community, i.e., its knowledge, is the experience of the reality of that deepest knowledge found between the spiritualized ancestors and the physically living thinkers within community.

(Kongo proverb)

—K. Kia Bunseki Fu-Kiau,
African Book Without Title

W. E. B. Du Bois, Arna Bontemps, Shirley Graham Du Bois, and others, Gunter's Studio, Phi Beta Kappa Fisk University, Nashville, Tennessee, 1958.

1
The Talented Tenth Recalled

They are unable to conceive of the workers as anything else but workers and therefore are unable to conceive of themselves as anything else but intellectuals. No intelligence in the world can enable a social grouping to think of itself as something
which must be abolished. In fact, up to a point, the more intelligent they are, the
worse for them.
　　　　　　　　　　　　　　　　　　　　　　　　　　　　　　—C. L. R. James
　　　　　　　　　　　　　　　　　　　　　　　　　　　　　　American Civilization

Referring to a select caste, C. L. R. James wrote pessimistical-
ly about the possibilities of American intellectuals to move
beyond the conservative functions of elites.[1] Nevertheless, this
Trinidad-born radical, deported in 1953 by the U.S. government, believed that Americans could build a new society based
on "a democracy of equals, with relations of a subtlety and inti-
macy" previously unknown.[2] The uniqueness of this new,
democratic society, according to James, would be its unity of
thought and action in which "the worker as such and the
thinker as such will disappear."[3] James was relatively uncon-
cerned with whether or not intellectuals as a caste supported or
opposed this process. He believed that "the mass seeking to
solve the great social problems which face them in their daily
lives" would be the creative impetus toward change.[4] The intellectual activities of millions of workers dealing with economic,
political, and cultural realities, James asserts, would be recog-
nizable to intellectual elites "only when they see and feel the
new force."[5] This new force or mass movement toward democratic renewals would herald the demise of intellectuals as an elite
that historically promoted its agency through (clerical, educational, or managerial) relationships of social power contingent

15

upon the existence of a "passive subordinate mass." James's optimism about social transformation, in which intellectual elites as such "will be undergoing liquidation in the very action of the mass which will be creating a totally new society, an active integrated humanism,"[6] shaped his ideas for progressive leadership. In the post-World War II era, other prominent black leaders in the United States theorized about democratic race leadership to echo James's ideology on American civilization and organizing. It took W. E. B. Du Bois nearly half a century to democratize the Talented Tenth in the militant spirit of James's radical observations made in the 1950s.

American intellectuals rarely discuss James's comments about our conservative roles as elites within state structures. Unsurprisingly, we infrequently reference the agency of radical, nonelite intellectuals. Our reflections on Du Bois's evolving ideology repudiating elites and the Talented Tenth are likewise muted.

The Talented Tenth

Since Reconstruction, African-American race leadership has been identified with the training of black elites based on the model of privileged, white educational institutions. In a society where intellectual ability denotes college or university training and socialization, intellectualism is tied to academe. Consequently, it has been aligned with a corporate, conservative sphere that is traditionally geared to middle-class (white) males. (Today only thirty percent of whites and fifteen percent of blacks have college or university degrees.) Classism and elitism were endemic to the identity of the university-trained American intellectual. The mythology surrounding academic and institutionalized intellectualism worked to valorize the elites being socialized and trained.

Contemporary understandings of black intellectualism are traceable to late nineteenth-century liberalism and its conventional antiracism. The phrase *Talented Tenth*, generally associated with Du Bois's 1903 essay of the same title, originated in 1896 among Northern white liberals of the American Baptist Home Missionary Society (ABHMS), which established Southern black colleges to train Negro elites. Evelyn Brooks-Higginbotham describes how the year after Booker T. Washington's infamous 1895 Atlanta Compromise speech, Henry Morehouse, who had twice served as ABHMS executive secretary, developed the phrase "the Talented Tenth" to distinguish his liberal arts education programs and their students from the "average or mediocre" black intellect that aligned itself with Washington's ideology of vocational education for race advancement.[7]

The Christian missionary founders and funders of black higher education, who included women in their construction of race leadership, prioritized race management. Morehouse's Talented Tenth were to provide a racial class buffer zone between unprivileged blacks and white society.[8] Consequently, ABHMS disapproved of black Southern students relocating to Northern colleges, believing that educational migration weakened the links between elite race leaders and poor and working-class African Americans.

In the nineteenth century, ABHMS college-trained blacks "sought to subvert the power of illiterate [black] leaders by privileging the written word."[9] In the twentieth century, conventional academics gauge black intellectual ability by literacy and publications. Today's Talented Tenth seem more ideologically and socially split from nonelite blacks than their predecessors were. Perhaps this is partly due to the integrationist successes of previous generations. The select of the Tenth work at elite institutions and live in places vastly different from those of their nineteenth-century counterparts or contemporary peers teaching in urban or vocational schools. Distance, or even estrangement, from black communities does not negate the contributions of elite black intellectuals. However, as Brooks-Higginbotham and Cedric Robinson have noted, historically the conservative, managerial function of such an educated elite formed an intellectual and political leadership scrutinized and regarded with suspicion by nonelites. Like their predecessors, most contemporary black intellectuals rarely ask to what extent they intentionally or unintentionally fulfill the nineteenth-century missionary mandate for race management.

Although ABHMS elitist constructions remain the acknowledged or unacknowledged conceptual cornerstone for current debates on the black public intellectual, most academic writers rarely refer to the Talented Tenth's origins in the race ideology of white liberal missionary societies and the black elites they schooled. Critical examinations of elite leadership in black emancipation projects are indispensable, so why do so few black intellectuals deconstruct the Talented Tenth? Failing to analyze Du Bois's growing dismissal of university-trained African Americans as *de facto* social justice agents, academic intellectuals as a select caste shape a discourse on race leadership that often uses Du Bois to validate the Talented Tenth as inherently progressive. Or, paradoxically, privileged intellectuals may minimize his later, radical thought; in this manner, Henry Louis Gates Jr. and Cornel West in *The Future of the Race* position themselves as more democratic and inclusive than (a somewhat reified) Du Bois.[10] In collective amnesia, many either overlook or underestimate Du Bois's later repudiation of black elites as reliable leaders for an oppressed people. Race memory misleads as it fails to recall that the greatest promoter of black elite agency became, in time, its most severe critic.

Du Bois's Rejection of Black Elite Leadership

> Some years ago I used the phrase "The Talented Tenth," meaning leadership of the Negro race in America by a trained few. Since then this idea has been criticized. It has been said that I had in mind the building of an aristocracy with neglect of the masses. This criticism has seemed even more valid because of emphasis on the meaning and power of the mass of people to which Karl Marx gave voice in the middle of the nineteenth century, and which has been growing in influence ever since. There have come other changes in these days, which a great many of us do not realize as Revolution through which we are passing. Because of this, it is necessary to examine the world about us and our thoughts and attitudes toward it. I want then to re-examine and restate the thesis of the Talented Tenth which I laid down many years ago.
>
> —W. E. B. Du Bois

Discussions of contemporary U.S. black leadership are foregrounded by, and sometimes frozen in, Du Bois's early construction of black intellectualism embodied in the Talented Tenth, of a progressive leadership of responsible Negro elites dedicated to black development.[11] His 1903 essay, "The Talented Tenth," describes how this elite represent African-American ability and resistance to racism. Initially, the Harvard Ph.D. formed an "identity politics" of black elites as intellectuals and political leaders. His select, a "new" Negro nobility, disproved the alleged inferiority of black Americans. As elite educators of the black masses, they served as models of Negro gentility for the dominant white society and subordinated blacks. With their talents honed by college and university training, as the vehicle for black uplift and the vanguard to democratize U.S. society, Du Bois's Tenth countered the image of black incivility and inhumanity. Later political crises would radicalize Du Bois's thoughts about the ABHMS construct of an elect few promoting race uplift through race management.

Like the ABHMS, Du Bois included women in the Talented Tenth. His referents were generally male; Du Bois did not always use *men* as a generic reference to both sexes. In the 1903 essay, the word signifies males developing in a socially constructed *manhood*: "The training of men is a difficult and intricate task," writes Du Bois, "Men we shall have only as we make manhood the object of the work of the schools."[12] Still, by identifying women as members of the *public*, political race leadership, Du Bois's sexual politics were advanced for his era.

But gender inclusiveness does not in itself democratize the Talented Tenth. Despite the presence of women, this construction of black agency remained elitist and undermined democratic leadership. Intraracial inequality was endemic to this concept of race leadership. Du Bois's academic training in Greek classicism infuses his 1903 model of Negro leadership with a Platonic hierarchy of enthroned philosopher kings/ queens. Consistent with the Platonic mandate, those most suited for (benevolent) leadership, or rule, are identified, nurtured, and educated as befits their station. All others, in various lower ranks, are trained to follow the philosopher kings/ queens who serve for the greater good. Exploring Du Bois's concept of second sight, Thomas Holt uses Plato's allegorical narrative or parable of the cave, writing that neither white nor black workers "looking through a glass darkly . . . can see each other clearly." Whites (whom Holt refers to as the "outside leaders") are incapable of leading "the entombed." Consequently, in Du Bois's ideology, writes Holt, the recourse for "those within the cave is to organize their inner resources— material and spiritual—to create a base from which the entire edifice can be reformed. Being black—thereby, capable of gain-ing strength, discipline, and solidarity from their oppression—the cave dwellers are blessed with a second-sight into the promise *and* the broken promises of America."[13] However not all cave dwellers, in Du Bois's estimation, were equally gifted in sight. His original Talented Tenth, with its exalted estimation of the visionary abilities of privileged blacks, presupposed a shortsightedness and moral as well as intellectual stuntedness on the part of impoverished blacks.

For Du Bois, race leadership is an issue of necessity and expediency as well as ability; the desperate conditions African Americans faced mandated the formation of an elite to oversee a community in crises, a community whose majority he did not then trust to provide its own leadership. The "Negro race, like all races," writes Du Bois, "is going to be saved by its exceptional men." Consequently, Negro education must further the Talented Tenth, as Du Bois viewed it, given the critical "problem of developing the Best of this race that they may guide the Mass away from the contamination and death of the Worst, in their own and other races."[14]

"The Talented Tenth" essay asks: "Can the masses of the Negro people be in any possible way more quickly raised than by the effort and example of this aristocracy of talent and character?" Du Bois rejects any democratic conjectures by his quick response with a rhetorical question: "Was there ever a nation on God's fair earth civilized from the bottom upward?" At the turn of the century, for this social architect, the answer was clearly "No." The nobility determines past, present, and future progress: "It is, ever was and ever will be from the top downward that culture filters. The Talented Tenth rises and pulls all that are worth the saving up to their vantage ground."[15] Disquietingly, though, those whom the Tenth did not carry in their wake of Ascension were deemed superfluous. Du Bois's contemporary Anna Julia Cooper took a less Darwinian approach to racial uplift a decade before the publication of "The Talented Tenth" essay. Her 1892 *A Voice from the South,* known to Du Bois, argued for a different standard for African-American success, one that did not easily consign those hampered by multiple oppressions from ascension—black women laborers—to the status of not "worth the saving."

Over the years, Du Bois revised his views on African-American agency. Departing from his 1903 essay, he writes that at one time he had "believed in the higher education of a Talented Tenth who through their knowledge of modern culture could guide the American Negro into a higher civilization."[16] He recalls that he had felt that in the absence of such elites, "the Negro would have to accept white leadership, and that such leadership could not always be trusted to guide this group into self-realization and to its highest cultural possibilities." Gradually, black working-class activists surpassed elites in Du Bois's estimation of political integrity and progressive agency. He democratized his concept of race leaders through the inclusion of the radicalism of nonelites.

As their elite class formulations faded, the democratic intent and content of his later essays rival if not surpass that of Cooper's 1892 treatise-autobiography. His evolving thought was influenced by different sources and experiences. Battles with Washington and academia infused his developing concept of race leadership and agency. His activism allowed him to revisit his political thoughts on agency. Co-organizing the Pan-African conferences beginning in 1903, coordinating the short-lived Niagara Movement (1905–1907) and mobilizing the long-lived NAACP (1909–) while serving as editor of *The Crisis,* the NAACP national magazine, all profoundly influenced Du Bois's understandings of political agency and democratic development.

Du Bois's political experiences gave him a difficult schooling in the flaws and infidelities of the elites designated to redeem both the souls of black folks and the American soul. For example, his university tenure dashed any idealization of an intellectual nobility shaped by meritocracy and service with unwavering dedication to social justice. As an academic, Du Bois endured decades of marginalization. Despite exemplary research, publications as well as pioneering conferences at Atlanta University, he was eventually encouraged to leave the university. His studies on black Philadelphians were insufficiently appreciated and underfunded by the University of Pennsylvania, his previous employer. He was also marginalized within and alienated from black colleges and universities. Wilberforce State University in Ohio reproved him for insufficient acculturation to academic mores, such as its social conventions for chapel. As a consequence of his rivalry with Booker T. Washington, Du Bois was barred from teaching at Tuskegee Institute (and possibly other African-American institutions). Du Bois's radical formulations of agency, progressivism, and black leadership were likely conditioned by these confrontations with institutional intellectuals and academics.

Du Bois's battles with Tuskegee's elite, state-anointed Negro leadership—the prevailing model of black vanguardism—also provided early, sobering lessons in machine politics as he attempted to define, redefine, and realize an ideal black leadership. Du Bois would later recount that the Tuskegee Machine's strong-arm tactics and ideological differences widened the chasm between himself and Booker T. Washington. David Levering Lewis disputes Du Bois's interpretation, positing ego clashes as the source of contention: "Contrary to what Du Bois later claimed, the initial conflict with Washington had been professional and then bitterly personal before it became ideological."[17] Regardless of the chronology and origin of their antagonisms, the Du Bois–Washington ideological divide centered on their debates and attempts to determine who, and what, qualifies as race leader and racial uplift in early twentieth-century Afro-American leadership. Du Bois characterizes these conflicts in *Dusk of Dawn* (1940), which he describes as "not so much my autobiography as the autobiography of a concept of race, elucidated, magnified and doubtless distorted in the thoughts and deeds which were mine."[18] In this memoir, he rejects what he defines as the "Washingtonian position": race leadership ideology that equates material acquisition or economic wealth with moral and political leadership. This reference to the Tuskegee president also alludes to the federal government, which elevated the conservative Georgian as national spokesman for black Americans.

In *Dusk of Dawn*, Du Bois writes that previously his "panacea" for racial inequality constituted a "flight of class from mass through the development of a Talented Tenth."[19] He reflects on the shortsightedness of his earlier stance: "The power of this aristocracy of talent was to lie in its knowledge and character and not in its wealth. The problem which I did not then attack was that of leadership and authority within the group, which by implication left controls to wealth—a contingency of which I never dreamed."[20] In its theoretical reflections on experiential politics rather than race rhetoric in liberation leadership, *Dusk of Dawn* retracts Du Bois's construction of black elites as a cure for white racism and black poverty. By 1940, having been rejected by academe, censured by Washington's black conservatives, frustrated by NAACP white and black liberals, the archetype of antiracist intellectualism and leadership departs from his earlier view of elite agency. Revisiting the Talented Tenth, he critiques the class elitism inherent in the original concept and argues for the unique role black workers can play in social justice. Given the global economic changes in the post-Depression, World War II era, writes Du Bois, "mass and class must unite for the world's salvation. . . . We who have had least class differentiation in wealth, can follow in the new trend and indeed lead it."[21]

This internationalist anticapitalist retained a refined elitism, though: Mass and class are to unite, but caste remains. Now only the materially privileged who also possessed *noblesse oblige* qualified as "leadership and authority within the group."[22] At this stage, Du Bois was not willing to demobilize the elite vanguard. In the reformulation of the Talented Tenth, *Dusk of Dawn* would inch toward democratic reform yet still identify black elites as "natural" leadership. Rather than call for the abolition of an aristocratic black vanguard, the memoir merely differentiates among the aristocracy, distinguishing between those with material wealth (the "Washingtonian position") and those with the "existential wealth" of political and moral leadership. Nevertheless, Du Bois would continue to whittle away at elitism in black leadership.

Eight years after the publication of *Dusk of Dawn,* he intensified his criticisms of elitist black leadership. Addressing Wilberforce State University alumni nearly half a century after his first formulation of the Talented Tenth, Du Bois made a radical departure from his previous position on black agency. In "The Talented Tenth: Memorial Address," delivered August 12, 1948, at the Sigma Pi Phi's nineteenth convocation at Wilberforce, Du Bois recanted his race leadership dogma. Reworking the 1903 essay's title, he subverted his original ideology, dismantling old leadership and appealing for new with a double entendre: Memorial means burial and commemoration as well as a petition to an authoritative body. Du Bois bestowed upon his audience of elite race men an authority that he simultaneously denied them as an inherent attribute of their social status as university graduates. The Wilberforce Address both buries and resurrects the Talented Tenth. Before men whose education and social achievement marked them as ideal candidates for his original aristocratic race leaders, Du Bois disbanded the old club.

The address places the concept of race leader in an international struggle for economic and racial justice. Du Bois thereby radicalizes the concept of black agency and leadership. His speech credits the work of Karl Marx with enlightening him to the moral and political agency of workers and laborers. The memorial also refers to the "Americanization" of the black middle class. This deradicalization process, according to Du Bois, occurs when more privileged African Americans (re)align themselves to function as a middle class interested in individual group gain rather than race leadership for mass development. Asserting that the New Tenth must remain connected to the mass, he highlights a new leadership in conflict with an assimilated or assimilating African-American elite. In his reminiscences, Du Bois notes that as a young idealist he had never considered the fragility of a bond strained or severed by self-interest and ambitious desires on the part of black elites. Here he offers a much harsher criticism of elites than he was prepared to make in 1940.

Du Bois told his university audience that the lynchings, economic exploitation, and social violence that black Americans faced at the turn of the century shaped his earlier concept of the Talented Tenth. As a student and worker at the time of his seminal essay, he believed that American Negroes would achieve "salvation through intelligent leadership." Du Bois recalls: "And for this intelligence, I argued, we needed college-trained men. Therefore, I stressed college and higher training. For these men with their college training, there would be needed thorough understanding of the mass of Negroes and their problems; and, therefore, I emphasized scientific study. Willingness to work and make personal sacrifice for solving these problems was of course, the first prerequisite and *sine qua non*. I did not stress this, I assumed it."[23] Youth and idealism, his audience of elites were to understand, no longer obscured how selfish self-interest and individualism eclipse sacrifice and service in black elite leadership within the political thought of the older Du Bois.

For the Wilberforce black bourgeois and petit-bourgeois male audience, the mature, pragmatic Du Bois proceeds to evoke the image of revolutionary, antiracist economic struggles as the vehicle of black agency and emancipation. Reflecting the "revolutionary thought" of moral leaders, prophets and reformers, he instructed that Marx argued: "The poor need not always be with us, and that all men could and should be free from poverty."[24] Embracing Marx and referring to economic and labor struggles, the keynote speaker advocated that the best form of civilization had "a wide human base." At this wide human base, the philosopher kings/queens yield to the economic revolutionary, the radical worker-intellectual. Positing antiracist "intellectuals" developing in coalitions with workers, Du Bois grounds the New Talented Tenth in a mass formation, writing that it "must be more than talented, and work not simply as individuals." The new leadership would find that: "Its passport to leadership was not alone learning but expert knowledge of modern economics as it affected American Negroes; and in addition to this and fundamental, would be its willingness to sacrifice and plan for such economic revolution in industry and just distribution of wealth, as would make the rise of our group possible."[25]

The Wilberforce Address is foregrounded by two world wars, the consolidation of the Soviet Union and its regional empire, and decolonization movements against European and U.S. imperialism. The New Tenth manifests an international perspective. At its most developed stage, its internationalism posits that "races" are only cultural groups and that political coalitions are essential. Elevated and projected into global politics, as agitators for a decolonized world, the New Tenth forms broad alliances among colonized peoples. The "new idea for a Talented Tenth" would be based on "group-leadership, not simply educated and self-sacrificing, but with a clear vision of present world conditions and dangers, and conducting American Negroes to alliance with culture groups in Europe, America, Asia and Africa, and looking toward a new world culture."[26]

Implementing an agenda for progressive cultural coalitions required replacing a black vanguard intelligentsia with a mass "special organization," one that necessarily "calls for more than a tenth of our number."[27] For Du Bois, agency belongs neither to elite nor race within the context of revolutionary internationalism.

Du Bois was both optimistic and realistic regarding the extent to which the Talented Tenth could be democratized and radicalized. In his address he declares, "We can do it. We have the ability. The only question is, have we the will?"[28] Du Bois apparently did, as evident in his discard of his early, ABHMS-inspired theories on black agency and leadership. Several years after the Wilberforce Address, at the height of anticommunism, his query to black Americans—"Have we the will?" for radical, international struggle—found both disappointing and reassuring replies. In 1948, at the beginning of the Cold War, Du Bois had advocated that American Negroes ally themselves with postwar independence movements, the same movements that the United States and its allies, European colonial powers, opposed. The McCarthy era's reactionary campaigns of intimidation and repression targeted Du Bois precisely for the peace activism and internationalism that embodied his "new idea for a Talented Tenth."

In 1951, Du Bois ran for the U.S. Senate on the American Labor Party ticket; he received 250,000 votes. In 1950–51, he was indicted and tried as an unregistered foreign agent. This personal and political crisis solidified his theorizing on the essentialism of a mass base for progressive movements. According to David Du Bois, his stepfather's most thorough rethinking of the Talented Tenth occurred during these years of government persecution. Du Bois's struggles with state repression sharply delineated his allies. His black middle-class support largely dissipated via its fears, political timidity, and conservatism. Du Bois's support among workers who actively opposed his prosecution grew. The efficacy and militancy of workers and laborers agitating for his exoneration dispelled all specters of black elites as ideal race leaders. The memoir *In Battle for Peace* (1952) recounts betrayals by African-American middle-class colleagues as well as new alliances with working-class African Americans. "While most of my educated and well-to-do Negro friends—although by no means all—were scared by the [anti-Soviet] war propaganda and went quickly to cover," Du Bois writes, "an increasing mass of Negro working class, especially the members of the so-called left-wing unions, rallied to my side with faith and money."[29] His own dependency on militant black workers brought the final transformation to his ideology on political leadership and agency: "My faith hitherto had been in what I once denominated the 'Talented Tenth.' I now realize that the ability within a people does not automatically work for its highest salvation ... naturally, out of the mass of the working classes, who know life in its bitter struggle, will continually rise the real, unselfish and clear-sighted leadership."[30]

Workers not only share positions of leadership ideologically held previously by professional intellectuals. They also, by virtue of their confronting labor conditions that necessitate radical resistance, constitute a more courageous and committed cadre of organizers. Workers' and radicals' agitation likely kept Du Bois from imprisonment. For the elder leader, the development of "the ability within a people," its "real, unselfish, and clear-sighted leadership" was no longer an attribute of privilege; the grass-roots bore progressivism.[31]

Having been dependent upon working-class radicalism, Du Bois's later autobiographical reflections on the Talented Tenth reveal an increasing reflexivity or self-reflection on the deradicalizing aspects of his privilege that interrogate his middle-class status in African-American communities. Even without wealth or economic status, Du Bois's education and employment placed him solidly in the black elite. Education marked him as a member of the old Talented Tenth; yet, political sensibilities, self-sacrifice, and radical vision identified him as a member of the New Tenth.

Contemporary Reflections on the Talented Tenth

Writing that "little more is passed on to our youth today of W. E. B. Du Bois than the elitist concept of black leadership," David Du Bois wryly observes that the African-American "tendency to want to hold on to this Talented Tenth elitist concept of black leadership has existed in the most unlikely places."

Illustrating his point, Du Bois recalls that in 1972, after a twelve-year African sojourn from U.S. racism, he welcomed Black Panther Party newspaper editor Erika Huggins's invitation for a feature article on his stepfather. Considering this an excellent opportunity to educate about W. E. B. Du Bois's rejection of an elite Talented Tenth, the younger Du Bois wrote of "Dr. Du Bois' conviction that it's those who suffered most and have the least to lose that we should look to for our steadfast, dependable and uncompromising leadership." When his article appeared in the Black Panther paper's December issue, all references to the senior Du Bois's rejection of the Talented Tenth were deleted, according to David Du Bois, who suggests that the Panther leaders sought to hold on to vanguard elitism.[32]

Not only marginalized black militants reasserted the mask of Du Bois as the patriarch of elite race leadership considered the vehicle for black liberation. Today many references to and representations of Du Bois disregard his evolving radicalization of agency. Some of the "most unlikely places" for a Talented Tenth fetish are located in the literature of cultural studies, critical race theory, feminism, black postmodernism, and Afrocentrism. Such writing excises Du Bois's democratic radicalism and his conviction that those with the least to lose, and therefore the most to gain, are most likely to provide exemplary leadership in liberation struggles.

Some of the most recent writings on the Talented Tenth express strong criticisms of black elitism. Consider Kevin K. Gaines's *Uplifting the Race: Black Leadership, Politics, and Culture in the Twentieth Century* which focuses on the first fifty years of this century in which a racial uplift ideology infused with classism became normative. Gaines, who states that he is interested in how black elites responded to white supremacy and the ways in which racial uplift ideology used the appeal of a "better class of blacks" to represent black success at assimilating as a so-called civilized group, critiques historical black leaders such as Anna Julia Cooper for their anti-labor unions stance and somewhat sycophantic attitudes toward white elites. "The attempt to rehabilitate the image of black people through class distinctions," Gaines writes, "trafficked in claims of racial and gender hierarchy."[33] Focusing on the early Du Bois, Gaines devotes one chapter to analyzing *The Philadelphia Negro* (1899).[34]

He closes this chapter with the observation that, by the time of the 1908 riot in Springfield, Illinois, antiblack violence and race riots had transformed Du Bois from an academic to an agitator (the following year Du Bois helped to found the NAACP).

The Future of the Race also offers a critique of black elitism, including the elitist thought of the early Du Bois. Du Bois's transformation into an activist is not central to this discussion. Although Du Bois grew into militant activism, Henry Louis Gates Jr. and Cornel West do not focus on this evolution in their reflections for postmodern times in which many, including perhaps the authors, believe that the development and stability of black intellectualism rest on the transformation of the agitator into the academic. Gates and West have different perspectives for the future of the race, departing from or modifying Du Bois's 1903 formulation of a Talented Tenth, but not necessarily rejecting the racial uplift ideology which Gaines critiques. Referring to themselves as "grandchildren" of Du Bois's intellectual elite, the Harvard academics discuss their felt "responsibilities . . . to the larger African-American community, past, present, and future."[35] They offer a strong injunction for black intellectuals to renew their commitments to progressive causes: "It is only by confronting the twin realities of white racism, on the one hand, and our own failures to seize initiative and break the cycle of poverty, on the other, that we, the remnants of the Talented Tenth, will be able to assume a renewed leadership role for, and within, the black community."[36] Urging public stances against all forms of antiblack racism, Gates and West also make political assertions such as the following: "to continue to repeat the same old stale formulas, to blame 'the man' for oppressing us all, in exactly the same ways; to scapegoat Koreans, Jews, women, or even black immigrants for the failure of African Americans to seize local entrepreneurial opportunities, is to neglect our duty as leaders of our own community."[37] To the extent that this passage censures black apathy, indolence, demagoguery, and bigotry it is well noted; however, simplistic assumptions appear to be embedded in its generalities. Are we to assume that if black intellectuals do not blame "the man" then they are absolved from a critique of the state? Surely the critical analyses of black radicals and revolutionaries concerning the intersections of capitalism, imperialism, racism, patriarchy and state violence (via police agencies, the military, courts, and institutional poverty) are not yet stale, although the reductionism of such analyses into opportunistic sloganeering and performance must be tired and old. But equally dated is an uplift ideology in which black enterprise, free enterprise, for small business owners is seen as generally viable in a transnational age of NAFTA, cottage industries, sweatshops, and prison labor. Somehow in this discussion of the future of the race which advocates that we rise above Du Bois's 1903 ABHMS articulations of race leadership, it seems that blacks progress only to end up back in time, with the truncated vision of a postmodernized version of racial uplift. Gaines's observations about twentieth century black leadership remain useful for the twenty-first century: "Only through a recognition of those ways in which black middle-class ideology, as a product of the most nightmarish aspects of our history, has affected African Americans for the worse can black elites and intellectuals redefine uplift not just in those narrow, racial, masculinist, and class-specific terms, but as an ongoing project of social emancipation—self-help in the truest sense."[38] Maintaining that acknowledging the contradictions within uplift ideology should not obscure "the potential within uplift ideals for democratic visions. . . rooted in an ethos of social kinship,"[39] as Gaines does, still does not mitigate analyses of structural oppression in the U.S., where the state has not historically sided with oppressed peoples and where its interventions on behalf of racial and economic justice are whimsical at best.

Without a notion of uplift embedded in bourgeois ideals (and illusions) that ignore structural, racialized economic oppression, earlier writings by black intellectuals followed in the steps of the mature Du Bois; constructing agency and leadership as a mass rather than an elite phenomenon, they explore the democratic visions and social kinship ethos of black radicalism. For instance, *Black Marxism: the Making of a Radical Tradition* reviews the limits of elite black intellectualism. Cedric Robinson spends considerable effort in detailing Du Bois's growing radicalism and his repudiation of black elites as effective leaders of oppressed blacks. Angela Davis's *Angela Davis: An Autobiography* also democratizes intellectual ability, breaking from the philosopher kings or queens of the ABHMS's and Du Bois's early Talented Tenth. Reflecting on her autobiography's democratic and communal aspects, Davis notes that its "real strength" comes from an "honest emphasis on grassroots contributions and achievements," which counters the common notion "that history is the product of unique individuals possessing inherent qualities of greatness." For Davis, assigning political agency largely to "great actors" tends to erase the role of unnamed activists who through collective organizing secured gains attributed to prominent individuals. Davis illustrates her argument by citing the skewed perceptions and romanticism concerning her trials and political leadership during the early 1970s: "Many people unfortunately assumed that because my name and my case were so extensively publicized, the contest that unfolded during my incarceration and trial from 1970 to 1972 was one in which a single Black woman successfully fended off the repressive might of the state."[40] Iconoclastically she writes that history, theory, and resistance are attributes of an expansive community of peoples seeking and demanding freedom from oppression and political repression.

Like Du Bois, Davis was inspired by Marx. As black radicals began studying Marx's writings, political community took on international proportions. Marx's concept of workers resisting exploitation on a global level presented a unifying vision for Du Bois's "new" Talented Tenth. In similar fashion, Marx and Engels's vision in the *Communist Manifesto* of a society not polarized by economic exploitation greatly influenced Davis's concept of a democratic black liberation movement. Reinforcing her belief in the democratic nature of the international dimensions of oppressed peoples' struggle, *The Manifesto* also led her to assess antiblack violence and black middle-class agency: "Like an expert surgeon this document cut away cataracts from my eyes."[41] It gave perspective to the violence and poverty of Southern blacks known in her youth. "What had seemed a personal hatred of me, an inexplicable refusal of Southern whites to confront their own emotions, and a stubborn willingness of Blacks to acquiesce," she writes, "became the inevitable consequence of a ruthless system which kept itself alive and well by encouraging spite, competition and the oppression of one group by another."[42] Oppression manifests as driven by economic greed: "Profit was the word: the cold and constant motive for the behavior, the contempt and the despair I had seen."[43] Black liberation struggles in her political thought were seen as inherently structured by class oppression and economic exploitation. With this radical rethinking of race and class, the concept of black leadership would also be revisited and revised: Davis writes in her autobiography that she realized that despite her initially "superficial aversion for some of the social activities of the black middle class" she still "had been depending on" a Talented Tenth to lead the unemployed poor as well as impoverished black workers "to freedom."[44]

Race Memory

Memory can be the trickster. Marginalized by anticommunism and racialism, the memory of Du Bois's important contributions to American democracy and intellectualism is largely shrouded. When unmasked, there is a selectivity about what we choose to remember about him and which fragments of memory we emphasize. Unmasking, we find that Du Bois's treatment of intellectual elites reveals the deceptive workings of memory. For instance, as race leader, communist, Pan-Africanist, profeminist, Du Bois struggled for decades against myriad oppressions. Forging a praxis of intellectuals as radical actors, his continuous reformulations of African-American agency understood the greatest intellectual development to be tied to service. Given that both conservatives and progressives have ignored Du Bois's repudiation of an intellectual aristocracy of class-based elites, most infrequently remember his radical rethinking of the Talented Tenth and his repudiation of black elites.

When William Edward Burghardt Du Bois died in Ghana, on August 27, 1963 the thousands gathered at the Lincoln Memorial for the March on Washington gave silent tribute. Tribute continues to this day. In a 1993 Black History Month *CROSSROADS* editorial, Frances Beale, a former SNCC activist and Third World Women's Alliance founder,[45] praised Du Bois as a "scholar and activist; mystic and materialist; advocate of human equality and believer in the unique contributions of

Black people to human society; unfettered scholar and Marxist; intellectual and fighter who tackled all injustices and paradoxes that confront the African American people."[46] Those recognizing Du Bois's extraordinary service testify to a popularity gauged by the magnitude of his intellectual and political contributions. Like the race leaders to follow, Malcolm X and Martin Luther King Jr., Du Bois revealed a dynamic, evolving analysis that eventually underscored the importance of class and the primacy of the agency of militant workers. Honoring Du Bois's gifts, many build on his work to confront injustices. The failure to recognize and recall the work of marginalized intellectuals amid distorted memories that promote leadership as elite-driven eviscerate Du Bois's democratic legacy. Recalling black agency as an attribute of nonelites, in the spirit of Du Bois's unmasked legacy, may become the cornerstone of expanding democratic leadership, as well as a foundation for radicalizing black leadership.

W. E. B. Du Bois after a lecture, Negro History Week, Holy Trinity Episcopal Church, Brooklyn, New York, February 1954.

Profeminism and Gender Elites
W. E. B. Du Bois, Anna Julia Cooper, and Ida B. Wells-Barnett

By expanding critical theoretical frameworks, Du Bois de-mystified racism and class elitism. Unfortunately, at the same time, he also mystified the agency of African-American women. Du Bois's sexual politics suggest that he navigated between increasingly nonclassist and democratic ideologies and a mori-bund gender progressivism into a quagmire of contradictory progressive and paternalistic racial-sexual politics. Attempting to better understand the contradictions of Du Bois's profemi-nist ideology, we see an analogy with antiracism. Like some types of antiracism, certain forms of feminism and profemi-nism are disingenuous. Consider that antiracist stances guided by a Eurocentrism that presents European (American) culture as normative inadvertently reproduce white dominance; this rein-scription of white privilege occurs despite the avowed racial egalitarianism. Likewise, despite their gender progressivism, antisexists or profeminists whose politics unfolds within a meta-paradigm that establishes the male as normative reinforce male dominance. For Du Bois, the African-American male was the paradigmatic black intellectual.

Du Bois's profeminist politics clearly marks his opposition to patriarchy and misogyny. Still, a masculinist worldview influences his writing to diminish his gender progressivism. Du Bois rejected patriarchal myths about female inferiority and male superiority. Yet he holds on to a masculinist framework that presents the male as normative. Since masculinism does not explicitly advocate male superiority or rigid gender social roles, it is not identical to patriarchal ideology. Masculinism can share patriarchy's presupposition of the male as normative without its antifemale politics and rhetoric. Men who support feminist politics, as profeminists, may advocate the equality or even superiority of women. For instance, Du Bois argued against sexism and occasionally for the superiority of women. However, even without patriarchal intent, certain works may replicate conventional gender roles.

Du Bois's fictional portraits of African-American women emphasize and romanticize the strength of black women. They thus differ from his nonfiction writing regarding individual African-American women. Although Du Bois makes no chauvinistic pronouncements like the aristocratic ones characterizing his early writings on the Talented Tenth, his nonfiction minimizes black female agency. Without misogynist dogma, his writings naturalize the dominance of black males in African-American political discourse.

Du Bois's Profeminism

> The uplift of women is, next to the problem of the color line and the peace movement, our greatest modern cause. When, now, two of these movements—women and color—combine in one, the combination has deep meaning.
>
> —W. E. B. Du Bois

In the above quote from his 1920 essay "The Damnation of Women," Du Bois cites three "great causes": the struggles for racial justice, peace, and women's equality.[1] His use of the phrase "next to" does not refer to a sequential order of descending importance. Concerns for racial equality, international peace, and women's emancipation combine to form the complex, integrative character of Du Bois's analysis. With a politics remarkably progressive for his time (and ours), Du Bois confronted race, class, and gender oppression while maintaining conceptual and political linkages between the struggles to end racism, sexism, and war. He linked his primary concern, ending white supremacy—*The Souls of Black Folk* (1903) defines the color line as the twentieth century's central problem—to the attainment of international peace and justice. In his analysis integrating the various components of African-American liberation and world peace, gender and later economic analyses were indispensable. Exploring Du Bois's relationship to that "deep meaning" embodied in women and color, we examine his representation of African-American women and his selective memory of the agency of his contemporaries Anna Julia Cooper and Ida B. Wells-Barnett.

Du Bois's writings champion women's rights, denounce female exploitation, and extol women as heroic strugglers. But while condemning the oppression of African-American women, Du Bois veiled the individual achievements of women such as Cooper and Wells-Barnett from the political landscape. In his profeminist politics, he obscured black women's radical agency and intellectualism. Here *feminist* refers to women's gender-progressive politics, and *profeminist* denotes male advocates of women's equality. In examining the contradictory aspects of Du Bois's profeminism, we should consider his political actions on behalf of women's rights, his representations of black women, and the place of African-American women in his non-fictional essays and political autobiographies. In theory and practice Du Bois opposed women's subjugation. But his political representations of and relations with influential female leaders reflect a considerable ambivalence toward black women's political independence.

A vocal supporter of women's equality and a tireless critic of patriarchy, Du Bois provided important advocacy for ending women's oppression. He consistently emphasized the equality of females with the least rights—African-American girls and women. Bettina Aptheker, a pioneering feminist scholar and interpreter of Du Bois's profeminism, notes that Du Bois began his scientific studies of Africans and African-Americans "in an era when predominant scientific and theological opinion held the Negro to be an inferior, if not subhuman, form."[2] As "a pivotal figure in the struggle for human rights," writes Aptheker, Du Bois was also "strikingly advanced in his views on women . . . a conspicuous theme in much of his work is the subjugation of women, especially Black women."[3]

The theme of women's subjugation is dominant in "The Damnation of Women." The essay argues for the liberation of females from domestic exploitation: "Only at the sacrifice of intelligence and the chance to do their best work can the majority of modern women bear children. This is the damnation of women"(164). Such declarations by Du Bois are often highlighted by those who note his profeminist activism. Aptheker documents that through *The Crisis,* Du Bois celebrated women in the "Men of the Month" column popularizing race leaders. (David Levering Lewis notes how white women were initially privileged by Du Bois in this column.) He also condemned lynching, violent attacks, and sexual assaults against black women as well as white men's violence against white women. An advocate of women's enfranchisement, Du Bois was invited to address the predominantly white National American Woman Suffrage Association.[4] In January 1906, African-American women in New York state formed a women's Du Bois Circle. Charter members of this group, an auxiliary to the male-dominated Niagara Movement, formed in 1905, gathered to support and popularize the work of Du Bois. They also organized around social issues and sex education.[5] Despite opposition from some of the original all-male organization, such as Monroe Trotter, Du Bois successfully worked to ensure the inclusion of women in this leadership group. He also organized, unilaterally, a Massachusetts Niagara Women's Auxiliary.[6] These and other efforts attest to his standing as a profeminist; however, as we shall see below, Du Bois's profeminism proved problematic.

Holding exceptionally progressive positions on gender equality, sexual violence, and the victimization of women and girls, Du Bois condemned sexual assaults and endorsed initiatives waged by the women's movement. His profeminist positions censured white society's denigration of African Americans. In a strong denunciation of white males' sexual violence against black females, he wrote: "I shall never forgive, neither in this world nor the world to come ... [the white South's] wanton and continued and persistent insulting of the black womanhood which it sought and seeks to prostitute to its lust."[7] Here, Du Bois eloquently condemns the hypocrisy of the prevailing sexual politics that legitimized violence against women: "All womanhood is hampered today because the world on which it is emerging is a world that tries to worship both virgins and mothers and in the end despises motherhood and despoils virgins."[8]

With references to Du Bois's essays on women's oppression, Lewis compares the familial patriarch with the public advocate of women's rights, describing Du Bois as a "theoretical feminist whose advocacy could erupt with the force of a volcano."[9] But Du Bois's condemnations of sexism and racial-sexual violence appear skewed by this "theoretical feminism" that simultaneously condemns social injustice and reproduces gender dominance. For Lewis, Du Bois's progressive sexual politics strongly emerge in his fiction, particularly his first novel, *The Quest of the Silver Fleece* (1911):

> *The Quest* reflected the force and sincerity of Du Bois's feminism, his credo that the degree of society's enlightenment and of the empowerment of disadvantaged classes and races was ultimately to be measured by its willingness to emancipate women—and, above all, black women. What he would later affirm with pistol-shot accuracy was found on virtually every page of the novel: that the race question is "at bottom simply a matter of the ownership of women; white men want the right to own and use all women, colored and white, and they resent any intrusion of colored men into this domain."[10]

Through his writings, we easily ascertain that Du Bois's response to the query "Should women be emancipated?" is an emphatic "Yes!" Answering the question "By whom?" is more difficult. His nonfiction presents vague and generalizing portraits of the agency of his female contemporaries. As Lewis notes, Du Bois largely reserves detailed depictions of specific black women leaders for fictive characters. In his nonfiction essays and autobiographies, Du Bois withholds from his female contemporaries the recognition given his invented women.[11]

Feminist Assessments of Du Bois's Representations of Women

Rather than providing a critical analysis of Du Bois's profeminist politics, accepting them at their face value seems to be the norm. A few scholars analyze gender relations to offer a more critical assessment of Du Bois's sexual politics. For example, Patricia Morton and Nagueyalti Warren demystify Du

Bois's symbolic treatment of black women, analyzing the ways in which his contributions paradoxically reproduced male elites or gendered black intellectualism. For Morton, Du Bois "was a pioneer in the transformation" of antiblack woman stereotypes "into empowering symbols of worth."[12] Through his literary representations of black women, Du Bois rewrote the place of African-American women in history. His representations obscured women's political agency with symbolic imagery that undermined the pragmatic politics of his profeminism. Consequently, Morton argues that, given the black tradition of "idealized and ambivalent images of black women"[13] that informed his work, Du Bois's challenges to denigrating stereotypes of African-American females failed to "reconstruct black women as full human beings in history."[14] In idealizing the "black mother" as community and family caretaker and linking femininity to motherhood, Du Bois's "emphasis on the primacy of women" and his "feminized symbolization of the virtues he attributed to the Negro race" led him to employ the "all-mother" as "both the controlling metaphor of his vision of black womanhood" and "his mystique of race."[15] Morton contends Du Bois's reading of history discerned a "legacy of survival and strength" rooted in the African-American woman "epitomizing and nurturing the ability of her race to move ahead into the future."[16] His historical works praise women such as Sojourner Truth and Harriet Tubman but focus on male leaders.[17] For Morton, his writings venerated "a not more worthy, but a finer type of black woman" who embodied, in Du Bois's words, the delicate "beauty and striving for self-realization which is as characteristic of the Negro soul as is its quaint strength and sweet laughter." Illustrating how his romanticization obscured political specificity and women's radical agency, Morton quotes Du Bois's description of Mary Shadd in *Darkwater*: "a refined, mulatto woman" of "ravishing dream-born beauty" whose "sympathy and sacrifice" were "characteristic of Negro womanhood." Morton points out that Shadd was also a confrontational abolitionist noted for independence, strength of character, and intelligence.

Du Bois's casting of black women as types, maintains Morton, transformed antiblack female stereotypes or caricatures such as the "mammy" into that of the black Christian martyr.

However, the icon of black female martyr or noble sufferer, redeemed through crucifixion, cannot accurately depict the defiant militancy of race women such as Wells-Barnett. Nagueyalti Warren examines how Du Bois's fiction depicts African-American women as victims and survivors. Surmising that his representations mythologize female victimization as well as agency, Warren argues that Du Bois's *Darkwater* uses "the Black Madonna or messianic symbol" as a "literary archetype" to project "a covert image of powerlessness"; this "canonizing of virginity and immaculate conception" strips the woman of "the power and control of her body."[18] For Warren, the "strength of the positive, strong African American woman" paints her as "invincible" as this strength is "mythicized to the almost total exclusion of her victimization."[19]

Both profound strength and deep suffering exist in Du Bois's depictions of African-American women. In general, his writings present varied and contradictory relationships with African American women. He reveals a symbiosis with his fictional female protagonists and admiration for the generic, composite symbol of womanhood in African-American women's suffering and strength. Du Bois's writings also show a reverence for his mother, familial women as well as personal friends and acquaintances, profeminist politics, and a censorious revisionism in obscuring the pioneering works of Cooper and Wells-Barnett. The diverse and conflictual nature of these relationships point to a "double consciousness" muddled with the contradictions of his gender politics.

Undoubtedly, the multiple oppressions and brutalities that women of African descent battled moved Du Bois to empathy and outrage. His 1914 poem "The Burden of Black Women" pays tribute to the trials of African-American women:

> Dark daughters of the lotus leaves that watch
> the Southern sea,
> Wan spirit of a prisoned soul a-panting to
> be free;
> The muttered music of thy streams, the
> whispers of the deep
> Have kissed each other in God's name and
> kissed a world to sleep[20]

This poem echoes the sensibilities of "The Damnation of Women": "To no modern race does its women mean so much as to the Negro nor come so near to the fulfillment of its meaning."[21] Despite the moral sentiment and political commitment, those women, including the ones informing his politics, largely remain nameless in Du Bois's nonfiction. African-American women were an essential cause to be championed for Du Bois. Still, those black women leaders, whom Du Bois did not create as fictional characters, would have a difficult time finding themselves in his writings.

Educational Elites:
Anna Julia Cooper and Du Bois

Just as it is disingenuous to minimize Du Bois's significant contributions toward women's equality, it would also be deceptive to ignore his problematic representations of and political relationships with independent, influential African-American women activists.

The writings and political works of Cooper and Wells-Barnett are so significant in the life-struggles of their era that they compel juxtaposition with the work of Du Bois. Both Cooper and Wells-Barnett worked with, were influenced by, and influenced Du Bois. At times all three were members of the same organizations. Each struggled with and critiqued white supremacy and the conservative segments of African-American leadership. Eventually each leader was isolated from mainstream African-American leadership for his or her radical commitments. They were also alienated from one another. Du Bois rebuffed Cooper's and Wells-Barnett's independently made overtures to work with him. Neither woman left a record of having sought the other out as colleague and supporter.

Hazel Carby observes that black American history commonly perceives the turn of the century "as the Age of Washington and Du Bois." Such a view, writes Carby, marginalizes black women's political contributions during "a period of intense intellectual activity and productivity" marked by the development of black female-led institutions and organizations. In the "Age of Washington and Du Bois," Cooper was a well-known figure among black leaders. One of three African-American women invited to speak at the World's Congress of Representative Women in 1893, she later presented a paper, "The Negro Problem in America," at the 1900 Pan-African Congress Conference in London. Cooper had helped to organize that first Pan-African conference and served as a member of its Executive Committee, working alongside Du Bois, another prominent conference organizer. She cofounded the Colored Women's YWCA in 1905, the same year that Du Bois founded the Niagara Movement. Widowed as a young woman, and childless, she worked as a lifelong activist in African-American liberation. As principal of the prestigious M Street (later the Dunbar) High School in Washington, D.C., Cooper, who had a graduate degree from Oberlin, structured a curriculum enabling her students to be admitted to Harvard, Yale, and other prestigious universities. As a result of her successes, outraged European Americans and alarmed African Americans on the school board forced her out of the principalship. Racism and unsubstantiated rumors of sexual impropriety were the basis of the dismissal.[22] Continuing her activism as an educator, she obtained her Ph.D. from the Sorbonne in 1930 at the age of sixty-six. As an elder, Cooper assumed the presidency of Frelinghuysen University, an independent school known as the "College Extension for Working People" for employed working-class African Americans in Washington, D.C.[23]

In advocating liberal arts education for African Americans and criticizing Booker T. Washington's race-based ideology of vocational training, Cooper became an important ally of Du Bois. As a response to Cooper's urging and her declaration of support for financing and distribution for such a publication, Du Bois embarked upon writing that led to *Black Reconstruction* (1935); however, he never acknowledged Cooper's request that *The Crisis* serialize her biographical sketch of Charlotte Grimke, the prominent activist-intellectual.[24] He nevertheless drew upon Cooper's intellectual resources more than once. Paula Giddings writes that Cooper's 1892 political autobiography, *A Voice from the South*, provides a "treatise on race and feminism ... [that] anticipated much of the later work of W. E. B. Du Bois."[25] Du Bois's later democratic revisions of the Talented

Tenth adapt Cooper's gender critique and expand upon her assertion that elite African Americans were neither the panacea nor standard for black liberation.

In *A Voice from the South,* Cooper calls for a mass, female standard for evaluating the effectiveness of African-American praxis, a decade before Du Bois penned his concept of "The Talented Tenth." Cooper's standard to gauge the efficacy of African-American praxis is defined by the mass of black people: "Is it not evident then that as individual workers for this race we must address ourselves with no half-hearted zeal to this feature of our mission [the lives of the masses and women]. The need is felt and must be recognized by all."[26] Rejecting the idealized "great leader" and the premise that the lives and (real and potential) contributions of elites were more consequential than those of laborers, she set new criteria for race leadership. Dispensing with black intellectual male elites as representative of black freedom, Cooper reasserted the whole, starting with the bottom, as the measure for liberation. Emphasizing the conditions of working-class and poor black women, she writes, "our present record of eminent men, when placed beside the actual status of the race in America today, proves that no man can represent the race." For Cooper, "Only the black woman can say, 'when and where I enter, in the quiet, undisputed dignity of my womanhood, without violence and without suing or special patronage, then and there the whole *Negro race enter with me.'* "[27]

Quoting Cooper's now-famous "When and where I enter" sentence in "The Damnation of Women," Du Bois fails to mention her by name, prefacing his remarks with the proprietary phrase: "As one of our women writes."[28] Du Bois's selective quotations curtail Cooper's full argument; the passage preceding the quote more accurately reflects the critical mandate for black leadership echoing throughout *A Voice from the South.* When Cooper argues "we must address ourselves with no half-hearted zeal to this feature of our mission,"[29] she refers to the uplift of the masses of African-American women. Du Bois's failure to name Cooper renders her anonymous. With no attributed source, his citation allows Cooper to disappear as her words appear. In her absence, readers were unlikely to juxtapose Du Bois with Cooper. Nor would they fully benefit from her own gender analyses. Her anonymity allows Du Bois to appear as a transgender representative for the entire vilified and oppressed race. Mary Helen Washington contextualizes this erasure of Cooper's name within masculinist and patriarchal thought. "The intellectual discourse of black women of the 1890s, and particularly Cooper's embryonic black feminist analysis," she writes, "was ignored because it was by and about women and therefore thought not to be as significantly about the race as writings by and about men."[30] This "embryonic black feminism" maintained that the criterion for African-American progress centers on the emancipation of black women, who labor the longest for the least wages under the most numbing and exploitive conditions. Du Bois himself suggests this position by using her quote. Sharing Cooper's advocacy for the struggles of impoverished black women, he detaches from her depiction of leadership as the attribute of black female elites.

Cooper's gender politics revolved around poor black women's struggles and elite black women's agency. But Du Bois's evolving class politics allowed him to, theoretically, attribute greater agency to *poor* black women workers and laborers. Du Bois's later writings surpass Cooper's 1892 work in democratizing agency. Cooper repudiates masculine elites, or privileged black male intellectuals. However, her repudiations do not extend to feminine elites, or privileged black female intellectuals. Cooper countered the dominance of male elites with that of female elites and remained somewhat oblivious of the limitations of her caste and class-based ideology. Cooper's 1892 book failed to argue that the intellectual and leadership abilities of black women laborers equaled those of black women college graduates, whereas Du Bois's later revisions of the Talented Tenth included nonelite black women and men. In this respect, we see that Du Bois's maturing politics were less hampered by the cultural conservatism of bourgeois notions of respectability for (black) women. Black women elites such as Cooper "had a great stake in the prestige, the respectability, and the gentility guaranteed by the politics of true womanhood."[31] Conforming to standards of white, bourgeois respectability, black female elites sought a shield from racial-sexual denigration. The class-biased strictures placed upon middle-class African-American women were partly self-imposed. Du Bois had written critically of this "cult of true womanhood" in bourgeois femininity and white society's racialized gender hypocrisy. Cooper's embrace of conventional femininity led her to minimize and evade the leadership that nonbourgeois black women could offer to their elite counterparts.

Not all middle-class race women were trapped by rigid social conventions. In the same year as the appearance of Cooper's *A Voice from the South,* Wells-Barnett's *Southern Horrors: Lynch Law in All Its Phases* was published. The antilynching crusader embodied race militancy and intellectualism. Her manifest responsible womanhood both reflected and rejected the cult of true womanhood. Wells-Barnett's treatment of the volatile racial-sexual politics of lynching deals with issues of race, sex, and violence unmentioned in *A Voice From the South*'s pioneering discussions of sexual violence. As the lioness of the antilynching crusades, Wells-Barnett endured death threats, the destruction of her Memphis press by a lynch mob, and decades of exile from the South. Transgressing the notions of feminine gentility and masculine courage, she traveled extensively, armed with a pistol, to document and organize against lynchings.

Frayed Alliances: Ida B. Wells-Barnett and Du Bois

Lynchings had a tremendous impact on black intellectuals and academics during Du Bois's, Cooper's, and Wells-Barnett's era. Both Wells-Barnett and Mary Church Terrell lost friends in the 1892 Memphis lynching and were radicalized by the murders. Wells-Barnett's posthumously published memoir, *Crusade for Justice,* recalls how the lynchings of her associates and friends in Memphis brutally disabused her of her initial belief that lynching was a preventive measure to protect white female virtue from black male sexual savagery.

Du Bois's desire to respond effectively to the atrocities left him disaffected with academic life. Lynchings transfigured Du Bois, politicizing him into a militancy that left the Harvard Ph.D. ill-suited for academic society and liberal institutions. Du Bois's *Darkwater* short story about lynching, "Jesus Christ in Texas," speaks to his profound pessimism concerning racist violence. Two decades later, *Dusk of Dawn* describes how racial atrocities haunted and transformed his early adult life: "Lynching was a continuing and recurrent horror during my college days: from 1885 through 1894, seventeen hundred Negroes were lynched in America. Each death was a scar upon my soul, and led me on to conceive the plight of other minority groups."[32] The pressing need to confront racist violence furthered Du Bois's disaffection for and alienation in academic life.[33] Du Bois writes eloquently of his first encounter with lynching: "There cut across this plan which I had as a scientist, a red ray which could not be ignored, I remember when it first, as it were, startled me to my feet; a poor Negro in central Georgia, Sam Hose, had killed his landlord's wife." Having drafted "a careful and reasoned statement concerning the evident facts"[34] for publication in the Atlanta *Constitution* and en route to deliver his editorial to the newspaper, he recalls: "I did not get there. On the way news met me: Sam Hose had been lynched, and they said that his knuckles were on exhibition at a grocery store farther down on Mitchell Street, along which I was walking. I turned back to the University."[35] Shaken and galvanized by this close proximity to a lynching victim, Du Bois writes that thereafter he resolved that "one could not be a calm, cool, and detached scientist while Negroes were lynched, murdered and starved."[36]

The late nineteenth-century and early twentieth-century antilynching campaigns included and directly affected more African Americans than the university education campaigns of Du Bois and Cooper. Only a small percentage of African Americans attained university educations. But all were susceptible to the violence of a lynch mob; poorer blacks tended to be more vulnerable to racial violence. Du Bois and Wells-Barnett, a former schoolteacher, participated in both the liberal arts education campaigns and the antilynching crusades. Advocating liberal arts education for African Americans, Wells-Barnett became a proponent of Du Bois's social thought. *Crusade for Justice* recounts how influential black and white leaders at a Chicago meeting debated the merits of *The Souls of Black Folk*, although most of those present, writes Wells-Barnett, were "united in condemning Mr. Du Bois's views."[37] Ida B. Wells-Barnett, and husband, Ferdinand, championed Du Bois's critique of Booker T. Washington's promotion of industrial education as a panacea. Wells-Barnett's stands in the educational debates, which placed her in the line of Washington's fire, were consistent with her outspoken opposition to lynching. The failure of Du Bois's memoirs to mention her work in the educational campaigns is in tandem with his silence about her extraordinary antilynching activism. Despite Wells-Barnett's exemplary research and publications,[38] her political courage and radical analysis of the sexual politics of lynching, Du Bois's autobiographical writings on antilynching mostly ignore Wells-Barnett.

As one of the most significant human rights campaigns in postbellum United States at the turn of the century, the antilynching crusades generated a black liberation movement in which black women were prominent public leaders. African-American women initiated the first major antilynching campaign in 1892. They embarked on this extremely dangerous work without the backing of any influential, multiracial organization such as the NAACP, which was not formed until 1909. With uncompromising demands for justice, women such as Florida Ruffin Ridley and Mary Church Terrell and Wells-Barnett exposed and challenged the U.S. "red record" of African Americans brutalized, imprisoned, and murdered at the whim of whites. Skeptical that media, court, or mob prosecution was motivated by the desire to end sexual violence, black women created a legacy of investigative reporting and social analyses to ascertain facts distorted or denied by the media or legal institutions.

Wells-Barnett demystified the racial-sexual politics of interracial sex and exposed the duplicity of the legal system and its complicity in lynchings in language few male or female race leaders dared to use. Her writings discredited the apologists for lynchings by noting that the rape charge was used only in a fraction of lynchings and was generally used against men innocent of sexual assault. Her arguments paraphrase Frederick Douglass's critique of postbellum rationalizations. (Like Du Bois, she did not always credit her sources; *Crusade for Justice* does not fully acknowledge Douglass's influence on antilynching activism or the contributions of other activists.) Wells-Barnett's unique contribution to the antilynching movement was her documentation and incendiary rhetoric on the hypocrisy of American sexual politics in which white men were the predominant assailants of white and black females, yet masked their violence, as well as their attempts to politically and economically dominate blacks, with racist terrorism.

Du Bois built on and benefited from the political and intellectual radicalism of Wells-Barnett without fully acknowledging his indebtedness. By refusing to name Wells-Barnett and her dynamic leadership, his writings erase her contribution much as he renders Cooper anonymous. Given their incendiary tone, Du Bois likely could not use Wells-Barnett's words, as he had Cooper's, without sharing her stigma and isolation as too combative in antiracist activism. Failing to document Wells-Barnett's antilynching agency, Du Bois obscures both her individual contributions and the range of antiracist militancy and radicalism. Consequently, Du Bois forgoes a critical examination of Wells-Barnett's political thought and so misses an opportunity to analyze the "deep meaning" of the lives of radical African-American women activists.

Though neither as prolific a writer nor as formally educated as Du Bois, Wells-Barnett was widely influential in her day. With the decline in mob lynchings, her prominence waned while Du Bois's prestige increased in the first part of the twentieth century. As Du Bois's writings were increasingly "mainstreamed" through the NAACP, her work was marginalized. In part, this occurred because of her uncompromising politics and opposition to Booker T. Washington. In retaliation to the Barnetts's political independence and vocal critiques, Washington used his influence over the Afro-American press to cripple the publishing and journalistic careers of the Barnetts.

Although Wells-Barnett and Du Bois were radicalized by lynchings, antilynching organizing unraveled rather than cemented the ties between them. In August 1908, white race riots and the lynchings of blacks in Springfield, Illinois, led progressive European Americans and African Americans to form what would become the NAACP. As founding members, Du Bois and Wells-Barnett were active in the first meetings at New York City's Cooper Union. From the floor, Wells-Barnett urged the assembly not to compromise its agenda with that of the Tuskegee machine.[39] Seated on the dais, Du Bois wielded influence behind doors in closed meetings of the nominating committee for the organization's initial leadership. Unlike Wells-Barnett, Du Bois was not isolated by white and black NAACP liberals for his radicalism and opposition to Washington as an accommodationist.

Du Bois's autobiographical record of the founding of the NAACP omits any reference to Wells-Barnett being ostracized at the NAACP founding conference. He writes: "The members of the Niagara Movement were invited into the new conference, but all save [William Monroe] Trotter and Ida Wells-Barnett came to form the backbone of the new organization."[40] *Dusk of Dawn* does not explain Wells-Barnett's absence from a key organization formed to fight a crusade she had pioneered. Nor does Du Bois refer to maneuvers to bar her from NAACP organizational leadership. One of two African-American women signing the Call for the National Negro Conference in 1909 that led to the formation of the NAACP, Wells-Barnett's name was left off of the list of the Conference's Committee of Forty assigned to develop the NAACP. According to her memoir, in seeking a representative from the Niagara Movement, Du Bois substituted for her name that of an absent Dr. Charles E. Bentley. Wells-Barnett also speculates that Mary White Ovington's friendship and influence with Du Bois led to "the deliberate intention of Dr. Du Bois to ignore me and my work."[41] Ovington, who later chaired the NAACP, was on less than cordial terms with Wells-Barnett. Lewis minimizes Wells-Barnett's account to argue that philanthropist Oswald Garrison Villard's aversion to radicalism and anti-Tuskegee activists bears the primary culpability for Wells-Barnett's isolation. Yet Du Bois, also a radical and an outspoken critic of Washington, was not similarly censored. Lewis writes that Du Bois attempted to achieve moderate representation in leadership and so "was probably motivated far less by personal animus than by well-intentioned (though possibly sexist and perhaps mistaken) calculations."[42] Whatever the motivation, this slighting marginalized the era's most effective antilynching militant. After the restoration of her name to the Committee of Forty, following protests by herself and others, Wells-Barnett joined NAACP national leadership in name only. Holt notes: "The singular irony of her career is that Wells-Barnett, the most prominent voice opposing lynching over the preceding decade and the most persistent advocate of a national organization to combat racial oppression, was not among the leaders of the NAACP."[43] Wells-Barnett's bitterness must have been edged with a sense of betrayal. For years she had been an avid supporter of Du Bois and a critic of Washington, and, as a consequence, she suffered the backlash of the Tuskegee machine.[44] She consistently supported Du Bois until their break at the NAACP founding conference; her support was never reciprocated.

The most glaring omission by Du Bois regarding the significance of Wells-Barnett's antiviolence activism occurs in *Dusk of Dawn*. Here, in his depiction of the Steve Greene and Pink Franklin cases, he erases her unparalleled contributions to countering lynching. In 1910, Steve Greene arrived in Chicago, wounded from a shootout with a white Arkansas farmer who tried to indenture or enslave him on his farm. Greene was extradited to Arkansas, ostensibly to be lynched. However, Wells-Barnett's Negro Fellowship League raised money and organized a defense committee that safely spirited Greene to Canada. Lewis comments on Du Bois's selective recollection: "Curiously, Du Bois's coverage of the dramatic events behind Greene's removal from the clutches of his Arkansas warders omitted any mention of Wells-Barnett and her Negro Fellowship League."[45] Several months earlier, in a similar case, the NAACP had struggled and failed to save Pink Franklin from a legal lynching. Franklin had shot and killed a white farmer breaking into his house in order to return Franklin to sharecropping. Such "curious omissions" concerning Wells-Barnett are not aberrational in Du Bois's autobiographies.

After military service in World War I, African-American soldiers returned with raised expectations for racial equality, economic opportunity, and democratic politic. Instead, they were met with a white backlash. Lynchings increased, particularly in the South. *Dusk of Dawn* refers to the September 1917 military lynchings in Texas of soldiers in the Twenty-fourth Colored Infantry who participated in an armed rebellion against the repressive acts of local whites.[46] One-hundred armed black troops, stationed in Houston, in response to racist assaults, marched on the city. The resulting confrontation left sixteen whites and four black soldiers dead. Following the revolt, the U.S. Army executed nineteen soldiers and court-martialed and imprisoned fifty. Du Bois makes no mention of Wells-Barnett's campaign to stop the executions and free imprisoned members of the Twenty-fourth Infantry. Wells-Barnett describes the soldiers as "martyred." Her agitation for the release and pardon of the Twenty-Fourth Infantry was so noteworthy that Secret Service agents threatened her with charges of wartime sedition and imprisonment if she continued demonstrating on behalf of the prisoners. Despite government threats, she extended her organizing and remained free of incarceration.

Dusk of Dawn forgoes relaying information about Wells-Barnett's activism to detail the expansion of NAACP organizing against lynching. In 1919, notes Du Bois, the NAACP leadership was instrumental in two thousand antilynching public meetings and a government investigation of the Chicago riot; it also convened a national conference on lynching in New York City, which issued an address to the nation signed by prominent officials, including a former U.S. president and a then current chief justice. Du Bois writes: NAACP organized African-American political power to "make it influential and we started a campaign against lynching and mob law which was the most effective ever organized and eventually brought the end of the evil in sight."[47] Reconstructing NAACP activity as *the* antilynching movement, he writes that "Mary Talbert started the antilynching crusade, raising a defense fund of $12,000," and that NAACP Secretary James Weldon Johnson forcibly brought the Dyer Anti-Lynching Bill before Congress in 1921.[48] In his singular validation of NAACP antilynching activism, Du Bois deflects from the work of the Negro Women's Club Movement, Wells-Barnett, and other antilynching activists whose radicalism and analyses laid the foundations for later NAACP campaigns.

While describing or embellishing upon NAACP antilynching activism, Du Bois refers to the organization's internal contradictions, inefficiency, and its ideological liberalism. "Revolution," the final chapter of *Dusk of Dawn,* closes his memoir by expressing disappointment over the increasing ineffectiveness of the NAACP, an organization to which he had devoted decades of his lifework. His regrets echo those of Wells-Barnett.[49]

This antilynching crusader reflects in her own autobiography that had she been more active in its national leadership, the NAACP would have been more responsive to the dire conditions of African Americans. Lacking allies for radicalizing organizational leadership (it would seem, allies with the tenacity and militancy of Wells-Barnett), Du Bois recalls that by 1930 he had increasing doubts about the viability of NAACP liberalism. For him the organization's ideology advocated "a continued agitation which had for its object simply free entrance into the present economy of the world, that looked at political rights as an end in itself rather than as a method of reorganizing the state; and that expected through civil rights and legal judgments to reestablish freedom on a broader and firmer basis."[50] This ideology, wrote Du Bois, "was not so much wrong as short-sighted."[51] He argued that liberalism, legalism, and an inadequate economic program led the NAACP to miss an essential opportunity "to guard and better the chances of Negroes" to earn an adequate income. Du Bois in 1934 resigned as editor of *The Crisis* and from the NAACP national board. It is uncertain if a successful Du Bois/Wells-Barnett alliance might have influenced NAACP national leadership towards civil rights radicalism and a program for economic justice. In any case, such an alliance was apparently undesirable on Du Bois's part.

Despite his distance from Cooper and Wells-Barnett, Du Bois's increasing radicalism led him to develop a structural analysis of black oppression. The later writings of Du Bois, who worked until his nineties, address economic exploitation, capitalism, and state oppression, issues that Cooper's and Wells-Barnett's analyses largely ignore.

Nonspecificity and Erasure in Du Bois's Profeminism

Specificity entails detailed accounts of agency and includes identification of subjects or political actors in accord with their deeds. The lack of specificity contextualizes Du Bois's profeminist and later proworker stances. This absence inadvertently highlights the black vanguardism that he eventually repudiates. Perhaps Du Bois's early, progressive views on women shielded him (in his own self-reflections) from criticism. This shield may blind us to the fact that his writings about African-American women noticeably erase women's political agency. Specificity and erasure inform Du Bois's gender politics. In their lack of documentation, his autobiographical records choose a generic rather than an empirical study regarding the achievements of his female and working-class contemporaries. We need not suggest that Du Bois should have written his memoirs with the impressive detail found in *Black Reconstruction*. We should only note that he reserves specificity in his memoirs and essays for fellow elites. His autobiographies privilege activists who were personal friends or acquaintances: African-American men such as Monroe Trotter and James Weldon Johnson, as well as European Americans Joel Spingarn and Mary White Ovington. In the process of democratizing black leadership, Du Bois inadvertently reinscribed the primacy of elites through his representations of political agency. Nonelite blacks and black women appear largely without specifics or names. Du Bois frequently withheld the attribute of political agency from those who had earned a place in political history.

If we address black women as a generic topic without their specificity, we obscure the radical dimensions of black politics and history. If we portray African-American women in an aggregate as victims, icons, or the embodiment of a cause, we project the notion that political change transpires without black female independence and leadership. If we assert black women's leadership in theory but minimize the empirical record of African-American women leaders, we masculinize black agency and implicitly elevate men to a superior status as intellectuals.

In studying Du Bois's treatment of women activists, we see that nonspecificity and erasure overlap to some degree. Nonspecificity promotes the disappearance of the detailed historical or empirical record. In some respects, it erases subjects, deeds and events, while simultaneously discussing them. Nonspecificity promotes erasure. With the solo appearance of the generic, the category becomes surrogate for the individual: The "black woman" replaces Wells-Barnett. The generic also supplants historical or empirical data in representation: Black women's victimization stands in place for the uniqueness of their political praxes in the suffragette movement or antilynching crusades. The documentary writer controls representation and memory in his or her use of nonspecificity and generic representations. With specificity in representation, the historical subject appears to put forth her own ideas; at times, she may interrupt the chronicler with her own voice. That intervention or corrective is no longer possible if her words are appropriated and her identity obscured (as happened with Du Bois's use of Cooper's intellectualism). If we understand "erasure" as the complete absence of representation, the refusal of agency and identity altogether, it seems obvious that representations that fail to reference marginalized groups promote the erasure of those groups in political discourse. Erasure and exclusionary bias also appear when we discuss disenfranchised peoples without the specifics of their historical and contemporary political leadership.

Some contend that Du Bois's nonspecificity regarding black women in his political writings implies no bias or attempt to elide the significant contributions of a marginalized group. To be consistent, those who argue this position must also maintain that the use of generalizing and vague discourse concerning the achievements of males and elites is a common and acceptable practice. Engaging in nonspecificity and erasure misrepresents intellectual ability and political agency and detracts from comprehensive and progressive political analyses. Gender erasure reconstructs politics as the purview of male elites. Whether the elites are determined by race, gender, or education and wealth, dominance is reasserted when racially, sexually, and economically marginalized groups are presented as categories or characterized in symbolic and abstract terms. The distance between attentiveness to black women as a category and disinterest in their political praxes creates a void in which progressivism disassembles itself.

The Heirs of Du Bois

Building upon the gift of sight that Du Bois bequeathed to progressives, we better comprehend the deep meaning that manifests when two movements for justice—women and color —combine. Evaluating our inheritance from Du Bois, as well as our own antiracist sexual politics, we can strategize for a gender progressivism that unpacks this legacy to transcend the limits of Du Bois's profeminism. Doing so requires addressing the profeminist politics in the writings of present-day progressive intellectuals.

Given the racial and sexual biases that inform our concepts of political, intellectual, and moral ability, it is unsurprising that black male intellectuals intentionally or inadvertently reproduce sexist thought. Du Bois, his profeminism notwithstanding, proved no exception to the norm. Profeminism permitted Du Bois to include women in democratic struggles; paternalism allowed him to naturalize the male intellectual. Like their predecessor(s), today's male thinkers infrequently cite or analyze African-American women's intellectual and political productivity. Contemporary African-American political thought reflects both Du Bois's profeminist politics and his gender amnesia. Gender conservatives resist while gender progressives embrace and expand upon his profeminist politics. The trickster in Du Bois's legacy though suggests that his profeminism, both its advocacy for gender equality and its erasure of radical black women's agency, might be a cornerstone in the construction of the contemporary black intellectual as male elite. In current works by black males, we encounter writings on black politics and history in which black women disappear or have only token inclusion; we also find writings that extol black women's political and intellectual power while excising the details of their radicalisms.

Regarding the erasure of radical women from black history, both feminist and profeminist writers seem to have inherited Du Bois's penchant for selective memory. Contemporary writers diminish the significance of black women activists and intellectuals with various objectives in mind. For example, both profeminists and feminists may elide women's agency in order to reify black women's status as victims of black male dominance. Minimizing the presence and impact of black women's radicalism on black liberation struggle promotes generalizations about black patriarchy. Some writers condemn patriarchal political history that ignores women only to highlight women's contributions in ways that further ignorance of African-American women's radical agency. In this sense, their progressive works are wedded to male elitism and sexist censorship. The following chapters focus on feminist erasures of black women's militant agency; here it is useful to explore Du Bois's male lineage among academics.

Some contemporary profeminist writings, while reductively universalizing black male leadership in African-American politics, offer a subtle erasure of black radicalism in their generally progressive sexual politics. The privileging of males in black intellectualism produces male elites. Hence, male leadership is naturalized as universal and normative in the history of black thought and politics. Patriarchal myopia deradicalizes, as does a profeminism that obscures the roles of women in political and intellectual movements. Deleting the contributions of black women from African-American political thought and radicalism is a fairly common practice that produces flawed historiography and political analysis. Consider how Paul Gilroy's *The Black Atlantic* fails to discuss the prominent African-American women activists-intellectuals who also crossed the Atlantic—Jessie Fauset, Anna Julia Cooper, Ida B. Wells, and Mary Church Terrell.[52] These female contemporaries and colleagues of Du Bois either studied or organized in Europe. Their histories, and with them much of black history, disappear in Gilroy's depiction of cultural hybridity and migratory intellectualism. (This male-biased account of Afro-American intellectualism is compatible with the larger antiradicalism of his project, which decontextualizes Du Bois and African-American culture from radical politics to argue for the primacy of European influence on Du Bois's thought and African-American culture.[53]) Gilroy's academic scholarship on blacks renders black women invisible. (David Roediger's *Wages of Whiteness* also provides an example of the erasure of women; citing Du Bois as a major influence on his understanding of race in class formations, Roediger fails to reference women workers in his study of Irish [American] workers.)[54]

Contrary to Gilroy, other black male writers draw attention to the masculinist (historical) erasure of black women. Manning Marable's commentary offers one example. Given the pervasiveness of male elites, it is unusual for African-American male intellectuals to discuss black paternalism or sexual opportunism vis-à-vis black females. Counter to the norm, Marable's essay "Grounding with My Sisters" denounces the erasure of African-American women from political texts and memory. Although increasingly we find similar writings by black male profeminists, Marable's 1983 text was one of the earliest statements of such politics. Describing "Black social history" as "profoundly patriarchal" and shaped by male bias, Marable writes: "The sexist critical framework of American white history has been accepted by Black male scholars; the reconstruction of our past, the reclamation of our history from the ruins, has been an enterprise wherein women have been too long segregated."[55] A decade before the 1990s explosion in literature published on black Americans, Marable flagged a critical weakness that led to not only gender-distorted notions of political agency but also skewed scholarship.

Marable's own profeminist contributions offer an interesting corrective. "Groundings With My Sisters" describes patriarchy in the black liberation movements and the limits of some feminisms. Marable quotes Michelle Wallace's observation that: "Every black male leader of the 1960's accepted and perpetuated the idea of Black Macho, the notion that all political and social power was somehow sexual, and that the possession of a penis was the symbol of revolution."[56] He notes that this statement is accurate concerning tendencies; patriarchy and misogyny existed within the black movement, yet, machismo politics cannot be generalized to all male leaders. Former Student Nonviolent Coordinating Committee leader James Forman's autobiography, the *Making of Black Revolutionaries*, praises Ruby D. Robinson and acknowledges Ella Baker's pivotal leadership role in the civil rights movement. Radical women active in the movement do not use such a broad brush to paint the gender politics of movement organizers. Assata Shakur describes how sexism and elitism led her to leave the Black Panther Party, yet writes of her coactivist Zayd Shakur: "I also respected him because he refused to become part of the macho cult that was official in the BPP. He never voted on issues or took a position just to be one of the boys."[57] The Montgomery Women's Political Caucus organized the 1955 bus boycott with E. D. Nixon and chose the politically inexperienced Martin Luther King Jr. as its titular leader for appearances of respectability and authority tied to middle-class male clergy. Although women constituted a good part of the civil rights leadership, Wallace suggests black civil rights leadership as uniformly sexist. Profeminists may follow this feminist message that diverges from women activists' own accounts of the complexity of gender struggles within the movements and promotes erasure of women's leadership. Yet, African-American women activists cannot be reduced to mere gender victims or subordinates in a movement they designed and waged.

Interventions that call attention to black male abuses in political leadership and male privilege in historiography are essential. Interventions that diminish the significance of black female activism in order to project images of black female victimization offer problematic profeminist politics. While eliding black female militant leadership to characterize black women as politically paralyzed by black male dominance makes points about black patriarchy, it also reinscribes male elitism into black intellectualism and radical politics. Furthering the elision of black female militants, truncating notions of black agency and intellectualism, some black feminist writings offer ahistorical deconstructions of black women radicals that prove compatible with the erasures of profeminist writers.

Ida B. Wells with Betty Moss, widow of lynching victim Thomas Moss and children (one is likely the
Moss's daughter Maurine, who was also Wells's god-
child), Memphis, Tennessee, circa 1892.

3

Sexual Politics
An Antilynching Crusader
in Revisionist Feminism

[In] this war against Negro progress is the substitution of mob rule for courts of justice throughout the South. Judges, juries, sheriffs, and jailors . . . are all white men,
and thus make it impossible for a negro to escape the penalty for any crime he com-
mits. Then whenever a black man is charged with any crime against a white person
these mobs without disguise take him from the jail in broad daylight, hang, shoot or
burn him as their fancy dictates.

—Ida B. Wells-Barnett
Crusade for Justice

By waging the antilynching campaigns as resistance to both
racial and sexual violence,[1] crusaders such as Ida B. Wells-
Barnett established a political language to critique U.S. racial-
sexual politics and the duplicity of the white press, courts, and
police. Transforming the meanings of lynching, countering
repressive violence, African-American women led the antilynching campaign by deconstructing the myth of the black
rapist.[2] For instance, in *Southern Horrors* and *A Red Record*, Ida
B. Wells-Barnett documented that the overwhelming connection between most interracial rape cases and lynching was that
black women and children were raped prior to and during
lynchings, as well as lynched with black males who assisted
them in resisting or avenging rape by white males.[3] Women
pointed out that by inverting the reality of racialized sexual
violence, whites grossly exaggerated the likelihood of black
male assaults on white women. A rare phenomenon for white

women, interracial rape was a constant nightmare for black women. Most interracial rapes in the United States were (and remain) committed by white males.[4] Logically, if a rational connection between lynching and the prosecution of sex crimes existed, the majority of lynch victims would have been white men.

Today, using the historical, black female-led campaigns to reflect on contemporary politics surrounding (interracial) sexual violence, black feminists offer diverse responses to the campaigns and the women who led them. Conflicting depictions of antiracist activism and speech regarding charges of interracial sexual violence surround the figure of Wells-Barnett. As the icon of the antilynching crusade, she has come to represent a type of militant black womanhood immersed in controversy.

For instance, Alice Walker and Valerie Smith represent Ida B. Wells-Barnett by filtering the image of the antilynching crusader through revisionist feminism, in order to explore the racial-sexual politics of interracial rape. Walker's short story "Advancing Luna—And Ida B. Wells"[5] reconstructs Wells-Barnett's sexual politics to portray her as blinded by race-paranoia and cowed by racist violence into irrational denials concerning black males' assaults of white females. In an equally novel but harsher depiction, Smith's essay "Split Affinities"[6] represents Wells-Barnett as embittered with antiwhite resentment, a counterfeminist whose hostility toward white women reinforced moral indifference to sexual violence. In their respective portraits of Wells-Barnett, neither writer offers much in terms of historical specificity. Reconstructing Wells-Barnett, and by extension the women-led antilynching campaigns, in order to represent a form of antiracist radicalism embodied as gender regressive, Walker and Smith argue against a type of female race militancy. For each womanist/black feminist, Wells-Barnett exemplifies the race woman misled by black identity politics into reactionary sexual politics.

In the following varied portraits of Wells-Barnett—as radical activist, paranoid race woman, and antiwhite counterfeminist—her sexual politics becomes the touchstone for debates about venality, black feminist intellectualism, and radicalism regarding the intersections of race, sex, and violence.

Wells-Barnett the Militant Activist

In the black female militancy of the antilynching crusades,[7] Wells-Barnett deconstructed the rationalizations for white terror: Negro domination of whites through the vote; Negro race riots; black male sexual assaults of white women. The last charge proved to be as specious as its predecessors but the most incendiary and tenacious. Wells-Barnett argued that although there was no record of a white female sexually assaulted by a black male during the Civil War,[8] and although the charge of rape was used in only a fraction of lynchings, this accusation became the general rationalization for racist violence. With this charge, Americans who considered themselves above the mob acquiesced to lynchings as a "necessary preventive measure" to protect white women; at the same time, they turned a blind eye to the more prevalent problem of white male sexual violence.

To demystify the belief that white men enforced written or unwritten laws for the protection of white women, Wells-Barnett's critique of lynching apologias exploded their psychosexual mythology and moral hypocrisy. Any chivalry toward women, writes Wells-Barnett, garners "little respect from the civilized world, when it confines itself entirely to the women who happen to be white."[9] In 1895, noting the duplicity of white men's prosecutorial performances, she wrote:

> To justify their own barbarism they assume a chivalry which they do not possess. True chivalry respects all womanhood, and no one who reads the record, as it is written in the faces of the million mulattoes in the South, will for a minute conceive that the southern white man had a very chivalrous regard for the honor due the women of his own race or respect for the womanhood which circumstances placed in his power.[10]

During this era, whites defined voluntary sexual relationships between white women and black men as sexual assaults, reconstructing consensual relations as the rape of white women. These voluntary interracial sexual associations were punishable by the death of the black male lover or sexual partner. Although white women were ostracized, institutionalized, and beaten for such alliances, they could repudiate the relationship with the charge of rape. African-American males had no such escape clause.

African-American women activists reasoned that ending lynchings both eradicated racist terror cloaked in chivalry and diminished malfeasant prosecutions of rape. Seeing the prosecution of rape as determined by the social status of the woman assaulted and that of the accused male, they pointed out the rarity of this type of interracial sexual violence, rather than categorically, and irrationally, deny that black men assault white women.

Female crusaders demanded that society acknowledge that the lynchings of African Americans had very little to do with rape and that the barbaric murders deflected attention from the prevalence of sexual violence against black women and social contempt for their sexual safety. Late nineteenth-century African-American women recognized that the myth of black (sexual) pathology excused rape. The mythology masked sexual violence against black women, and the reality that the rapists of white women were overwhelmingly white men. As a caste, white men were the moral and legal prosecutors of sexual violence, yet were, particularly if affluent, the least prosecuted and censured for sexual violence.[11]

By demystifying the idea of lynching as rape prevention and prosecution, Wells-Barnett broadened the base of anti-lynching activism to establish a foundation for moral and political resistance to American violence. Discrediting the belief that white men enforced written or unwritten laws for the protection of white women, she waged a radical campaign against lynching apologias.

Her condemnations of lynchings both electrified and offended the American public. Because of white America's refusal to end lynching, the crusade became an international one. A passage from Wells-Barnett's April 9, 1894, Liverpool special correspondence for the *Inter-Ocean* typifies what some considered to be inflammatory rhetoric and others understood as antiracist militancy: "The machinery of law and politics is in the hands of those who commit the lynching," writes the author, who proceeds to argue that "it is only wealthy white men whom the law fails to reach."[12] In contrast to the virtual immunity of the white male elite, Wells-Barnett observes: "Hundreds of Negroes including women and children are lynched for trivial offenses on suspicion and in many cases when known to be guiltless of any crime . . . the law refused to punish the murderers because it is not considered a crime to kill a Negro."[13] She concludes the passage: "Many of the cases of 'Assault' are simply adulteries between white women and colored men."[14]

Despite her polemical writings, Wells-Barnett did not categorically deny that black men assaulted white women nor did she advocate that others make such denials. The body of her work, in which the word "many" is generally used to describe false accusations of rape, makes it clear that she makes no assertion of universal innocence. (Her memoir's reprint of an 1894 letter by Florida Ruffin Ridley, excerpted below, best reveals her position.) However, Wells-Barnett demanded that white society acknowledge that actual rape had very little to do with the lynching of African Americans: "With the Southern white man, any mesalliance existing between a white woman and a colored man is a sufficient foundation for the charge of rape."[15] She argues further that in "numerous instances where colored men have been lynched on the charge of rape, it was positively known at the time of lynching, and indisputably proven after the victim's death, that the relationship sustained between the man and woman was voluntary and clandestine, and that in no court of law could even the charge of assault have been successfully maintained."[16] Noting that the "Southern white man says that it is impossible for a voluntary alliance to exist between a white woman and a colored man, and therefore, the fact of an alliance is a proof of force,"[17] she excoriated the state and vigilantes for punishing voluntary sexual relationships between white women and black men as sexual assaults while ignoring de facto sexual violence against black women. The punishment of African-American men for real and imagined sexual violence against white women was a given while the prosecution of any male for sexual violence against African-American women was an anomaly. The myth of the black rapist and interracial rape accusations and cases increased the likelihood of, and social indifference to, lynching as well as deflected attention away from the more prevalent intraracial sexual violence. (Today, FBI statistics report that currently over ninety percent of rapes are intraracial, that is, occur within the same race or ethnic group.)[18]

Wells-Barnett's analysis of the psycho-sexual politics of lynching proved relentless and ruthless. Demystifying the rationalization of lynching as rape prevention and prosecution (for white women), she helped to make antilynching activism respectable. Her analyses influenced and shaped resistance to racist violence justified as a war to counter sexual violence. At the same time, this controversial figure was stigmatized as an apologist for rape. As Wells-Barnett's one-time colleague and later rival Mary Church Terrell noted, an "error on the subject of lynching consists of the widely circulated statement that the moral sensibilities of the best negroes in the United States are so stunted and dull, and the standard of morality among even the leaders of the race is so low, that they do not appreciate the enormity and heinousness of rape."[19] In contemporary black feminism that revisits and revises the sexual politics of Wells-Barnett, we find depictions of the antilynching militant as having been morally crippled by her antiracism.

Although mob prosecution gave way to legal executions, the most severe punishments for rape were, and are, disproportionately reserved for black males.[20] Some feminist critics argue that by focusing on the use of lynching to terrorize black men, Wells failed to note the impact of violence on women. Yet, she saw that courts which considered only interracial sexual violence against white women truly heinous enough to warrant the death penalty inevitably treated sexual assaults against black females lightly. During the lynching (and post-lynching) era, the racist application of the death penalty for sex crimes reflected the different values the state and society placed on white and black lives as well as white and black sexuality. Consequently, female antilynching crusaders positioned themselves as both race leaders and (proto)feminists.

Joanne Braxton describes Wells-Barnett as such, as a radical female icon for social justice. Arguing that Wells-Barnett's activism created a matrix for "womanhood" formed by race, gender, and class, Braxton writes that her leadership in the black women's club movement created the "fusion of powerful influences: black feminism and black nationalism."[21] This fusion created "a race-centered, self-conscious womanhood" represented in the black women's club movement; consequently, Braxton argues, for women such as Ida B. Wells-Barnett, "a blow at lynching was a blow at racism and the brutally enforced sexual double standard that pervaded the South. It was a defense of the entire race."[22] Historically, the dominant society stigmatized black and white women antilynching activists as sexual deviants, expressing contempt and opprobrium for women advocating fair hearings and trials regarding interracial sexual assault cases. In spite or perhaps because of her militancy, Wells-Barnett was able to provide progressive leadership for both black and white women. Braxton writes that Wells-Barnett "forged a legitimate black feminism through the synthesis of black nationalism and the suffrage movement, providing a useful model with race, not sex, as a point of departure."[23] This model, according to Braxton, served not only the NAACP but also the antilynching activism of white women and feminists such as Jessie Daniel Ames in the Association of Southern Women for the Prevention of Lynching. Other black feminists give starkly different readings of the antilynching crusader's sexual politics.

"Advancing Luna—And Ida B. Wells" and the Paranoid Race Woman

Fiction and autobiography are the most noted literary forms of African-American women. When literary creativity supplants research and analysis to offer itself as political thought or political autobiographies are treated as "fiction" problems arise. In both instances, invention becomes surrogate for political substance and historical specificity. Wells-Barnett's autobiography, *Crusade for Justice,* has become a classic for understanding the life of a heroic African American and the antilynching crusades. The importance of the work is underscored by the fact that Wells-Barnett's daughter Alfreda Duster worked extensively with scholar John Hope Franklin to edit, document, and verify the accounts of this posthumously published memoir. (Duster also struggled for thirty-five years before finally finding a publisher who recognized the significance and historical accuracy of the work.) Even cursory studies of Wells-Barnett reference her memoir to legitimize their political stances.

Alice Walker references *Crusade for Justice* to historicize her narrative in "Advancing Luna—And Ida B. Wells." The story centers on the relationship between a white woman, Luna, and a black woman, the nameless narrator, and the narrator's relationship to her ancestor Ida B. Wells. Walker's story characterizes the fears shaping black women's responses to interracial rape cases and the uneasy alliances between black and white women. Throughout the story line the narrator offers unflattering observations of Luna, while recounting their friendship, which began in 1965 when they became roommates in Atlanta as civil rights activists and ended after they left the movement and briefly roomed together in New York City. After moving into Luna's apartment, the narrator is informed by Luna that during their stay in Atlanta she was raped by Freddie Pye, a black man. The narrator immediately thinks of the "rapist-revolutionary" writings of Eldridge Cleaver and LeRoi Jones (Imamu Baraka) whose "misogynous cruelty . . . was habitually lost on black men (on men in general, actually), but nearly always perceived and rejected by women of whatever color."[24] She also disdainfully recalls Pye: "He was coarse and spoke of black women as 'our' women. . . . He was physically unattractive . . . with something of the hoodlum about him."[25] Asking Luna why she did not scream and receiving the reply, "You know why," the black woman thinks of Emmett Till, a fourteen-year old black youth lynched in Mississippi years earlier for whistling at a white woman.

Disturbed by Luna's revelation, the narrator begins to write a novel about "such a rape." In preparation, she converses with the antilynching archetype, Wells-Barnett, confiding that she has read her memoir three times "as a means of praying to her spirit to forgive me":

> My prayer, as I turned the pages, went like this: *"Please forgive me. I am a writer. . . . I cannot write contrary to what life reveals to me. I wish to malign no one. But I must struggle to understand at least my own tangled emotions about interracial rape. I know, Ida B. Wells, you spent your whole life protecting, and trying to protect black men accused of raping white women, who were lynched by white mobs, or threatened with it. You know, better than I ever will, what it means for a whole people to live under the terror of lynching. Under the slander that their men, where white women are concerned, are creatures of uncontrollable sexual lust.*[26]

The betrayal that weighs heavily on the narrator's conscience is truth-telling. She assumes that Wells-Barnett, feeling betrayed by writings that might contradict her own stance, will reprove the young woman for her audacious honesty.

Transferring the fearless investigation that characterized Wells-Barnett's activism onto the narrator's intellectual aspirations as a novelist, literary production supplants political deeds; now, political courage is symbolized by a literary act embodied in the narrator's allegedly transgressive fiction. Walker's narrator neatly reduces Wells-Barnett's activism to a life spent "trying to protect black men accused of raping white women" from lynching. In fact, in the most memorable historic cases around which Wells-Barnett agitated—the 1892 Memphis lynchings, the 1918 East St. Louis riots, and the 1917 executions of black soldiers at Camp Grant—sexual violence against white women was not alleged. Rather, racist fears against independent blacks, economic greed, and political ambitions motivated these attacks.

In the dialogue, the narrator shifts responsibility for her own naivete concerning racial-sexual violence onto Wells-Barnett:

> *"You made it so clear that the black men accused of rape in the past were innocent victims of white criminals that I grew up believing black men literally did not rape white women. At all. Ever. Now it would appear that some of them, the very twisted, the terribly ill, do. What would you have me write about them?"*
>
> Her answer was: *"Write nothing. Nothing at all. It will be used against black men and therefore against all of us. Eldridge Cleaver and LeRoi Jones don't know who they're dealing with. But you remember. You are dealing with people who brought their children to witness the murder of black human beings falsely accused of rape. People who handed out, as trophies, black fingers and toes. Deny! Deny! Deny!"*[27]

The theatrical exhortations uttered by Walker's Wells suggest an unrestrained emotionalism and disingenuousness among antilynching activists. Using the barbarity of white supremacy, as the argument goes, these activists excused black moral cowardliness in regard to sexual violence. The short story's Ida B. Wells is determined by a hysteria not discernible in her writings, which speak of her rage at, rather than fear of, racist violence and public acquiescence. Death threats likely contributed to

Wells-Barnett's fearfulness in probing the rape issue as a race issue; yet fear did not hinder her investigative work. Walker's story overshadows Wells's meticulous accumulation of data on lynchings with emotionalism concerning antiblack violence.

"Advancing Luna—And Ida B. Wells" thus allows the black woman writer to morally triumph over her ancestor, as the narrator rejects Wells's fictive counsel:

> And yet, I have pursued it: *"Some black men themselves do not seem to know what the meaning of raping someone is. Some have admitted rape in order to denounce it, but others have accepted rape as a part of rebellion, of 'paying whitey back.' They have gloried in it."*
>
> *"They know nothing of America,"* she says. *"And neither, apparently, do you. No matter what you think you know, no matter what you feel about it, say nothing. And to your dying breath!"*
>
> Which, to my mind, is virtually useless advice to give to a writer.[28]

The narrator-writer commends herself for a sincerity and valor seemingly lacking in Wells-Barnett. Here, the antilynching crusader's moral timidity highlights in juxtaposition the narrator-writer's relentless pursuit of the truth. The narrator seems uninformed about the specificity of Wells-Barnett's praxis. Wells-Barnett was also a writer "guilty of wanting to know"; one of her mottoes was "To tell the truth—freely." She often did so at the risk of her own life as she painstakingly documented lynchings. An investigative reporter and a skilled polemicist, Wells-Barnett was adept at uncovering what "life reveals" in its most gruesome details. Walker's construction reduces this organizer to a cowering defensiveness and ignores her stance on armed self-defense for blacks, and her personal working relationships and friendships with prominent whites who likely would not have been on equal terms with Walker's semiparanoid race woman.

At the beginning of the twentieth century, most African Americans would have censored any black person who advocated sexually assaulting white women and who thereby promoted the imago that antilynching activists risked their lives to dispel. Whereas at the end of the twentieth century, black Americans take multiple contradictory stances toward the image of the sexual savage, in Wells-Barnett's time such performances had deadly consequences. It is more likely that

Wells-Barnett, in dialogue with a contemporary black feminist writer, would express contempt for racialist misogyny antithetical to black safety and beneath black dignity. She had publicly challenged or condemned prominent blacks and whites for any behavior she considered detrimental to black emancipation, and she did so irrespective of the costs to her career and safety.

Yet, Walker's revisionism allows the narrator a moral triumph over a denial-ridden, fearful Ida B. Wells who shields black rapists in order to protect black communities. Although the narrator states that she repeatedly read Wells-Barnett's autobiography, she misses the substance of the activist's political thinking. Somehow, the story appends defensive sentiments held by some contemporary black women onto the historical radicalism embodied by Wells. Walker's narrator extends her narrow representation of Wells-Barnett to black women in general: "Whenever interracial rape is mentioned, a black woman's first thought is to protect the lives of her brothers, her father, her sons, her lovers. A history of lynching has bred this reflex in her."[29] This insight is not easily generalizable today: Not every black woman considers the historical dangers of lynching, legal or extralegal, to be a contemporary problem. Not all black women perceive all black men with the protective sympathy they might extend to their brothers, father, sons, or lovers. And black women who survive sexual abuse from their brothers, fathers, or lovers may have decidedly unsympathetic responses to rightly or wrongfully accused male kin.

The short story's endings "Afterwords, Afterwards: Second Thoughts" and "Postscript: Havana, Cuba, November 1976," politicize Luna's assault to a level of state violence. In "Afterwords," the narrator and a black male friend express conflicting emotions while condemning the attack as "morally wrong" and "politically corrupt." The narrator notes their shared concerns: "As we thought of what might have happened to an indiscriminate number of innocent young black men in Freehold, Georgia, had Luna screamed, it became clear that more than a little of Ida B. Wells's fear of probing the rape issue was running through us, too."[30] In the "Postscript," after reading "Luna" to African-American artists-activists who like herself are visiting Cuba, the narrator argues with an Afro-American muralist. As the fiction writer offers different endings for the story, the muralist discourages the one in which Pye is contrite by stating she neither understands evil nor the need to eradicate it. Evil, he continues, does not refer to Pye as an individual rapist, rather, "'Freddie Pye' ... was probably raping white women on the instructions of his government."[31] Recalling the FBI's COINTELPRO, the muralist invokes the assassinations of black activists by U.S. agents, admonishing the female writer: "Even though you know by now that blacks could be hired to blow up other blacks, and could be hired *by someone* to shoot down Brother Malcolm, and hired *by someone* to provide a diagram of Fred Hampton's bedroom so the pigs could shoot him easily while he slept, you find it hard to believe a black man could be hired *by someone* to rape white women." He argues, then considers "the perfect disruptive act," noting that: "Enough blacks raping or accused of raping enough white women" would doom "any political movement that cuts across racial lines."[32] Warning that greater "forces are at work than your story would indicate," the impoverished artist reveals that such "forces"—or the government—offered him money, probably her tax dollars, to assault white women in order to disrupt civil rights organizing.[33]

Using the muralist to introduce state complicity in violence, Walker moves beyond individual motive and black male misogyny to underscore the ambiguity of the narrative and the complexities of racial-sexual violence. The postscript ends with the narrator's observation about the muralist: His look "implied I would never understand anything about evil, power, or corrupted human beings in the modern world. But of course he is wrong."[34] Walker leaves it to the reader's imagination to determine why.

Valerie Smith, on the other hand, agrees with the muralist's assessment of the narrator's ignorance, but for entirely different reasons as she retells "Advancing Luna—And Ida B. Wells" eliding the ambiguities and contradictory images of Walker's postscript and narrative. Smith's essay "Split Affinities" reviews representations of interracial rape in Walker's short story as well as "journalistic discourse" surrounding the Central Park Case in which African-American and Latino youths were convicted for the brutal assault and rape of a white woman.[35] With selective, decontextualized passages that distort Walker's story, Smith revises the historical politics of antilynching activism as well as Walker's fiction to reflect on black women's gender venality. "Split Affinities" uses "Advancing Luna—And Ida B. Wells" to support its thesis that the divided loyalties of black women create their split affinities in interracial rape cases. Smith, like Walker, notes that given the historical use of rape charges to justify racist violence, African Americans view accusations of rape "as a way to terrorize innocent black men." For Smith this reasoning "may lead to the denial of the fact that some black men do rape."[36] The stances of black females on interracial rape cases are "particularly vexed," according to Smith, who also notes that given society's greater indifference to violence against black women, African-American women's "identification with white women is problematic." Smith writes that as "members of communities under siege," black women "may well sympathize with the black male who stands accused" while "as women they share the victim's sense of violation."[37] She expands this position with a historical perspective that argues that Wells-Barnett was a counterfeminist hostile to white women abused by black men. Smith uses Walker's fictitious characters as representative of historical and contemporary black women. She does so without mentioning the liabilities of using contemporary fiction, rather than historical or sociological research, to represent the politics of nonfictional African Americans. Smith's argument has merit; in interracial rape cases, divided loyalties can reduce some African-American women to reactionary, counterfeminist politics leading them to pained or vindictive positions on interracial rape that support black males who rape rather than their white victims. Yet their counterprogressive politics can neither be generalized to all contemporary black women nor facilely appended to historical, black female antilynching radicals.

To make her generalizations plausible, Smith transforms "Advancing Luna" into a black and white polemic between a venal black counterfeminist and an equally abstract, heroic white feminist. Inconsistent with Walker's narrative, she paints political stances absent in the story to portray the narrator as determined by nationalist sensibilities. In the story, the black narrator first temporarily leaves a prestigious, white Ivy League women's college, Sarah Lawrence, for a summer commitment to civil rights activism. Then, in somewhat dilettante fashion, she departs midsummer from her organizing project in Georgia to take advantage of a travel grant to Uganda. Her writing about this African sojourn reveals a decidedly nonnationalist consciousness: "I was taken on rides down the Nile as a matter of course, and accepted all invitations to dinner, where the best local dishes were superbly prepared in my honor. I became, in fact, a lost relative of the people, whose ancestors had foolishly strayed, long ago, to America."[38] Militant, race-nationalists do not casually refer to the Middle Passage, enslavement, and genocide as hapless wandering. Smith inserts the antiwhite, black militant race woman into Walker's story, and then drapes this persona over both the fictive narrator and the historical crusader to disparage both as counterfeminists.

Smith begins three consecutive paragraphs with the phrase: "The narrator's hostility to Luna." Referring to the sexual jealousy that marks interracial relationships between some male-identified heterosexual women, she argues that the black woman's ill will "points to a thinly veiled sexual competitiveness between the black and the white woman which may more generally problematize the discourse of interracial rape."[39] Walker's story offers no evidence for Smith's interpretation of female sexual competition. Smith's story synopsis and sleight of hand in retelling the tale alter the intent of the narrative; this suggests a systemic misreading of "Advancing Luna—And Ida B. Wells" to advance the split affinities/black gender venality thesis.

The ambiguity of Walker's text seems to be reconstructed as an issue of the veracity of the rape charge. "Split Affinities" maintains that Pye, "who Luna states raped her or who raped Luna," spends the night in Luna's bedroom illustrates the "ambiguity of the story and its open ended interpretation." The ambiguity is not whether or not Pye raped Luna: The narrator recognizes Luna's account as true. The short story asserts the rape as a fact. The ambiguity lies in the responses of black and white women to the rape.

Smith's depiction of split affinities among black women implies that the narrator must choose between black men and white women in interracial rape cases. Yet Walker's narrator follows her own conscience, identifying with rape victims as well as lynching victims. "Split Affinities" deploys a dichotomy that alters "Advancing Luna" to contend that the narrator "instead of identifying with the silenced woman victim ... locates herself in relation to the silenced black male victim of lynching."[40] It is difficult to read this position into the story. Rather than blind race loyalty or black male identification, Walker's narrator exhibits a grim determination to protect the innocent, expressing concern for nameless, unimplicated black men, rather than a guilty Freddie Pye. Presenting identification as shaped by an exclusive choice between accused black males or white female survivors, Smith ignores the possibility that the narrator might believe that black criminals should pay for their crimes, including crimes against whites; this essay fails to acknowledge the possibility that African Americans critical of racist prosecutions may still be supportive of survivors. Although African-American women's positions on interracial rape cases span from the reactionary to the radical, Smith's argument splits progressive gender and racial politics.

Having so represented the narrator's racial consciousness, Smith proceeds to illustrate the black woman's gender insensitivity. She offers as example the narrator's failure to understand why Luna is disturbed after the black woman invites two men to spend the night, one on the couch and the other in the narrator's bedroom. Without knowing the short story, and the racialized sexual preference of each woman, we might assume from Smith's essay that the men are black and be appalled by the narrator's obtuse indifference to any presence that would remind Luna of her attacker and further her emotional and psychological distress. However, Walker's protagonist is not that insensitive. Smith fails to convey that Luna and the narrator desire their ethnic opposites: The black narrator prefers white men, particularly "ethnic exotics" who look like the singing cowboy film star Gene Autry; white Luna sleeps with black men. Both men who sleep over by invitation of the black woman are white. Luna, who only has black lovers, is upset because she feels that the narrator slept with "the enemy." Cross or transracial preferences are lost to Smith's essay which provides only the line "Luna never told me what irked her so that Sunday morning [after the men had slept over], yet I remember it as the end of our relationship."[41] The lines completing Walker's paragraph, which Smith does not relay, dispel some of the mystery. Noting their "strange" assortment of friends, including Luna's friends who "especially were deeper than they should have been into drugs,"[42] the narrator expresses concern and uncertainty about their deteriorating relationship; she reflects: "It was not, as I at first feared, that she thought my bringing the two men to the apartment was inconsiderate. The way we lived allowed us to *be* inconsiderate from time to time."[43] In Walker's short story, unlike Smith's essay, the complex frailties of black-white women's relationships are not generated by black women's antiwhite sensibilities.

Building upon the image of Luna's rape, Smith recreates Luna to symbolize both white feminism and white victimization at the hands of black men and women. Depicting a traditional feminine virtue, compassion, as absent in black women's positions on interracial rape cases, "Split Affinities" applies Walker's reconstruction of Wells-Barnett as fearful, denial-ridden, and protective of black males against the narrator herself. Luna is traumatized not only by the black rapist but also by the black woman she befriends, as Smith superimposes Walker's portrait of a frightened, disingenuous Wells-Barnett onto the narrator.

Wells-Barnett the Counterfeminist

The recasting of Walker's story whose first "metatextual moment," according to Smith, occurs when the narrator theorizes "about the exclusion of black women from the discourse surrounding rape," is the prelude to revising the praxis of Ida B. Wells. Rather than excluded from the discourse surrounding rape, Wells-Barnett reshaped it, through the Afro-American press, black organizations, and antilynching campaigns. With other African-American women activists, she forced public discourse on sexual violence to pursue a new agenda. Accomplishing what most whites in the United States would not do, and what black males could not do, black women created the counterdiscourse to lynching as rape prevention, changing the politics of that discourse from an apologia to a condemnation, or at least a questioning, of lynching.

"Split Affinities" severs contemporary black feminism from Wells-Barnett's analyses and black women's historical antiracist radicalism; it simplifies the complex relationships between the antilynching crusader and white as well as black female leaders. Offering no specific information about Wells-Barnett's organizing with white feminists, diagnosing Wells-Barnett as harboring a personal dislike for white women, Smith psychologizes the crusader to dismiss the antilynching campaigns as counterfeminist and antiwhite. Whereas Walker presents Wells-Barnett as reduced by anxieties of racist violence into a paralysis of irrational disavowals, Smith depicts her as infused with both a hostility toward (female) whites and an indifference to sexual violence. Reducing Wells-Barnett's militant opposition to racist violence to a personal acrimony against women in a racially oppressive caste, she contends that Wells-Barnett bequeathed a legacy and praxis unsuitable for feminism (the essay uses this representation of Wells-Barnett as a counterfeminist to discuss the Central Park case.)

Omitting any reference to the role of white women's racism or moral reticence in false accusations of rape, Smith reminds us of "Wells's own discrediting of the testimony of white victims." Wells-Barnett's investigative reporting discredited not so much the testimony of victims but the barbaric use of the rape charge in false accusations against African-American men and the general demagoguery of using rape as a pretext for racist violence. Smith criticizes Wells-Barnett for her "focus on the unreliability of white rape victims" which she constructs as an attack on white women victims. "Victims" is somewhat of a misnomer here. Wells-Barnett did not view white women in lynchings collectively as rape victims. *A Red Record* reports that most who voluntarily or reluctantly claimed to be rape victims, to sanction lynchings, were not sexual-assault victims or were not victimized by African-American men. Smith fails to examine three vital facts concerning Wells-Barnett's era: The overwhelming number of rapes were intraracial; the charge of rape was used only in a fraction of the lynchings; and whites had defined all consensual sexual relationships between white women and black men as rape. Blurring distinctions between research and fiction (problems arise when the latter is taken as a more accurate guide for assessing the politics of this African-American antilynching activist), Smith writes that Wells-

Barnett's "opposition to lynching as a practice requires her effectively to deny the veracity of any white woman's testimony against a black man."[44]

Smith claims that a logical reading of passages from *Crusade for Justice* reveals Wells-Barnett "effectively blaming white women for the lynching of black men."[45] All white women? If so, then Wells-Barnett's political and personal friendships with prominent white women—such as Susan B. Anthony and other suffragettes, "halfway house" movement leaders, British antilynching supporters, and NAACP founders—are inexplicable. If Wells-Barnett had been contemptuous of sexual violence in white women's lives or uniformly condemned all white women, as Smith implies, she would have alienated most of her white female supporters.

The progressive analyses of contemporary black feminisms are rooted in and indebted to the earlier critiques of black women antilynching crusaders who recognized the interrelatedness of racial and sexual violence. Although it would be useful to examine with specificity how, and under what conditions, African-American women choose to subordinate sex to race and vice versa, we cannot logically infer a uniform practice of subordinating sexual oppression to racial oppression in African-American women's challenges to lynching, particularly since the historical antilynching campaigns were also waged as antisexual violence campaigns.

Other problematic areas arise as Smith interchanges the terms "accusations" and "instances" when referring to interracial rape, rendering accusations synonymous with factual assaults. She also confuses the prosecution of rape with the crime of rape to write that Wells-Barnett's formulations "subordinate the sexual to the racial dimension of interracial rape, thereby dramatizing the fact that the crime can never be read solely as an offense against women's bodies."[46] Wells-Barnett's critique did not, as is asserted, "subordinate" the sexual to the racial; rather it connected the sexual to the racial to counter racist depictions of black sexuality. Wells-Barnett's journalism refers to the prevalence of white men not prosecuted for raping black women and children. The state did not perceive rape as a crime that could be "read solely as an offense against women's bodies." Nor did it prosecute it as such given that no generic woman exists under white supremacy, capitalism, and patriarchy. The prosecution of rape is, to quote Smith, never "read solely as an offense against women's bodies," given a hierarchy of bodies based on race, class, and sexual orientation.

Unaware of the historical roots of her own feminism, Smith advocates a multitextured black feminism over a monodimensional Eurocentric one, describing the former as a more competent framework for analysis: "Black feminism presumes the 'intersectionality' of race and gender in the lives of black women, thereby rendering inapplicable to the lives of black women any 'single-axis' theory about racism or sexism."[47] This "new" analysis is in fact based on a paradigm articulated a century ago. Race and gender intersect (with class and sexuality) not only in black women's lives but also in all women's lives. Smith defines the very foundation of black feminism as one which presumes the "intersectionality" of race and gender in the lives of black women; this definition is also based on a position articulated and fought for by nineteenth-century African-American women in campaigns largely initiated by Wells-Barnett.[48] Delineating the impact of race in white women's lives and their complicity in white supremacy as well as racial-sexual violence, Wells-Barnett applied this intersectionality more consistently than Smith does in her essay. (Down-playing what Wells-Barnett underscored—white women's complicity in white supremacy and racial-sexual terror—Smith never raises the issue of white women's split affinities.)

Rather than generalize that black women's antiracism privileges males, we might note the complexities involved. Women recognize that racist violence terrorized women and children, in addition to men; women most vulnerable to violence could also prove the most vocal advocates for stiff prosecutions. Some African-American women prove highly unsympathetic to accused black males (particularly now that black males are the primary source of sexual violence against African-American females). Still others, outraged by the sexual violence as well as the racist prosecution of the accused, may identify with both survivor and defendant(s), embracing dual rather than split identities, with the understanding that just-legal prosecutions of sexual violence supersede simplistic dichotomies.[49]

Castigating the Crusader

Historical revisionism and historicism based in selective and skewed information concerning Wells-Barnett's sexual politics elide or distort the praxis of past radicals in order to shape perceptions and depictions of present-day race politics. Erasing the specificity of past radicalism promotes a doctrine of evolutionary leadership in which contemporary political or feminist leadership is uniformly taken to be more progressive than its predecessor. Consequently, many may assume that late twentieth-century black feminism is inherently more advanced than its nineteenth-century counterpart. Feminist revisionism regarding Ida B. Wells naturalizes that assumption. Using ahistoricism, feminist elites may diminish the contributions of historical women in order to argue for the primacy and superiority of their own gender ideologies and forms of agency.

Writers may construct contemporary womanist or black feminisms as more (gender) progressive than the views of women such as Ida B. Wells-Barnett who led the antilynching campaigns. Walker's reading of Wells-Barnett as intimidated by racist violence into fearful denials and Smith's reading of Wells-Barnett as a counterfeminist place contemporary black feminist thought above the political thought of historical activists. This evolutionary ascent toward the black feminist writer counters traditional notions of public intellectual as engagé; it allows the contemporary to transcend her predecessor in progressive agency, as the writer replaces the activist. In fictional dialogues between ancestor and progeny, the contemporary heroine, as moral and political agent, consistently triumphs over her militant race-woman predecessor. In our postmovement era the postmodern, professional writer and/or academic reigns as an intellectual. Validating progressive gender and race ideology in the symbolic analyst, one may supplant the activist with the commentator-essayist as representative of ideal political leadership.

Perhaps some gender specific criticisms and caricatures found an easy target in the persona of Wells-Barnett, who unlike antilynching leaders Frederick Douglass, Du Bois, or Terrell vociferously challenged the racial-sexual apologies for lynching to trample the twin myths of white (female) sexual purity and black (male) sexual savagery. Outrage led Wells-

Barnett to take risks and cross over the line of conventional antiracist rhetoric. She rejected the discourse of civility. Her abrasive militancy distanced her from those who maintained the importance of conciliatory rhetoric in resistance struggles. As her isolation grew so did her vulnerability to attack and misrepresentation. Although she transgressed the civility that the Talented Tenth were presumed to embody and was isolated by elites for her assertiveness, Wells-Barnett bequeathed a legacy of skepticism concerning state-accounts of and prosecution of racialized sexual violence through the press, police, and courts; of risk taking in investigative journalism; and of willingness to directly confront the state and elite society to stop violence. This legacy influenced later generations of women such as Rosa Parks and Ella Baker who organized in the 1930s around the Scottsboro Boys trial in which black youths were incarcerated in Alabama for raping two white women although one woman later admitted that there had never been a sexual assault.

Walker's and Smith's historiographies of Wells-Barnett, and by extension black women antilynching crusaders, argue against antiracist commitments that undermine progressive gender politics. Yet, Countering black chauvinism/reactionary sexual politics with a revisionist lens distorts radical agency.

Black feminisms both illuminate and obscure radical agency and gender politics in black intellectualism. How they imagine and image historical African-American women activists-intellectuals shapes visions of contemporary antiracist radicalism and black female leadership. Some black progressives' representations of African-American leadership discredit the radical. Others alter her appearance. In both discrediting and (dis)appearing acts, we lose radical black praxis for consideration, and consequently are more likely to only validate nonradical elites, the conventional Talented Tenth, as the most viable form of leadership.

Mississippi Freedom Democratic Party delegates singing at rally on Atlantic City Boardwalk at 1964 Democratic National Convention. Fannie Lou Hamer, Eleanor Holmes Norton, and Ella Baker are in the foreground.

Disappearing Race Women and Civil Rights Radicals

Strong people don't need a strong leader.

—Ella Baker

Civil rights radicals' ability to analyze, advocate, and agitate for social justice brought new meanings to the concept of the Talented Tenth. African-American women's activism and courageous resistance qualified them as activists-intellectuals. Amid conflicting intellectual modes, radical women offered a model of intellectualism that suggests that the political actor, rather than spectator, is best rooted to resist co-optation and intimidation. Some overlook the contributions of such intellectuals to democratic praxis given the racial, gender, and ideological biases of American historiography. Elites have a long history of muting radical voices, particularly those of militant black women,[1] as they simultaneously mask radicalism while managing crises. That most do not routinely offer the names of women activists in the role-call of black civil rights leaders reflects the consequences of this masking.[2] Recovering the work of race women and civil rights radicals, such as Ella Baker, reveals other forms of agency.

Transcending the Talented Tenth: Miss Ella Baker

By virtue of her college degree, Baker technically qualified to join the ranks of a Talented Tenth intelligentsia. She approached political thinking and organizing with a radicalism that both distinguished and marginalized her from most of her liberal counterparts and contemporaries.[3]

When Ella Baker died in New York City on her birthday, December 8, 1986, writers and human rights activists paid tribute, praising Baker in their remembrances as a "major force behind the civil rights movement"; "the godmother of SNCC"; and a "midwife" to SCLC and SNCC. One year after her death, the New York-based Center for Constitutional Rights held a reception to initiate its "Ella Baker Student Intern Program." Former Student Nonviolent Coordinating Committee (SNCC) activists recalled Baker as a "hero of the civil rights movement [who] devoted her adult life to social change." SNCC members or supporters preserve the memory of Baker. Activists, political students, writers, filmmakers, and artists keep her memory alive; their tributes attest to the incredible power of Baker's intellect, and a politics rooted in communal relationships and spirited counsel to younger activists. For example, Sweet Honey in the Rock founder Bernice Johnson Reagon worked with Baker in SNCC and later composed "Ella's Song" with a quote from her mentor: "Until the killing of black men, black mothers' sons, is as important as the killing of white men, white mothers' sons, we who believe in freedom cannot rest." Described by *Eyes on the Prize* documentarian Judy Richardson as a political "long distance runner," for nearly half a century Baker established a praxis for black liberation movements.

Writers who recognize Baker's historical significance, brilliance, and passion for democratic politics may recall only her leadership in the Southern civil rights movement in the 1950s and 1960s. Her political insight and militancy, shared with the Southern civil rights movement, were initially formed through her interactions with black workers and laborers. Baker worked as a labor organizer and journalist in New York City in the 1930s. Like Du Bois she was radicalized by the agency of black workers. Serving as NAACP field organizer in the 1930s and 1940s, Baker acquired political experience and contacts that allowed her to emerge as one of the most astute strategists in the movement. After working as the first de facto director of the Southern Christian Leadership Conference (SCLC) in the late 1950s, she convened the 1960 student conference that lead to the formation of the Student Nonviolent Coordinating Committee, which she served as advisor. That Baker, working as a "facilitator" rather than a spokesperson, did not seek to establish herself as a "public intellectual" outside of a community of radical activists underscores the anonymity of black women's intellectualism that prioritizes the collective.

Baker recounted her role in black liberation struggles for a 1968 interview with John Britton. Shunning self-promotion, she remarks: "In my organizational work I have never thought in terms of my 'making a contribution.' I just thought of myself as functioning where there was a need. And if I have made a contribution I think it may be that I had some influence on a large number of people."[4] Baker's "organizational work" expanded U.S. democracy and radicalized the roles of civil rights intellectuals and activists. Her extensive FBI file marks her political significance. Baker transformed criticisms of racism into critiques of both capitalism and liberal acquiescence to oppressive state practices and channeled criticisms and critiques into political opposition via grass-roots civil disobedience. Merging black liberation rhetoric with mass mobilization of black people, she embodied both political worker and intellectual, with a model of black intellectualism that presented mass resistance rather than intellectual elites as indispensable for a true democracy.

Baker's influence on a large number of people extends to generations unfamiliar with her contributions yet shaped by her spirit and political legacy. As Charles Payne observes, her obscurity is as instructive as her political praxis: "That Ella Baker could have lived the life she did and remain so little known even among the politically knowledgeable is important in itself. It reminds us once more of how much our collective past has been distorted—and distorted in disempowering ways."[5] Part of the distortion stems from which actors are privileged in political memory. Reflecting the conservative or liberal bias that privileges men, whites, and the affluent, more than a few male civil rights leaders and contemporary civil rights historians deemphasized the role of African-American women in this movement. For most, leadership and agency have been described as primarily the attributes of male elites. It is not surprising that the contributions of black women radicals such as

Baker—who spoke and organized against racism, capitalism, and imperialism—are marginalized.

Even the knowledgeable may remember Baker's contributions in disempowering ways to deradicalize her politics. For some, Baker represents the "organic intellectual" described in Antonio Gramsci's *Prison Notebooks* as the strategist whose theorizing to end oppression forms the "ribs corseting the masses."[6] The organic intellectual as activist works with a theoretical *and* experiential political base, which is precisely how Baker positioned herself. However, Baker would likely reject as elitist any Gramscian characterization of her as vanguard leader. One of her often-cited quotes is that a "strong people don't need strong leaders." Baker, like C. L. R. James, argued that progressivism is furthered by the disintegration rather than the reform of a Talented Tenth that served as professional intellectuals and managerial race leaders.

Her democratic vision reveals a strong sense of social change determined by the "ordinary" people who wage political movements. A study of her political life, as well as her criticisms of SCLC male cleric elites, reveals the class, gender, and ideological differences simmering and erupting within the civil rights movement. Her relationships to impoverished and militant blacks forged political perspectives that identified African-American laborers and workers as political leaders. Such views on mass leadership shaped her facilitation of grassroots activism for the NAACP, SCLC, and SNCC, and led to her resignations from the NAACP and from SCLC. Baker saw the bureaucratic leadership of both organizations as uncommitted to grass-roots activism.

The mainstream press neither popularized nor vilified Baker's statements, as they had the ideas of her peers Martin Luther King Jr. and Malcolm X. Her organizing and political leadership would last generations beyond the tragically brief lives of her younger counterparts. Though Baker bequeathed a liberation praxis, with political thinking that set a fulcrum for radical antiracist leadership, her belief and practices in the commonness of political leadership promoted Baker's historical obscurity. (Writers who shared similar critiques of elite leadership but documented their own contributions in autobiographies did not generally share her anonymity.)

Baker criticized both male as well as female elite leadership. In his 1968 interview with Baker, Britton unfavorably compared his female contemporaries with Mary McLeod Bethune and other elite race women of a previous era. Responding to his query about the lack of "any similar strong leadership today from Negro women" and the absence of "more black women involved in the movement," Baker first differentiated the mass and confrontational character of the civil rights movement from previous struggles for racial justice in order to challenge Britton's implicit elitist concept of power and leadership. Previously, according to Baker, "You had the emergence of the individual as an articulate person, as one who could communicate between the masses to the Establishment." This spokesperson or translator depoliticized because the "articulate communicator," maintained Baker, "was basically an accommodating leadership with a great overtone of personal advancement involved."[7] For Baker, "another type of leadership which was no less strong and in fact was less assimilationist and co-opted" developed as an alternative to what she viewed as an egoistic caste of articulate communicators negotiating between agitating black masses and authoritative structural elites. Prominent, media-recognized leadership, Baker argued, was never desirable given that news media created a "cult of personality" that fostered passivity.[8]

Baker stressed that revolutionary democratic power is communal and requires direct mass action, and that progressive leadership is collective, identifying youth, women, and the poor as key figures in political leadership. This was her model for black democratic struggles, a model embraced by some and rejected by others. She exemplifies how black intellectualism can circumvent egoism, political acquiescence, and vanguardist notions of progressive leadership. The erasure of her life-story, conversely, highlights how black intellectualism can promote vanguardist notions of leadership and male privilege.

Unlike Du Bois and Wells-Barnett, Baker left no autobiography. Yet her lifework, mirrored in her few, obscure essays, touched many people. Still, many are unfamiliar with her political and intellectual contributions. Unfortunately, despite her long and productive public life, her name often doesn't appear in discussions of black intellectualism and civil rights. For instance, in the works of nonactivists, and academics who analyze race and class but not gender politics in civil rights organizing, Baker's political leadership disappears. Evading female radicalism, Jack Bloom's work on class formations in the civil rights movement does not mention Baker; the historiographies of David Garrow and Taylor Branch downplay her significance; while John Brown Childs's work on Afro-American intellectualism marginalizes her.[9]

The story of Ella Baker nearly disappears in civil rights historiography such as the academic writing of John Brown Childs which circumvents her contributions while highlighting her praxis. Childs's discussions of antidemocratic tendencies in black leadership begin with Du Bois and Booker T. Washington. Historically, Childs argues, vanguardism within African-American political leadership has crippled democratic movements. Using only masculine pronouns throughout his book, he mentions the political contributions of only one black woman to American social-political thought—Ella Baker. Childs traces the democratic agency (or "mutuality") for which SNCC became famous to Baker, but erases the political contributions of Baker and other women activists.

Childs highlights SNCC as the exemplary model of democratic organizing in the civil rights movement, in contrast to the hierarchical leadership styles of groups such as the Nation of Islam, SCLC, or Black Panther Party. Of SNCC's guiding mentor, he writes: "The indomitable Ella Baker played a key role in encouraging the mutualistic tendencies of SNCC."[10] Referring to the single woman he references merely once, and then only within a footnote, Childs conveniently transfers Baker's agency to the young Martin Luther King Jr. Offering a lengthy discussion of King, Childs writes that the "emphasis on the common man as star performer marks another mutualistic element in King's work." According to Childs, "mass action signified participatory action" for King who perceived the importance of participants developing in political organizing "as active participants through their cohesive cooperation with others."[11] Childs's argument is more realistic if restricted to the post-1964 King. Elitism and sexism marred the politics of the early King who battled with Baker and presided over a male-cleric SCLC hierarchy that relegated most of the early SCLC organizing to Baker and a few volunteers.

Compromising his discussion of democracy, Childs's analysis of antidemocratic tendencies and democratic agency within black liberation struggles fails to address male elitism and gender politics and so cannot fully assess vanguardism. Deploying a concept of agency via mutuality, he writes that the achievement of relationships based on respect and equality within a liberation struggle is a victory in itself. Ironically, the greatest practitioners of mutuality in the schools, churches, homes, farm fields, and neighborhoods—the sites for struggle in the movement—were women. As Kathlene Cleaver notes in "Sex, Lies, and Videotapes," when we look at the newsreel footage from the movement era, despite what male historiography tells us, we see scores of women in meetings, at demonstrations, in protest.[12] Activist women's stories and memoirs inform us of at least this much.

Repression and Women's Activism

The strongest, most gripping accounts of black radicalism usually surface in political memoirs. Women's civil rights autobiographies offer images of African-American female agency in black radicalism. These images remain marginal. This is partly because the most frequently read autobiographies of contemporary black radicals, for instance *The Autobiography of Malcolm X*[13] or George Jackson's *Blood in My Eye*,[14] are written by men. Historical accounts also tend to privilege black male radicalism. Frederick Douglass's autobiography, for example, is considered representative of heroic individualism while Harriet Jacob's narrative may be depicted as a lament against black female victimization.[15] Agency is ascribed most strongly to the former, not the latter. This perception is compatible with other gender generalizations. For instance, categorizing black women as essentially victims (of racism, patriarchy, poverty) in effect diminishes their agency. Both feminists and masculinists have offered reductionist depictions that veil the democratic power of women organizers.

Masculinist and patriarchal black writers often censure women who criticize sexism in African-American leadership.

(Men who offer similar profeminist critiques are less likely to be sanctioned, and more likely to be applauded for challenging male privilege.) The hostility or indifference directed at feminist works on black gender politics largely reflects machismo, misogyny, and racial and gender defensiveness. Sometimes, though, women's writings on black agency are disparaged not because of their stance against (black) sexism but because of their ahistoricism and reductive generalizations. Universalizing personal opinions or experiences as analytical and representational, some feminists have created problematic accounts of gender politics in black liberation movements.

Consider feminists Michelle Wallace's and Robin Morgan's critical appraisals of women in the civil rights movement. Wallace refers to the limitations of her early, controversial work, *Black Macho and the Myth of the Superwoman,* in a *Village Voice* essay in 1995.[16] Most readers may not be aware of Wallace's criticisms of this book or the extent to which her criticisms relate a more balanced history of sexual politics in the civil rights movement. Wallace's youthful reductive reading of African-American female agency was first published by *Ms.* In the turbulent wake of its release, prominent black writers, including former movement activists, "read" (or deconstructed) Wallace's early work while others legitimized and promoted it as informed and pioneering black feminism. Morgan, a prominent feminist and former *Ms.* editor, takes Wallace's account of black female victimization to extraordinary lengths in an antiviolence narrative that disparages revolutionary agency and armed resistance. Yet, the "mainstreaming" of Wallace's polemic diminishes antiracist radicalism and promotes the disappearance of political leadership.

For instance, Morgan's description of her own activism in New York City CORE (the Congress of Racial Equality) reduces political resistance to performance.[17] Her depictions of black women's activism prove to be even more problematic. In *Demon Lover: On the Sexuality of Terrorism,* she uses the analogy of a wife haranguing her husband to take out the garbage to discuss black gender relations in the (Northern) civil rights movement. Writing that black women had to "nag" black men into joining the movement, Morgan constructs a binary opposition between black females and males to polarize sexual and racial struggles and therefore women's and black liberation as mutually exclusive. Morgan reinscribes sexual-racial mythology into black radicalism. Portraying African-American women as stoically pacifist and passive in the movement, Morgan represents black women as uniformly hardworking, deferential, and dependent and thus curtails their civil rights agency and leadership. She also depicts black women in the movement as generally victimized by, as well as blind followers of, violence-prone black men. Beginning with Malcolm X, Morgan writes, African-American men corrupted and derailed the civil rights movement by introducing violence into it. *Demon Lover* offers no discussion of women's roles in the black tradition of self-defense against white violence. The autobiographies of movement women contest such stereotypes—remember that Wells-Barnett carried a pistol—by documenting black women's responses to racist violence during the movement.

The view that black males introduced violence into the civil rights–black liberation movements in the late 1960s and early 1970s evokes the images of the stereotypical violence-prone black male to deflect from both state repression and women's responses to violence. Examples of both are found in the memoirs of women movement radicals, such as Davis's *Angela Davis: An Autobiography,* Bernice Johnson Reagon's "My Black Mothers and Sisters or on Beginning a Cultural Autobiography," Anne Moody's *Coming of Age in Mississippi*, and Assata Shakur's *Assata: An Autobiography,* circumventing elitism and ideological bias in historiography.[18] Each woman embraced community development through organizations violently targeted by the Klan, police, and FBI, as well as plagued by internal factionalism and violence.

Although many civil rights activists embraced nonviolence as a deeply held philosophy, others, including Baker, saw nonviolence as a tactical strategy rather than a moral commandment. A few women activists analyzed the role of violence in revolutionary struggle. The responses of women civil rights activists to violence varied. Some went armed while others had bodyguards for protection. Moody, who found the experience of sleeping with weapons almost as nerve-wracking as the drive-by shootings by white racists, refused to arm herself in the SNCC freedom house although her young female friends and housemates did.

Moody's memoir describes the lynching of Emmett Till when she was a fifteen-year-old domestic worker for one of the "meanest white women" in her town. Warned by her mother not to talk about the murder with whites, when questioned by her employer about Till's death, Moody lies, stating she has never heard of Till. Her feelings on the murder, interrogation, and need to lie about racist violence before whites produced her first emotions of hatred. Moody writes: "I hated the white men who murdered Emmett Till and I hated all the other whites who were responsible for the countless [other] murders. . . . I also hated Negroes . . . for not standing up and doing something about the murders. In fact, I think I had a stronger resentment toward Negroes for letting the whites kill them than toward the whites."[19] Later in the 1960s, Moody entered Tougaloo College and was introduced to the civil rights movement by a white coed. Her memoir recalls how her mother begged her to leave the civil rights movement and warned her not to attend an upcoming NAACP convention in Jackson: "I got a letter from Mama with dried-up tears on it, forbidding me to go to the convention. It went on for more than six pages. She said if I didn't stop that shit she would come to Tougaloo and kill me herself."[20] Upon reading the letter, Moody realized that the sheriff and whites in her hometown, Centreville, knew that she was organizing in Tougaloo and that she could not return home; she also understood that her family could be harassed or endangered because of her political activism. Moody was, she recalls, "the first Negro from my hometown who had openly demonstrated, worked with the NAACP, or anything. When Negroes threatened to do anything in Centreville, they were either shot like Samuel O'Quinn or run out of town, like Reverend Dupree."[21] Violence shapes the pessimistic, despairing note upon which *Coming of Age in Mississippi* concludes. The toll that violence took on radical women has not been fully explored in civil rights historiography.

In her autobiography, Davis writes of children victimized by racist violence in her hometown. Years after Till's murder, on September 16, 1963, weeks after the civil rights March on

Washington, a black church in Birmingham was bombed. Angela Davis was completing her junior year at Brandeis by studying abroad in France. She describes her reactions to the deaths of four girls, Carole Robertson, Cynthia Wesley, Addie Mae Collins, Denise McNair, acquaintances or friends of her family and her younger sister, Fania: "Mother told me later that when Mrs. Robertson heard that the church had been bombed, she called to ask Mother to drive her downtown to pick up Carole. She didn't find out, Mother said, until they saw pieces of her body scattered about."[22] The "objective significance of the murders," Davis reasons, was that rather than aberrations they were logical and inevitable: "The people who planted the bomb in the girls' restroom in the basement of 16th Street Baptist Church were not pathological, but rather the normal products of their surroundings . . . this spectacular, violent event, the savage dismembering of four little girls . . . burst out of the daily, sometimes even dull, routine of racist oppression."[23] Davis's anger and grim remarks proved incomprehensible to her French companions: "No matter how much I talked, the people around me were simply incapable of grasping it. They could not understand why the whole society was guilty of this murder— why their beloved Kennedy was also to blame, why the whole ruling stratum in their country, by being guilty of racism, was also guilty of this murder."[24] Her observations also proved alien to most Americans, who were oblivious or indifferent to state complicity in antiblack violence.

Shakur, a former Black Panther Party member, who was a COINTELPRO target, criticizes militaristic vanguards who "thought they could just pick up arms and struggle and that, somehow, people would see what they were doing and begin to struggle themselves."[25] This desire to "engage in a do-or-die battle with the power structure in amerika, even though they were weak and ill prepared for such a fight" led some black militants to deny what she viewed as essential knowledge: "The most important factor is that armed struggle, by itself, can never bring about a revolution. Revolutionary war is a people's war."[26] Revolutionary war was not synonymous with violence. A "people's war," in Shakur's estimation, rejected militarist vanguardism for democratic collectives, political education, and critical consciousness.

Rewriting Women's Radicalism

Perhaps because discussions of black female stances on revolutionary struggle and violence are disquieting, few debate the full extent of women's antiracist radicalism. This seems especially true for academic texts, where even substantive discussions of black women's agency in civil rights organizing sometimes create nuanced evasions of radical agency. For instance, Pat Hill Collins's *Black Feminist Thought* offers an impressively detailed review of black women's ideologies, and examines the erasure of black women's experiences in academic studies.[27] Citing how "both traditional scholarship and its Afrocentric and feminist critiques" neglect black women's experiences, Collins writes that these omissions mirror "problems plaguing existing scholarly conceptualizations of power, political resistance, and political activism."[28] Black feminist scholarship, as Collins notes, provides essential information and analyses for the study of politics and theory.

Unfortunately, *Black Feminist Thought* also elides black female radicals. Reconstructing historical radicals as liberals, it deradicalizes militant women to generalize movement women activists as wedded to liberal politics. Collins redefines most forms of black women's antiracist work, including social work, as "radicalism." In doing so, her text serves as a primary example for the erasure of the black woman radical. Whereas Du Bois highlighted women as models while minimizing their radical agency, Collins emphasizes women's agency by supplanting historical radicalism with liberalism, a sleight of hand that she masks by renaming the latter "radical."

In *Black Feminist Thought*, Collins urges the study of black women activists and promotes the consideration of political activists as theorists and intellectuals. Rejecting the academic dichotomy between activism and the life of the mind (a catchall phrase representing any number of mental activities), she argues that the words and actions of political activists "have also contributed to the Black women's intellectual tradition" in an academic culture where African-American women artists and political activists "are typically thought of as nonintellectual and nonscholarly."[29] Collins rejects "a false dichotomy" between scholarship and activism, between thinking and doing: "Examining the ideas and actions of these excluded groups reveals a world in which behavior is a statement of philosophy and in which a vibrant, both/and, scholar/activist tradition remains intact."[30]

Amid its calls to bridge dichotomies and reconsider the political contributions of women organizers, *Black Feminist Thought* erases African-American women's radical or revolutionary politics in the civil rights movement. It therefore misrepresents the scale and political breadth of ideological praxis. Collins implicitly defines as revolutionary all black women who survive and thereby resist oppression, even if they do not engage in public activism or confrontation with the state. She does not mention women who engaged in revolutionary forms of activism through their participation in radical groups or underground movements; she refers to a few only in their post-movement professions as writers, academics, or intellectuals. Shrinking the ideological scale, Collins calls out the names of Baker, Reagon, and Davis. But she deletes any references to revolutionary or radical organizations such as the Student Nonviolent Coordinating Committee, the Communist Party USA (CPUSA), Soledad Brothers Defense Committee, the Black Panther Party, or the National Alliance Against Racist and Political Repression (NAARPR) from her discussions; these black women cited by her were affiliated with such groups. Among the civil rights organizations, SNCC and CORE personified street activism and confrontation with segregation and institutionalized racism. Although Baker left the Southern Christian Leadership Conference, then headed by Martin Luther King Jr, because of its inaction, elitism, and sexism, to help found SNCC, Collins associates her only with the less radical and better-known SCLC. Through SNCC, Reagon became a Southern movement leader. Davis worked with that organization and the Black Panthers on the West coast; she was also a member of the Soledad Brothers Defense Committee, and part of the national leadership of the Communist Party and the National Alliance Against Racist and Political Repression. Treating Davis and Reagon merely as writers, Collins elides female antiracist, radical leadership. Omissions that decontextualize to depoliticize revolutionary women reflect the antiradical tendencies in American historiography. This trend toward a national, cultural antiradicalism (and anticommunism) severs revolutionary organizations from the continuum of democratic politics. Radicals disappear only to reappear as writers, reconstructing the politics of a tumultuous era, redefine the liberal or centrist as "radical."

Decontextualized, militant historical black women's activism is recast in the image of the respectable middle-class black feminist or community worker as reductionism leads to simplistic readings of the African-American liberation struggle and those who waged it. In "Conceptualizing Black Women's Activism," Collins cites the informal leadership black women have exerted in the male-dominated black church (but fails to note the conservative roles black churches played in stymieing progressive struggles).[31] Significantly, Collins focuses her brief discussion of black women's activism on black female domestics, educators, and churchgoers. Although some women in their areas of employment, religion, or social work engaged in the civil rights movement as activists, not all of their acts can be generalized as "radical." Restricting radical political traditions to conventional occupations promotes the disappearance of the militant black woman activist.

Church women and teachers engaged in radical acts of resistance, yet Collins's text gives few specifics of political radicalism and no indication whether the women's relationships with radical or revolutionary groups were supportive or oppositional. For instance, what were their demands on the state? Their critiques of capitalism? Their stances on political repression? Their interventions on behalf of political prisoners? Their efforts in the "Free Angela Davis" campaign? Redefining black women's radicalism as a variation of liberalism, Collins masculinizes black radicalism and revolutionary politics, and thereby inadvertently suggests that only men engage in revolutionary struggle; only men have an understanding of violence and violent repression; only men hate their oppressors. In these gender truisms that relegate women to a loftier, more soothing role in resistance, we see the misrepresentation of female antiracist radicalism. On the question of violence, both feminist and nonfeminist mainstream accounts of the civil rights–black liberation movements are mostly silent about black women's agency in the face of state repression. Violence either intimidates political thinkers into paralysis or it acts as a catalyst. In the political autobiographies, women endure threats, arrests, beatings, and imprisonment. As targets, they were sometimes shunned by black communities, which feared their presence would incite violent reprisals from whites. In the civil rights movement, activists, facing violence from civil and state repression, brought new meanings to democracy.

Recovering Agency

According to Delores Williams, if progressive women uncover black women's roles in liberation, they will better understand the relation of black history to the contemporary folk expression: 'If Rosa Parks had not sat down, Martin King would not have stood up.' We can add that if Parks had not sat down and later organized with E. D. Nixon, and with Jo Ann Robinson and others in the Women's Political Caucus, as well as the Montgomery Improvement Association, the Montgomery Bus Boycott would not have emerged. Parks has become an icon, while Robinson and the Women's Political Caucus are barely known. Remembering the contributions of lesser-known women activists and radicals increases understandings of antiracist leadership and progressive change. Male-dominated podiums or pulpits cannot completely hide the democratic agency of grass-roots workers. The majority of these activists were and continue to be women working in churches, schools, neighborhoods, farm fields, and factories, seeking democratic power, liberation, and sustenance.

Corrective scholarship highlights the role of women in the civil rights movement. Civil rights activists Septima Clark, Jo Ann Robinson, and Rosa Parks have published their memoirs. Chana Lee's dissertation on and Kay Mills's biography of Fannie Lou Hamer are also part of the expanding literature in gender-inclusive civil rights historiography. Joanne Grant, whose documentary *Fundi: The Story of Ella Baker* provided my first encounter with Miss Baker, has a forthcoming biography on the civil rights radical, who one day may be more largely recognized as one of—if not *the*—most influential of the American radicals of the civil rights movement.[32]

The Present Future
Contemporary Crises and Black Intellectuals

Whoever believes or claims to believe that there is some possibility of emerging from the crisis on a world scale without blood, suffering, wearisome struggles, on a national and international scale, whoever says this is a charlatan or a fool.

—C. L. R. James
American Civilization

Tyson Stinson and church members inside the Immanuel Christian Fellowship church damaged by arson, Portland, Oregon, June, 1996.

On Racial Violence and Democracy

Hannah Arendt asserts in *On Violence* that democratic power is most severely tested and diminished by violence.[1] Only violence, maintains Arendt, can so thoroughly decimate a community that it destroys the collective unity and communal interactions necessary for the appearance of democratic power. Expanding upon her insights, we might add our own observations regarding black life in American democracy: Whether through economic exploitation, police brutality, Klan or racist burnings, or self-infliction, violence destroys the spirit of freedom and courageous resistance, and erodes the ability of black communities to raise intellectuals and political actors.

Arendt's insights into democratic power also entail confusing, contradictory positions on racism and citizenry.[2] For instance, although she condemned racial repression, she viewed 1957 civil rights protests in Little Rock, Arkansas, to end school desegregation as acts that destabilized rather than expanded democracy. Arendt's inconsistencies on racial justice and democracy mirror the confusion of a national culture that historically promoted democratic thought while it pursued racist politics.

In our movements for democracy, black activists and intellectuals have had to contend with the threat and reality of violence. In the aftermath of the Civil War, in the first aborted Reconstruction, white terror sought, with no little success, to disenfranchise newly emancipated blacks. A century later, in the second Reconstruction of the Southern civil rights movement, activists led the federal government to enforce the Thirteenth, Fourteenth, and Fifteenth Amendments of the previous century. As had their nineteenth-century ancestors, civil rights activists appealed to the federal government for protection. Unfortunately they had to contend with federal agencies, such as the Federal Bureau of Investigation, that waged their own forms of terror to destabilize antiracist organizing.

In the 1960s and 1970s, violence against civil rights and black liberation activists escalated through a national counterintelligence program, COINTELPRO. FBI director J. Edgar Hoover established the program in 1956 to disrupt the Communist Party USA. Later it was used to exacerbate factionalism and incite violence among revolutionary groups such as the Socialist Workers' Party, the Black Panther Party, and the Puerto Rican Independentistas and even among reactionary organizations such as the Ku Klux Klan. In 1967, the FBI extended COINTELPRO to include so-called black nationalist hate groups. Some scholars such as Kevin O'Reilly depict the abuses of the FBI as an aberration of Hoover's racist idiosyncrasies. However, others argue that the FBI's strategizing with agencies such as the CIA, National Guard, local sheriff and police to destabilize civil rights organizing suggests more than rogue operatives undermining law-abiding enforcement agencies.[3]

Under Hoover's counterintelligence program, the FBI sent anonymous communiques to Martin Luther King Jr. recommending that he commit suicide before he was exposed as a moral fraud. It also infiltrated and disrupted the SCLC, SNCC, CORE, the Nation of Islam, Malcolm X's Organization of Afro-American Unity (OAAU), and the Black Panther Party. In general, human rights activists were tied up in court litigations, detained as political prisoners, and criminalized as political dissenters. The most effective groups and leaders at mobilizing mass confrontations with government authorities were targeted by the FBI. Its March 4, 1968, memo dictates directives for COINTELPRO's "maximum effectiveness," recommending

that the agency prevent "true black revolutions" by block-
ing coalitions among black nationalist groups and the rise of
a black nationalist leader or "messiah."[4] The Black Panther
Party was undermined by violent state repression, as well as its
lack of democratic process. Joint operations between the
Chicago police and the FBI led to the murders of Black Panther
leaders Fred Hampton and Mark Clark. The Party was frayed by
internal divisions and government destabilization through
"dirty tricks" and legal repression. Party members died in
shoot-outs with police or were derailed from organizing by
legal battles. The government failed to obtain convictions in
most Panther trials, Joanne Grant writes, due to the increasing
numbers of blacks on juries and decreasing credibility of police
testimony: "Jurors seemed to hold the view that many political
trials had come about through the activities of *agents provocateurs* and police spies."[5] Black Panther attorney Charles Garry
asserts that twenty-eight party members were murdered by the
police (police worked in coordination with the FBI). The
Panthers were also torn by internal fratricidal politics, as the
line between Panther internal violence and FBI infiltration
and agent provocateurs blurred.[6] By 1974, the party was devastated.

African-American intellectuals have both rebelled and col-
lapsed when confronting repressive violence. Antiblack violence created a vortex for revolutionary thinking as well as
discouraged African Americans from engaging in radical democratic movements. A nation that barely refers to how its history of slavery and genocide normalized violence offers little in
the way of an explanation or an atonement for the destruction
of black activists. Likewise, we are hard-pressed to find discussions that address how violent repression and state collusion
or indifference make communities more susceptible to dema-
gogues' promises of protection. The appeal of militarist posturing from such diverse groups as the Panthers a generation ago
or the Nation of Islam's Fruit of Islam today expands or shrinks
in proportion to the intensity of antiblack violence in society.
The race rhetoric that declares a people to be "at war" with
their racialized oppressors renders democratic debate and decision a luxury if not a pernicious indulgence inside black

groups and thereby circumscribes democratic politics. How we manage to expand our critiques and confrontations with antiblack violence without resorting to militarist rhetoric and posturing is critical, yet, elusive. Black and American intellectuals who discuss and confront antiblack violence face the paradox of seeking recourse via state protection, despite the state's unacknowledged historical complicity in such violence.

Lynching—Meanings and Metaphors

Lynchings preoccupied black intellectuals in the postbellum era because they came to epitomize the ultimate right under white rule: arbitration over black life. The lynch rope became the American metaphor for deified and debased humanity, of both white executioners and black victims. Lynching, police malfeasance and brutality, and the indifference of the courts preyed upon all blacks, but particularly devastated the lives of poorer African Americans. Yet racist violence proved a catalyst for black intellectualism. It also served (and continues to serve) as a measure for determining intellectualism's relevance to African-American life. For instance, when William Patterson and the African American-led Civil Rights Congress petitioned the United Nations with *We Charge Genocide: The Crime of Government against the Negro People,*[7] citing lynchings with photographs of lynch victims, the document promoted the language and implementation of the 1948 *U.N. Convention on the Prevention and Punishment of Genocide.* Months before Rosa Parks sat down on the Montgomery bus in 1955, Emmett Till was lynched. Like the lynchings of James Chaney, Andrew Goodman, and Michael Schwerner nearly ten years later, his murder both haunted and mobilized Americans.

Contemporary black academics debate the relationships of earlier intellectuals to activism to end racist violence. Responding to a dispute over this issue at an academic conference, in 1995 *The Journal of Blacks in Higher Education* printed a brief paragraph with the banner "The Brutal Reason Why Racial Integration of American Colleges, Universities, and Secondary Schools Was Not the Principal Concern of Black Intellectuals in the Pre-World War II Period," and an accompanying photograph of a 1930 double lynching in Marion, Indiana.[8] In the photograph two black men hang from trees as a large crowd of smiling whites stands below their brutalized bodies. *The Journal* editors informed its readers that some black educators at a symposium "questioned our insistence that racial integration in education was not at the head of the agenda of black intellectuals during the Harlem Renaissance of the 1920s .... Here are 376 reasons why our statement is probably true." They then proceed to list over three hundred publicly recorded lynchings of African Americans between 1920 and 1935. *The Journal's* death count is based on *The Negro Almanac*: In 1920, fifty-three blacks were lynched; in 1921, fifty-nine died; in 1922, fifty-one; in 1923, twenty-nine were lynched; the numbers of victims fell to sixteen in 1924; increased to seventeen in 1925. In 1926, twenty-three died; sixteen were lynched in 1927; ten in 1928; seven in 1929; the numbers soared to twenty in 1930; fell again to twelve in 1931: diminished to six in 1932; exploded to twenty-four in 1933; subsided to fifteen murders in 1934; and rose again to eighteen in 1935.[9] Over a fifteen-year span, the number of ritual killings rose and fell only to rise and fall again, repeating their grisly cycle in a roller-coaster ride of terror for black Americans.

Today, the imagery rather than the act of lynching prevails. Antilynching crusaders risked their lives to change the meaning and the symbolism of the term. Through their efforts lynchings would constitute white rather than black guilt and depravity. A century after the historic, heroic struggles by antilynching crusaders, we freely use the term in curious ways. The most heinous form of racist violence has become a prop in black performance politics. Since blackness continues as the indicator of guilt in white American society, and lynching is the most visceral image of white victimization of blacks, the charge of lynching remains one of the strongest expressions of innocence by black males. Clarence Thomas, crying that he was a victim of a "high-tech lynching," used the term as a shield against sexual harassment charges in his 1991 Supreme Court confirmation hearings; he was supported by ultraconservatives who advocated the repeal of civil rights legislation.

Several years later, supporters of Ben Chavis denounced his removal from NAACP leadership for misappropriation of funds to settle a sexual discrimination suit by describing his ouster as a legal lynching.

But whites have also struggled to reclaim the meaning of this highly charged symbol. In the synonymy of blackness with violence, the specter of lynching appears as the expression of American rage and retribution. In the postbellum era, whites deployed lynchings to quell black independence and equality. At the end of the second Reconstruction, it was appropriated in the rhetoric of white (male) victimization. Ronald Reagan used lynching as a backdrop for the victim narratives of white men shaken by civil rights legislation redressing racial and sexual discrimination. Touring for his 1980 presidential candidacy, Reagan spoke in Philadelphia, Mississippi, the site of the 1964 triple lynching of civil rights activists Chaney, Goodman, and Schwerner. His speech failed to condemn the murders yet gave voice to the new racial victims, white males allegedly disenfranchised by civil rights and other progressive legislation. During his eight-year presidency, Reagan continuously inverted racial victimization to legitimize the claims by the dominant caste that they were harmed by the gains of racially and sexually subjugated peoples. This stance extended from domestic to foreign policies.[10] Inaugurating the conservative revolution, Reagan's Mississippi performance supplanted the symbol of martyred antiracists with that of "oppressed" whites or racists who opposed legal measures to end discrimination. Today, sixteen years after Reagan's presidential campaign in Mississippi, the nation is wracked by the sometimes violent campaigns of "angry white men"—Survivalists, Militiamen, Freemen—to address their outrage at their allegedly diminished status as racial and gender elites.

American idiosyncratic and cynical expressions of victimization, rage, and punishment invoke lynching as justified force against a violent, external threat personified by blacks. These expressions claim as well the racial-victim status for whites. For over a century, in the postbellum, civil rights, and war-on-crime eras, we have seen black-personified violence and the masking of institutional racial violence and white criminality. Such masking seeks to absolve a nation from confronting violence.

In the tragedy and cynical criminality of black scapegoating, the criminalization of blacks provides occasional opportunities for national chagrin. For instance, in 1989, after Boston police spent weeks detaining or strip-searching black men, ostensibly in search of the murderer of Carol Stuart, a pregnant white woman, her husband, Charles Stuart, committed suicide. The recipient of a large life insurance policy on his wife, Stuart had initially stated that an unknown black man shot and killed Carol and wounded him as they sat side by side in their car in Roxbury. Five years later in South Carolina, Susan Smith reported that an unknown black man had abducted her two toddlers in a carjacking. Her claims instigated a regional manhunt and widespread interrogation of black males. Later, Smith admitted that she drowned her children by locking them in the car and allowing it to roll down a bank into a lake. After Smith's confession, a national news magazine ran a cartoon depicting a pinafored Goldilocks confidently informing three frowning bears, glumly staring at empty porridge bowls, that "a black guy did it." Despite satirical commentary on racism, scapegoating remains pervasive as the racial myths used by individual white murderers mirror the images of white media.

Racial bias undergirded mainstream media reports of the April 19, 1995, bombing of the federal building in Oklahoma City, which occurred on the anniversary of the World Trade Center bombing and the Bureau of Alcohol, Tobacco, and Firearms (ATF)'s storming of the Branch Davidian compound in Waco, Texas. Immediately following the Oklahoma City bombing,[11] media terrorist experts, legitimized by the press as authoritative, characterized it as a "Muslim bombing." The U.S. profile of the national killer is the black; its profile for the international killer or terrorist is the Arab, imbued with blackness. The extensive manhunt after the bombing focused on men with "Middle Eastern" accents. Several days later, the police released composite sketches of white males. Within the week, Timothy McVeigh, a white man associated with the right-wing militia movement, was arrested for the bombing in which 167 people, including children, died.

At first, corrective press reports on the Stuart, Smith, and Oklahoma City tragedies discussed the ways in which media initially racialized manhunts. These reflections were sporadic and brief. Few media accounts dwelt on the racist imagery employed by Stuart, Smith, or the militia. Few press reports analyzed the racialized manhunts that dominated the first hours and days following the tragedies. Most national, mainstream coverage downplayed the racist ideology of the militia. (Although white extremists advocate the right to violence against a federal government in part because it allegedly promotes the rights of blacks, Jews, immigrants, women, gays, and lesbians, paradoxically, this argument is made at a time when national and state governments repeal legislation protecting the rights of disenfranchised groups under the mandate of a "new federalism.") Coverage depicted outraged whites demanding (for the white offenders) the "swift justice" of extralegal execution in the tortured death associated with blacks—lynching. White Americans were also cited in the national press calling for the lynching of Susan Smith and Timothy McVeigh.

Paradoxically, the rise of right-wing coalitions marks the use of black revolutionary struggle as an apologia for white fascists,[12] who, like social criminals Stuart and Smith, filter the responsibility for their savagery through the black image.

The Specters of Black Criminality and White (In)Security

African Americans have consistently, and with the greatest unity and outrage, battled racist violence. Responding to three waves of racist violence in the twentieth century—from turn-of-the-century lynchings through midcentury repression of civil rights activists to the late-century racialized prison industry, state executions, and new manifestations of police racism[13]—black intellectuals countered racial terror and fascistic movements within democracy. Historically, confronting racist violence, black intellectuals lectured, wrote, and organized institutions, coalitions and protests; more than a few fought back in armed self-defense. Today white mob terror is an anomaly in antiblack violence: The greatest threat of physical violence to blacks comes from black youths.[14] The dilemmas for black intellectuals today manifest in crime, the criminalization and imprisonment of blacks, and the role of the state in antiblack repression. In the criminalization of blacks and the racially biased death penalty exist the chimerical rights of poor and black peoples. Present in the punitive policies of the prison industry are the symbols of past servitude, embodied in forced labor camps and the return of chain gangs in Florida, Alabama, and Arizona.[15]

Boston Globe columnist Derrick Z. Jackson notes that although violent crime is at a record twenty-year low, and its most-likely victims are African-American teenagers, because of media coverage the (white) public perceives itself as besieged by black criminals: "In its blazing orange 'Murder' edition . . . *Newsweek*'s graphics department, not to be outdone by *Time*'s blackening of O. J. Simpson's mug shot, displayed the number of homicides in African-American liberation colors."[16] In current, common racial discourse, blackness remains the synonym for violent criminality. Whites are the greatest perpetuators of sexual and physical violence against other whites, yet as a group they remain the least likely to receive the death penalty for violent crimes. The group least likely to receive mandatory sentencing for drug abuse, white male suburbanites, constitute the majority of cocaine users. Linked with social pathology and sexual violence in the national psyche, blacks are viewed by many whites as contaminants in the political body. The use of blacks as national symbols for savagery diminishes concern for violence in general, especially in its nonracialized forms.

Propaganda around race and violence seems to exacerbate our lives in election years. In the last decade, despite their diminishing material conditions, many whites, particularly males, voted for candidates who passed policies and legislation benefiting the top five percent of the U.S. population.[17] Within a week of a House Ways and Means report, the *New York Times* informed on March 29, 1990 that economic gains from 1980 to 1989 were tied to property and higher corporate profits: U.S. personal savings rates of the net national income declined from 8.9 percent to 3.6 percent; average hourly wages decreased from $9.84 an hour to $9.66. At the same time, the percent of the working population rose from 59.6 percent to 63.3 percent. U.S. families, particularly the working class and lower-middle classes, earned more during the last decade because they worked more: Women wage workers were largely responsible for family income gains, as women holding two paying jobs moved from double to triple shifts. From 1989 to 1993, the average U.S. household annual income fell seven percent for a loss of $2,344.[18] Eroding standards of living promote scapegoating to deflect from declining economic conditions. Racialized and sexual resentment is evinced even among the affluent. In theory, college-educated, middle-class voters are less susceptible to racist demagoguery; in practice, the majority of votes for neo-Nazi David Duke in his 1992 Louisiana gubernatorial campaign came from middle class not poor whites. Candidate Duke capitalized on stereotypes of the black welfare cheat and criminal, although the largest financial thefts of public monies come from white-collar crime and the majority of public aid recipients are white.

Racialized resentments and fears are political tools to profit from the image of violence-prone blacks. Republican strategist Lee Atwater managed George Bush's 1988 campaign, and arguably secured his victory by playing to racial fears (the so-called "race card") through the Willie Horton television ad campaign which focused on a black convict on work furlough (Horton), who raped a middle-class white woman. Atwater's strategy for GOP electoral victories remains sound advice. The image of the black criminal and social parasite allows non-blacks to transcend their own class differences and interests to form a conservative bloc. This image also obscures the specificity of crime, violence, and economic dependency in the United States.

U.S. visual culture renders social violence, particularly sexual violence, synonymous with blackness. This legitimizes state violence in wars on crime or drugs against racialized-criminalized groups. Depictions of U.S. violence are usually racialized and so have been effective in mobilizing national support for the "three strikes" legislation of mandatory sentencing, expanding police powers, and the death penalty. Consider that in U.S. death sentencing, the race of victim and defendant are determining factors.[19] Between 1977 and 1986 nearly ninety percent of prisoners executed had been convicted of killing whites, although the number of black victims was approximately equal to that of white victims. In the 1970s, Georgia sentenced to death those convicted of killing whites eleven times more than those convicted of killing blacks. In the mid-1980s, the Supreme Court ruled this was an acceptable level of difference, given the past strides in racial equality. Overall those who killed whites were twenty percent more likely to receive the death penalty than those who killed blacks; and, in similar cases, black defendants would receive the death penalty more often than whites. Intellectuals such as John Wideman and Alice Walker have helped to mobilize national and international responses against the death penalty, and police malfeasance, by drawing public attention to the case of Mumia Abu-Jamal, a Death Row intellectual and author of *Live from Death Row.*[20]

Performing Revolutionary Violence

Audre Lorde's adage—"The master's tools can never dismantle the master's house"—has great relevance. Still, the image of revolutionary violence, the Fanonian reversals in which the oppressed use the violent tactics of the oppressor, retain currency.[21] Their strongest appearance lies in cultural performance. In its lyrics for "Rebel Without a Pause" on the album/CD *It Takes a Nation of Millions to Hold Us Back: Freedom is a Road Seldom Traveled By the Multitude,* Public Enemy identifies itself on this track as "a supporter of Chessimard"; Joanne Chessimard is Assata Shakur's "slave name." Various works that target police officers—NWA's "Fuck the Police," Public Enemy's "Arizona" music video on assassinating white racists in state government, Sister Souljah's music video featuring a black woman in a shootout with racist cops in a black neighborhood, and Ice T's group Body Count's "Cop Killer" video—have received condemnations. Censorship of these antipolice tracks may come from those indifferent to sexism and black-on-black violence in rap music. Images of black-on-black violence are "tolerable" but images of black violence against whites, particularly against police, are considered heinous. Paradoxically, while police violence against blacks is the occasion for searing national self-reflection on racism (especially in the aftermath of the 1992 Los Angeles riots), state violence against incarcerated blacks is deemed more acceptable.

Black political agency seems embedded in cultural performance with the performing revolutionary. The selling of black political culture suggests a race discourse abstracted from material struggles and radical agency, one that trivializes violence.

In recounting the struggles of revolutionary and radical activist intellectuals, some reduce agency to performance. Where performance reigns, vacuous renditions of black revolutionary struggles take center stage. Performing blackness reworks the history of radicalism to market "Black power" as a commodity. In 1995, black publications such as *YSB* (*Young Sisters and Brothers*) ran an advertisement for the "Panther Sweepstakes" of $1,000 of "personal empowerment money" to promote Mario Van Peebles's Hollywood movie *Panther*. When performing blackness pays in promotional book sales and other ventures, black intellectuals may glibly entertain by repackaging black radical struggles to appeal to commercial consumers. (For instance, in his 1994 National Public Radio, *Fresh Air* interview to promote *Colored People*,[22] Henry Louis Gates Jr. reminisced that as a youth, he found viewing the 1960s televised desegregation battles in Birmingham—where police used dogs, water blasts from fire hoses, and billy clubs to attack black protestors—to be akin to watching a basketball game: "The New York Nicks vs the Chicago Bulls."

In various evasions of antiracist militancy, conservatives and liberals may discredit radicalism that confronts racist violence as anachronistic to the romanticized 1960s. How black intellectuals construct a unified program for action amid repression, evasion, and the appropriation of black radicalism and resistance remains a monumental challenge for black progressivism.

Marian Wright Edelman (center) with youth activists and adult advocates at the June 1, 1996 march on Washington, D.C., organized by the Children's Defense Fund.

6
The Common Program
Race, Class, Sex, and Politics

Black intellectuals have historically argued for specific political agendas and the establishment of a common program for a broad-based movement. Responding to the critical need for a common program, some black intellectuals seek to organize multiracial formations of progressives. Often these formations advance effective policies to redress injustice. For instance, the political platforms of leaders such as Marian Wright Edelman unify both African Americans and Americans in general for progressive struggles.

In their lowest common denominator, though, shorn of critiques of institutionalized violence, racism/sexism, and economic exploitation, agendas can echo Rodney King's consensus-building plea—"Can't we all just get along?" Despite the lack of substantive strategies, the national preference for centrist politics, particularly in times of racialized turmoil, leads many to claim that only a politics of consensus matters.

In the quest for black unity for social justice, agency either bridges or splits along ideological differences and identity politics. Progressive African-American intellectuals and radicals have issued the call for a unifying, common program for black liberation struggles with detailed analysis and vision. For instance, intergrating feminist, antiracist, and socialist politics in the call to unity, Paul Robeson outlines a common program in his autobiography, *Here I Stand*.[1]

Paul Robeson emerged after World War II as one of America's most prominent cultural artists and intellectuals. By the late 1940s, Robeson was targeted by the U.S. government for his antiracist, pro-socialist and communist sentiments and activities. When the Truman administration denied the performer a passport in 1949, Robeson was marginalized and barred from both national and international media and cultural stages. Yet he continued to voice his political thoughts. Through the *Freedom* newspaper, which was published from 1951 to 1955, Robeson and other radical black writers, artists, and members of the National Negro Labor Council continued to challenge and shape American perspectives on race, class, and gender politics. In 1971, some twenty years after the founding of *Freedom* and his ban by the U.S. government, Robeson published his autobiography.[2]

Focusing on black economic power and self-determination in *Here I Stand*, Robeson writes that independent black organizations—such as churches, "fraternal orders, women's clubs, and so forth—will increasingly take the lead because they are closer to the Negro rank-and-file, more responsive to their needs, and less subject to control by forces outside the Negro community."[3] Emphasizing the role of black trade unionists, he notes, "We are a working people and the pay-envelope of the Negro worker is the measure of our general welfare and progress."[4] The "key to set into motion our power of organization," writes Robeson, "is the concept of *coordinated action*."[5] For him, coordinated action entails uniting the various black organizations "to plan and to carry out the common struggle."[6] Like Du Bois, Robeson ties the concept and practice of black leadership to service. "The primary quality that Negro leadership must possess," he writes, "is *a single-minded dedication to their people's welfare*."[7] Robeson emphasizes the importance of women's leadership in his memoir. In a chapter called "The Power of Negro Action," he advocates black women's agency as indispensable. "We need more of our women in the higher ranks, too, and who should know better," writes Robeson, "than the children of Harriet Tubman, Sojourner Truth and Mary Church Terrell that our womenfolk have often led the way. Negro womanhood today is giving us many inspiring examples of steadfast devotion, cool courage under fire, and brilliant generalship in our people's struggles; and here is a major source for new strength and militancy in Negro leadership on every level.[8]

Robeson's call for black unity encompassed more than workers, nonelites, and women; it crossed ideological and party lines. Referring to what he termed "our common viewpoint as Negroes," referencing the oppression that all blacks experienced on some level in a white-dominated society, Robeson advocated an inclusive, nonpartisan unity, devoid of factionalism. Robeson's transideological union is problematized by the rise of black Republicans in a neoconservative era, and the increasing splintering of black political consensus.[9] Still, for Robeson, the commonality of black oppression and African Americans' willingness to submerge individualism and personal gain for the collective good forged the binding ties: "A unified leadership of a unified movement means that people of all political views—conservatives, liberals, and radicals—must be represented therein. Let there be but one requirement made without exception: that Negro leadership, and every man and woman in that leadership, place the interest of our people, and the struggle for those interests, above all else."[10] Robeson repeatedly asserted the urgent need "to work out a *common program of action* for Negro Americans in the crisis of our times."[11]

The need for unified black movements that further an antiracist, socialist agenda that recognizes black female leadership concerned Robeson as well as other black intellectuals such as C. L. R. James, Angela Davis, and Manning Marable. Adding feminism and gay and lesbian rights to Robeson's formulations, Marable describes in *BLACKWATER* a Common Program agenda and principles for socialism, antiracism, and self-determination. Recounting African Americans' attempts to forge a common program for economic and social justice, Marable discusses black labor and Pan-African organizing, the 1972 National Black Political Assembly in Gary, Indiana, and the Congressional Black Caucus. For Marable, the common program differs from a coalition, and coalescing or consensus-building politics are not synonymous with radical agency. Attempting to bridge between dominant neoconservatives or reactionaries and marginalized progressives is like trying to unify a privileged white society that claims racism to be a thing of the past and impoverished, disenfranchised colored communities that experience racism as a daily assault. Those privileged to define the parameters of what constitutes legitimate consent and dissent tend to determine the objectives of consensus-building politics. For example, mainstream civil rights coalitions were routinely criticized for catering to the interests of their white influential members and financial supporters, to the disadvantage of their most desperate constituency, poor blacks.

Consensus building was a problem among black groups and leaders. Marable describes the divisions between black leaders and intellectuals during the demise of the black power movement in the early 1970s. The belief guiding the movement (and Robeson to some extent)—that all blacks shared similar interests and enemies—disintegrated during the infighting of black organizations,[12] in which, according to Marable, nationalists lost ground to integrationists. Black intellectuals during the civil rights-black power movements attempted to move beyond coalition politics toward a common program. For Marable the failure of black progressives to identify a common program as well as class stratification undermined "the Movement." We can add to Marable's argument that government destabilization and repression also crippled the movement. While poor blacks were set economically adrift, black elites became middle class or consolidated their status as middle class from gains made by social agitation; all the while, writes Marable, the progressive politics of a marginalized radical minority became coopted into the general society.

A quarter of a century ago, Martin Kilson's 1969 essay "The New Black Intellectuals" identified two types of black intellectuals in conflict and uneasy alliance.[13] Referring to working-class or lower-middle class urban street thinkers and community activists as "paraintellectuals," Kilson describes these "self-made intellectuals" as generally lacking formal education and employed within the underground economy of street selling and illegal activities. According to Kilson, both Malcolm X and Louis X (Farrakhan) developed as paraintellectuals through their associations with the Nation of Islam. This new urban black intelligentsia was in conflict with the traditional Talented Tenth of doctors, lawyers, and teachers, Kilson argued. Self-made intellectuals' greater proximity to and shared cultural experiences (including the negative experiences of police brutality) with the poorer blacks meant that they were more often chosen as spokesmen for nonelite blacks during the civil unrest of the 1960s.[14] Designated as the legitimate and *natural* leaders, paraintellectuals, Kilson maintained, accomplished what established mainstream black intellectuals had little desire or success in doing: They helped to politicize black urban masses in their critiques of black-white relations and their suggestions for policies to change these relations in ways beneficial to nonelite blacks.[15] The emergence of this urban leadership created a crisis among Kilson's established intelligentsia or the traditional Talented Tenth. To consolidate their status as black leadership, the formally educated elite could, Kilson notes, "leave militancy to the paraintellectuals" and concentrate on building the moderate, integration politics; or it could compete with street intellectuals by creating a "lower-class-oriented black militancy of its own"; or elites could form coalitions with the paraintellectuals "on the latter's terms."[16] Kilson makes some pessimistic observations: that an established black intelligentsia used the militancy of poorer blacks to argue for more access for African Americans, while the "natural" leadership amid the poor was bought off with jobs and structural placement. His recommendations for alliances between the two leaderships argue for a mutually beneficial pact: Paraintellectuals acquire the skills and political savvy "they badly need," while the professional politicians acquire both "legitimacy in the eyes of the black lower class" and "valuable political workers." Although some might view Kilson's 1969 marriage of convenience as a viable model for contemporary contracts, he fails to note the analyses held by that era's revolutionary black nationalists whose politics were circumscribed by neither the paraintellectual's nor the established intelligentsia's opportunistic accommodationism.

Revolutionary Black Nationalism and Nationalist Women

Progressive elements of black nationalism are traceable to the later thought of Malcolm X, who has come to symbolize

black resistance, independence, and revolutionary struggle.[17]
After the March 8, 1964, break with the Nation of Islam and its
political conservatism and alienation from the civil rights
movement, Malcolm X began to state political views that
brought him closer to radical civil rights activists.[18] This
Malcolm X inspires revolutionary nationalists (while the earlier Malcolm X appeals to cultural nationalists).[19] Malcolm's revolutionary nationalism expressed concern for black self-determination as well as for international liberation movements.[20]
Movement radicals, as internationalists, viewed the civil rights
movement as a decolonization struggle. Even before his departure from the Nation of Islam, Malcolm X supported decolonization movements in countries such as Cuba. His 1960 meeting with Fidel Castro in Harlem signals this revolutionary
internationalism reminiscent of Du Bois's Wilberforce Address.[21]
Once, in referring to Che Guevara, the Argentinean doctor
who fought in the 1959 Cuban revolution, Malcolm X stated,
"I love a revolutionary."[22] His affection for revolutionaries was
shared by other civil rights activists who, like Malcom X,
defined revolutionary politics within the context of black
nationalism. They also placed revolutionary nationalism within the context of black women's lives.

Malcolm's increasingly progressive gender politics and nationalism influenced and were influenced by radical black
women activists. Urging women to assume "the chief responsibility for passing on black cultural traditions to the children"
and to imbue black men with political militancy, Malcolm X
would quote an African proverb: "Educate a man and you educate an individual. Educate a woman and you educate an
entire family." On one level this manifests as a sexist homily to
further black instrumental politics.[23] On another level, radical
women embraced and shaped the political ideologies espoused
by black male intellectuals such as Malcolm X.

Bernice Johnson Reagon places black liberation and nationalism within the context of mothering. As a concept and practice, mothering evinces forms of community caretaking sometimes supportive of, sometimes antithetical to, radical black
intellectualism.[24] Contradictory images of mothering in black
resistance reflect the larger society's bipolar stereotypes of the
"good mother" and the "bad mother" (sometimes, the latter

represents the woman who counters violence with violence.)[25] Most mothers, rather than school their children in radical resistance to dominance, teach them to get along in order to survive, with coping strategies that create new forms of covert resistance to subjugation.[26] Still, mother-figures abide in black liberation struggles. Southern civil rights activists revered women leaders such as Annie Devine, Septima Clark, Rosa Parks, and Fannie Lou Hamer with the title "Movement Mammas." Such women "raised" white as well as black young activists in SNCC and Students for a Democratic Society and, later, feminist organizations, functioning in social and political struggles as birthmothers and midwives. In the Northern black liberation movement, Malika Mae Adams recounts that New York City Black Panther Party women moved from the title of "Guerrilla Woman" to that of "Mother Security." Women and men "mothered," understood as a feminine not female characteristic, youth and activists of all ethnicities into spiritual and physical survival/resistance to oppression.[27] Reagon's mothering includes the "spiritual art and political act" of nation building. For Reagon, whole families or communities perform the role of political mothering: "Whether it is from the mother or the grandmother or the aunt or the babysitter or the nursery, the first words that the child begins to speak, the first smells, the songs, the body stances, the tastes, come from the women part of the society."[28] Direct involvement in the reproduction of a people through nurturing future generations links black women to nationalism: "Black women are nationalists in our efforts to form a nation that will survive in this society, and we are also the major cultural carriers and passers-on of the traditions of our people."[29] Such women create "a black space" where African-American life can grow as "nationalistic, cultural, and also revolutionary." Reagon defines revolution within the context of black nationalism: as "the stopping" or "the turning around," the "radical change of direction" that entails "a lot of violence [and] a . . . cleansing process."[30]

Reagon worked with SNCC leader and Mississippi Freedom Democratic Party (MFDP) congressional candidate Fannie Lou Hamer, described by Malcolm X as "one of this country's foremost freedom fighters."[31] In her essay on women as cultural carriers, Reagon expands upon Malcolm's statements to describe black women's nationalism: "We are, at the base of our identities, nationalists . . . builders, carriers of cultural traditions, key to the formation and continuance of culture. We are the ones who touch the children first and most consistently."(81) For Reagon, women are at the center of black nation building because they provide "the most consistent concept of nationhood" among a people: "With black people in the United States, we understand that one of our responsibilities is to live and struggle so that there will be another generation of people. This makes us, Black women, as a group within the Black community, nationalistic."[32] The women shouldering the responsibility of black people's continuance, however, included more than cultural nationalists. Some were political revolutionaries.

Misogyny, homophobia, and ethnic chauvinism obviously existed and exist in some forms of black nationalism and its contemporary offshoots. However, gender-progressive women in the civil rights and black liberation movements, such as Reagon and Assata Shakur, were nationalists who reflected some of the most progressive elements of black intellectualism symbolized by Malcolm X's revolutionary ideology.

Rejecting nationalism as narrow or parochial, as did Malcolm X, Robeson, and Du Bois, black women radicals, advocated global solidarity in black liberation struggles and maintained the importance of black women's leadership. Stressing the liberating aspects of international politics, Shakur describes nationalism "without a truly internationalist component" as reactionary to argue against a construction of nationalism as inherently progressive: "Hitler and Mussolini were nationalists."[33] For Shakur, "Any community seriously concerned with its own freedom has to be concerned about other peoples' freedom as well. The victory of oppressed people anywhere in the world is a victory for Black people. Imperialism is an international system of exploitation, and, we, as revolutionaries, need to be internationalists to defeat it."[34] In revolutionary nationalism, the survival and liberation of a people connects with international alliances as this form of nationalism transcends isolationism to interact with a larger world, according to Reagon, who writes: "Being a nationalist may mean a centering in purpose inside oneself and then being sure of being everywhere so that as my nation goes, so will you, my enemy."[35] Assuming responsibility for black continuance through time, women worked as both cultural nationalists and political revolutionaries. The continuance of an entire community, rather than a gender or class within it, was the objective in the race leadership of this form of female black radicalism. But revolutionary nationalism, like black revolutionary feminism, appears to have little bearing on contemporary conflicts between black nationalists and black feminists.

Black Feminism and Black Nationalism

Black feminism is as ideologically diverse as black nationalism. There are conservative, liberal, and radical forms of each. However, black feminisms' calls for a common program—a black unity sans patriarch—are often labeled divisive by (gender-) conservative black nationalists.[36]

Challenging sexism in African Americans' pursuit of black unity through nationalist politics, black feminists' diverse ideologies have provided progressive and counterprogressive critiques. The progressive aspects manifested in calls to sexual equality and repudiation of heterosexism. The nonprogressive elements surfaced in various forms of elitism that disparaged black, nonelite political formations. Contemporary debates surrounding the Million Man March reflect some of the assessments Kilson made about the contest between black "paraintellectuals" schooled in the Nation of Islam and other urban, working-class formations, and the struggle between the intelligentsia, embodied in black professionals of the Talented Tenth. Given that black male elites (and some female elites) participated in or supported the Million Man March, the terrain of struggle appears to be more aptly defined by opposing constructs of black feminism and black nationalism.

The diversity of black women's criticisms of the 1995 Million Man March reflected various ideological stances.[37] Emphasizing the importance of coalitions and the centrality of black women's leadership in antiracist struggles, black women cited Frederick Douglass as a model of black male leadership that acknowledged women as peers in political agency. Some African Americans considered women who criticized the march as defecting from black communities and aligning themselves with a dominant, hostile white society. Misogynist attacks on black women who refused to support the October march reflected a debased political discourse among those who were preoccupied with female public criticism (through national [white] media) of an African-American male endeavor at unity, albeit an exclusionary unity. However, what the white media's sound-bite journalism did not provide, and what black press in its nearly uniform championing of the event would not grant, was a close scrutiny of the press statement titled "In Response to the Million Man March"[38] issued by the African American Agenda 2000, an ad hoc committee largely composed of black women academics and intellectuals. Unlike the women who issued the "African American Women In Defense of Ourselves" statement after the Clarence Thomas Supreme Court confirmation hearings, which was publicized through a three-quarter-page ad in the *New York Times*[39] and later reprinted in the *Black Scholar*,[40] these black women leaders did not ensure that their declaration appear in its entirety in black or white publications.

African American Agenda 2000 distributed its statement on the event at a press conference on October 12, 1995, four days before the atonement march to Washington. It received considerable coverage. Major media were generous in highlighting prominent black women who expressed reservations about the march (if the same women had called a press conference to give unqualified support, coverage might have been negligible).

The women who signed the statement wrote that they shared "the rage and pain and anguish that fuel" the march and saw the importance of black mobilization and the need to remind the nation of commitments to racial and gender justice and human rights. "But our needs are not served by men declaring themselves the only rightful leaders of our families, of our communities and of our ongoing struggle for justice," wrote the signatories, who asserted that a "march that excludes Black women and minimizes Black women's oppression" and attempts to counter racist stereotypes of black manhood with patriarchal, sexist images of black men promotes injustice:

> This call for men to take responsibility is not the solution to the rising plague of socially and economically engineered problems

that we face. We need to repudiate the Far Right's claim that *we* rather than racism are the cause of our problems, not echo their rhetoric. Rather than "atonement" for violence against women, it is time to commit to eliminating the sexism and oppression that spawns it. Instead of men marching to atone for their behavior, defend men's rights, and define women's roles, we the organizers of African American Agenda 2000 raise the call for men and women to come together and create an inclusive, well-organized social and political movement dedicated to combating racism, sexism and homophobia and to transforming the lives and conditions of our community.[41]

The African American Agenda 2000 passage cites homophobia. Some of the March organizers exhibited not only patriarchal paternalism, ethnic chauvinism, and bigotry, but also homophobia. The issues of women's and sexual minorities' rights have generally been ignored or disparaged in black nationalist discourse. Feminist, gay, lesbian, and bisexual antiracists and black nationalists as well as black gay and lesbian intellectuals have made extensive contributions to black emancipation. The rage against so-called sexual deviants, doubly rebounds against black gays, lesbians, and bisexuals. Apparently, a comprehensive common program for black unity would address not only racism, sexism, and economic exploitation, but heterosexism as well.[42]

Unfortunately, in the absence of a sustained dialogue between those who opposed the march and those who supported it, black intellectuals lost an opportunity to synthesize the progressive elements in each camp. Seizing such an opportunity might have minimized the stereotypes and polarization in which feminism and black nationalism were posed as mutually exclusive.

Black feminist reflections on the march (and the O. J. Simpson verdict that also occurred in October) were not uniformly progressive. When the *New York Times Magazine* published Kristal Brent Zook's 1995 "A Manifesto of Sorts for a Black Feminist Movement" as its black feminist response to black unity or nationalist discourse, it replaced what some considered to be an essentialist, antiwhite and antifeminist black narrative with an amblyopic, antiblack female diatribe.[43] The *Times* gave considerable exposure to a writer unknown to feminist or black organizations as a representative of the next wave of black feminism; predictably this manifesto garnered legitimacy via the *Times* and was subsequently used in university classes as a representative text on black feminism.

What may not have been discussed in those classrooms was its problematic content. Zook's claims about nonelite black women recycled antiblack caricatures to promote a black, postmodern feminist elite represented by Zook. First, it reprocessed the imago of the black Sapphire as Zook exhorts black women to "create public spaces along the way in which we can use our hardness, our meanness, our loudness, to challenge the models we've inherited." (This passage suggests that we should in fact first challenge the antiblack female stereotypes we have inherited and internalized.) The *New York Times* manifesto depicts an aggregate of colorful, emotional, naive black women. As a corrective to our negative inheritance of allegedly black female traits, it offers a model of feminism led by the elite of the new generation of enlightened feminists. Of the three young women profiled in photos as the black feminist "New Guard," among whom Zook presents herself, only one, a NAACP youth organizer, is connected to any organization with established ties to African Americans. This black feminist "New Guard," we are informed, supplants the previous generation's "antiquated queens" (depicted as Betty Shabazz, Myrlie Evers, and Coretta Scott King) and its "progressive bridges" (represented by Angela Davis, Jewell Jackson, and Kimberly Crenshaw).

This "new feminism" is most problematic because its primary spokespersons are largely young elites with tenuous ties to nonelite black communities and black organizations and reflects an inexperienced leadership alienated from black workers and neighborhoods, and mass political organizing. This movement manifesto does not inspire much confidence. Even if we were inclined to do so, it would be difficult to follow a leadership that makes the familiar point about African-American female complicity in misogyny with a diatribe on black women that crassly simplifies their diverse political thought. It is courageous to condemn sexism and homophobia in an ethnic group battling racism as a prime directive, as Zook attempts to do. Yet, the earlier antiracist critiques of sexism and homophobia provided by Audre Lorde, James Baldwin, and Essex Hemphill crafted nuanced depictions of black life and bigotry painfully missing in the "New Guard" manifesto; these critiques would be a useful study for any gender and sexual progressive leadership.

The limitations of the essay and its flawed scholarship on black historical figures such as Du Bois and Wells-Barnett reminded some black intellectuals of an alleged penchant of the *New York Times* to publish contentious articles about blacks (authored by blacks) that disparage African-American intellectual ability while simultaneously providing blacks as spectacles for the paper's largely white elite readership. Airing "dirty laundry" and black-on-black denunciations in white publications have transpired for years. Black women's politics are not exempt from criticism; but a (feminist) broadside hardly supplants a critique. What discourages progressives is not feminist rhetoric, but the venality of a generalizing discourse that suggests that black women consistently score below the national average in political intelligence. Manifestos have benefited greatly from reflexivity, savvy in African-American politics, and an exploration of double standards for elites and nonelites in race discourse. In addition, reflexivity in autobiographical reminiscence might lead black writers to consider to what extent their limited personal experiences with African Americans shape their portraits of blacks.

The manifesto offers no reflections on familial, educational, and community influences on the ideology of postmodern feminism. Ill-informed about contemporary black political history, the writer rejects an invitation to attend a National Political Congress of Black Women event to honor Coretta Scott King, Betty Shabazz, and Myrlie Evers-Williams, writing: "I couldn't bring myself to say so at the time, but to venerate women solely on the basis of the men they married is just inexcusably retro." The New Guard fails to realize that the Old Guard, as represented by King, Shabazz, and Evers-Williams, were and are more than the widows of assassinated black leaders; these women had organized for decades with working class and poor (black) men and women for social justice. Such political experiences novice and literary leaders have not achieved and perhaps, as intellectual elites, will not pursue.

This manifesto for a new black feminism raises interesting questions about double standards and opportunism in postmodern black feminism. For instance, the essay devalues beliefs held by, but not restricted to, nonelite black women when represented as black women's views but ignores the same sentiments as possibly debased when held by elites or the mainstream. In the *Times* essay, C. Delores Tucker's Afrocentric (or is it American?) admiration for Coretta King, Betty Shabazz, and Myrlie Evers-Williams as "our three queens" became their denigrating photo caption "The Three Queens." In the appropriation of this phrase one hears echoes of "Welfare Queen" lampooning poor black women and "Quota Queen" discrediting voting rights litigator Lani Guinier. One might note what both Zook and the *Times* did not: The veneration of political royalty, as well as the mothers and widows of assassinated leaders, is an American trait that is not peculiar to blacks. Such sentiments express a romantic longing for a time when a nation of people appeared to have more élan and purpose; it also illustrates our desire for public recognition of the significance of those idealized. Americans who reference the JFK administration as "Camelot" and revere if not idolize Jackie Kennedy Onassis for the role she played as wife, widow, mother (as well as editor-writer and arts advocate) are rarely ridiculed—at least not by most liberals. However, here, Tucker's esteem for black civil rights women is mocked.

A double standard for nonelite black women and elite black men measures the former group by a stricter code of conduct. For example, the manifesto criticizes black women as "supporters of Farrakhan" without noting that some black women who sent their sons to the Million Man March distinguished between "the message and the messenger" and welcomed any opportunity to diminish the high mortality rates in black neighborhoods stemming from black assaults and self-abuse. The new manifesto of sorts disapproves of black female support for the march; paradoxically, it repeatedly cites Cornel West as a model for progressive black intellectualism. Zook fails to mention that West supported, attended, and defended the March. In a similar move, she castigates a black woman juror and by implication her white, Chicano, and male counterparts who argued that the state did not make its case in the overblown O. J. Simpson trial. Henry Louis Gates Jr. cites West in a 1995 *New Yorker* article as affirming the verdict (and

Simpson's possible innocence).[44] West, like everyone else, has that right. It is hypocritical, though, to allow a Harvard University male professor to take unpopular positions without being dismissed as intellectually or morally deficient (in fact to celebrate his leadership and intellectualism) while simultaneously stigmatizing nonelite black females for similar stances. Somehow, Los Angeles District Attorney Garcetti's contemptuous complaint about black women's inability to reason resonates even within black feminism.

Since feminism is under attack on many levels, it is important to debate counterfeminist politics. However, ignoring the contradictions of feminisms, and progressive black women who do not call themselves "feminists," distorts the political reality and conflicting forms of agency that confront contemporary black feminists and their supporters. Recalling the incredible diversity of black women's activism, one notes the expansive visions for a national common program reflected in Marian Wright Edelman's Children's Defense Fund 1996 march for children's rights in Washington, D.C. One might also recognize Beth Richie's antidomestic violence project in New York City, Bernadette Cozar's community gardens in the Greening of Harlem, and Charlene Mitchell's leadership in the Committees of Correspondence. The work of tens of thousands of black women intellectuals and organizers in churches, schools, community centers, and prisons clearly suggests that many manifestos are being reworked, revised, and developed. Whether or not they claim the title or publish, progressives' and black feminists' contributions to transformative agency reveal that there are more of them engaged in political life than most people imagine. In their pursuit of a common program that grapples with the strengths and weaknesses of black agency and leadership, they provide a foundation to build on.

Assembly at the Black Women in the Academy conference, Massachusetts Institute of Technology, Cambridge, January, 1994.

7

Captive Theorists
and Community Caretakers
Women and Academic Intellectualism

Survival is not an academic skill.

—Audre Lorde
Sister Outsider

Women academics and intellectuals seek or shun roles in community caretaking or community-centered intellectual practice. Often such women find themselves pulled between expectations that they respond to the increasingly desperate conditions of nonelite blacks or conform to the mythos of objectivity and alienation set by academic elites.

University life generally privileges literary production by, and about, elites and the objectification of nonelites. Academic guidelines for intellectual achievement and career advancement invariably pose conservative constraints to academics' social justice organizing. Exploring and challenging the connections and intersections between community-centered and academic-centered intellectualisms, women embrace or rebel against roles as community caretakers. In doing so, they either reproduce or repudiate the class, race, and gender biases of academic elitism.

Recovering perspectives to redress racism, (hetero) sexism, and classism, black feminist thought functions as generally progressive within academe. However, it can also posture in the general society as an elite construct. Black feminism is not undifferentiated, although we often use the singular in referring to this body of work. Political ideologies contextualize varied (black) feminist consciousness. For instance, the black feminism of a law professor such as Anita Hill, who at least until the Clarence Thomas confirmation hearings was identified with neoconservative Republicanism, shares similarities with but fundamentally differs in its interpretations of the rights of oppressed peoples from the black feminism of Lani Guinier, a law professor identified with liberal Democratic policies. The politics of black feminism are neither monolithic nor equally oppositional to oppressive state politics. This becomes more apparent when we differentiate between liberal and radical black feminism. Examining the ways in which progressive intellectualism manifests itself within black feminism, we can explore black feminisms' promissory claims as a countersite to academic elitism and conservatism.

In their writings on academic intellectualism, bell hooks, Patricia Hill Collins, Elsa Barkley Brown, and Bernice Johnson Reagon project blacks into theory and intellectualism with different implications. Their varied responses to academic intellectualism, as black women progressives, reflect diverse stances on elitism and radicalism in black leadership. While hooks accepts hierarchical norms for black women academics and Collins ties the black woman intellectual to elitism, Brown and Reagon reject the deradicalizing tendencies of institutional education for an alternative intellectual model.

A Room of One's Own—
"Black Women Intellectuals"

In *Breaking Bread*, a "conversation book" coauthored with Cornel West, bell hooks's essay "Black Women Intellectuals" provides an alternative to the masculinist bias of West's companion piece, "Dilemma of the Black Intellectual."[1] Hooks personalizes and feminizes a theme also explored by West—the marginality and lack of support for black intellectuals; but unlike West, she references women's exploitation in unpaid household labor, and the constraints domesticity imposes on their intellectual lives, to demystify male intellectual elites. In her confessional essay, she describes her alienation as a black female intellectual, and recounts childhood traumas. Discussing the pain of youths labeled "freaks" because of their "brilliance of mind," hooks suggests that hostility in families directed at intellectually gifted girls constitutes a form of psychological child abuse.

Rejecting the historical role of women (particularly black women) as primarily caretakers, the essay encourages women to exempt themselves from reproductive labor. Rather than argue that the division of domestic labor be restructured, her essay advocates that the intellectual woman seek "a room of her own," that is, gain the same privileged status of male intellectuals exempt from primary roles in family and community caretaking. Consequently, despite its gender progressivism, "Black Women Intellectuals" offers a limited rethinking of intellectual life. Rather than democratize black intellectualism, it feminizes or demasculinizes elitist constructs; the intellectual modeled on the solitary male remains the lone individual of gifted abilities. Paradoxically, hooks's work transgresses bourgeois feminisms in its criticisms of capitalism and conventional culture only to reassert bourgeois, even aristocratic, notions of intellectual ability.

Like West, hooks acknowledges the multiplicity of nonacademic or nonliterary intellectual African-American traditions; but, the academic or literary intellectual is the subject of *Breaking Bread*. Perhaps this is because it is the form of intellectualism most familiar to academic authors, for whom the academician seems to represent the paramount intellectual. Paraphrasing Terry Eagleton's "Criticism, Ideology and Fiction,"[2] hooks defines the intellectual as academic-writer. In her assessment via Eagleton, an intellectual is primarily someone who "trades in ideas by transgressing discursive frontiers, because he or she sees the need to do that"; and secondly, "trades in ideas in their vital bearing on a wider political culture." Hooks notes that for Eagleton, who posits that critical openness "enables transgression," it is "essential that intellectuals be creative thinkers, explorers in the realm of ideas who are able to push to the limits and beyond, following ideas in whatever direction they might take."[3]

Hooks's description of Eagleton's work raises unanswered questions: Whose standards—or is it standpoint epistemology—determine whether an idea has a "vital bearing on a wider political culture"? Are ideas created independently of community? In addition, what is the significance of the image of an "explorer-settler" encountering and conquering "frontiers"? In what ways have individualism, commerce, trade, and the market shaped the notion of "intellectual"? Why "discursive frontiers" rather than oppressive political, economic, or state practices as the identifiable barriers calling for resistance and transgression? Where transgression is constructed as a rhetorical or literary "act," such questions may not be addressed.

Validating the intellectual as textual engagé, with little suggestion that political or community activists instruct intellectualism, "Black Women Intellectuals" posits communities as sites where an educated elite, one with a calling, researches and lectures. Recycling Du Bois's repudiated Talented Tenth, hook's version of elite race leadership unravels the ties of leaders and agency to traditional forms of political action.

Academic discourse or literary performance now supersedes organizing. Since academic intellectualism or literary production is inhibited by family and community caretaking, black women's academic performance is a central issue of concern in this construction of black intellectualism. With intellectualism as academic, hooks divorces community caretakers from intellectual production. Her concerns for liberating potential black women theorists from demanding families and communities lead her to assert that black women's failure to complete dissertations—"that graduate experience which best exemplifies the individualistic character of scholarly thought and work"— comes from their unwillingness or inability to "claim intellectual work as worthy of primary attention."[4] Having reduced intellectualism to academic intellectualism, the essay refers to the difficulties women have in prioritizing isolated, academic work over family, communal, and political ties and demands. Hooks suggests that the majority of black women who prioritize relationships over scholarship are anti-intellectual. Since political, civic, or church work are devalued as intellectualism in this construction, black feminists are urged to distance themselves from such work in the life of black communities and to opt for the life of the mind instead.

Rather than address the skewed value system of academic intellectualism that mandates hierarchies, individualism, and images of worth tied to the production of literary commodities, "Black Women Intellectuals" focuses on what are presented as deficiencies in black women's sensibilities. Describing fears of isolation from community or a sense of an unfulfilled social self as "a barrier preventing black women from wholeheartedly choosing intellectual [academic] work," it advocates that black women acclimatize themselves to alienation from nonelite, nonacademic black communities. Deemphasizing a critique of academic socialization and the privileging of scholarship based on exclusionary sexist and racist practices, hooks's transgressive discourse counsels conformity to the caste of professionalized thinkers. This counsel also promises that assimilation into what black feminists identify as Eurocentric, classist, and patriarchal institutions need not render black women academics social, political, or spiritual aliens in black communities. According to hooks, her most vital message for "young Black females who fear that intellectual work estranges us from the 'real' world" is that "when we do insurgent intellectual work that speaks to a diverse audience, to masses of people with different class, race, or education backgrounds, we become part of communities of resistance, coalitions that are not conventional. Intellectual work only estranges us from Black communities when we do not relate or share in myriad ways our concerns."[5] Hooks's theory ties literary production to liberation projects, thereby freeing the intellectual from the ethical bog that manifests in claims that political intent must be excised if our work is to function as theory, art, or scholarship. She thus shares Toni Morrison's criticisms when the latter writes that the word *political* is "a pejorative term in critical circles now: if a work of art has any political influence in it, somehow it's tainted."[6] Morrison continues: "My feeling is just the opposite: if it has none, it is tainted."[7]

Is hooks's insurgent intellectual work merely transgressive discourse in her constructions? If so, then she conflates literary production and liberation organizing. Furthermore, the authoritative discourse rests with the voices of elites who dominate the terrain of published discourse; lecturing outside classrooms does not democratize communication. Although disseminated as popular culture, the viewpoints of academic elite intellectuals need not reflect the concerns of nonelite communities. If these communities are reconstructed primarily as the audience or laboratory of academics, they have no parity or equal say in a dialogue. As nonelites, they are structurally prohibited from a counter discourse. With the lecture hall as the dominant stage, whether on or off campus, the autonomous or isolated individual theorizes what qualifies as revolutionary and who qualifies as insurgent. This new or neopolitical insurgent need no longer be dependent upon political action within nonacademic community work to further her reflections on the progressivism of black feminism. Accepting the dichotomy between theory and collective action, hooks prioritizes "theory" to argue that backwardness and anti-intellectualism have blinded nonacademic communities to the true value of the intellectual.

Here nonelite communities that talk back to black elites are considered not only unnecessary—they are also seen as, and in fact, are potentially debilitating or dangerous sites for those pursuing their individualized callings as elite intellectuals. These calls are legitimized by their claims that they are about more than individual desire. Here, elites are depicted as being informed, representative, progressive, and "authentic" via their claims to being knowledgeable of, or in service to, communities that are at least theoretically stripped of a cognitive ability to evaluate elite caretakers. Nonelites do talk back. However, those privileged in an intellectual hierarchy can from their vantage point dismiss the competing views of nonelites.

Just as Du Bois's rejected Talented Tenth mirrored platonic castes, hooks's black feminism evokes Plato's allegory of the cave: The enlightened philosopher sees the shadows on the wall as illusory, yet is ostracized and punished by the unenlightened cave dwellers for pointing to a larger, truer world. Portraying the intellectual as captive to the superstitions of communities of cave dwellers rationalizes the need for philosopher queens/kings, while valorizing those who engage in such a risky calling. She suggests that the distrust that activists hold for intellect severed from action is unsophisticated: "Within progressive political circles, the work of intellectuals is rarely acknowledged as a form of activism, indeed more visible expressions of concrete action . . . are considered more important to revolutionary struggle than the work of the mind."[8]

Although hooks's definition of black intellectualism is more expansive than the dominant norm, it entails simplistic dichotomies that sever the "work of the mind" from political action in order to reconstruct the former as the latter. The intellectual production in revolutionary struggles of political speeches, poetry, and theater belie a rigid dichotomy between political activism and literary production. To categorically accept literature "as a form of politics" need not mean that it functions as progressive activism. Furthermore, in progressive literature, the distinctions between literature that references other political events and actors and literature that references text or political rhetoric is an important one to maintain. If there is a distinction between speech that calls for action and text that is insular and rhetorical, then some writings offer specificity and strategies in their analyses of oppression while others produce liberation rhetoric. (What some call "speech acts"—unless all speech is to function as action—would seem to be restricted to the context of political organizing.)

Tied to dichotomies, "Black Women Intellectuals" engages in a philosophical reversal familiar to academe: Now the literary academic rather than the activist is designated the caretaker of political wisdom. The life of the mind becomes synonymous with political life since such constructions absolve the thinker from responsibilities to engage in everyday political struggles. They also skirt suggestions that comprehensive knowledge is better expressed through some combination of experiential or political action, reflection, and judgment. A theorist no longer constrained by or captive to the demands of nonintellectuals (or even Kilson's "para-intellectuals") is freed from the devastating conditions facing oppressed people. She or he also is freed from the criticisms of nonelites regarding the ineffectualness of black intellectualism in promoting economic and social justice. In this black feminist project, only the academic judges the commitments of *insurgency* void of political organizing. The phrase suggests insurrection, rebellion, and revolutionary movements that entail violent struggles. Hooks appends herself to the term by retracting it to revolutionary rhetoric. In this scaling-down process of a dematerialized radicalism, language defines revolutionary or radical outside the historical confrontations of revolutionary movements that gave these terms their political meanings.[9] (The term "insurgency" stems from military or war terminology; U.S. State Department or Pentagon news releases popularized the word in their discussions of liberation movements and counterinsurgency wars such as the Vietnam War and later CIA-backed contra wars in Nicaragua and Angola.)

Hooks is willing to claim a life as an activist who confronts issues of justice and ethics, despite the fact that more conservative academics and writers might consider these qualities irrelevant to literary and public life. Her body of work treats marginalized subjects, for instance, black women, sexual racism, misogyny, in accessible writing with an autobiographical voice. She thereby breaks a number of academic house rules associated with theory, or at least academic high theory. The span of her interests is impressive; even her definition of feminism is broader than most definitions. However, elitism diminishes the democratic intent of her political writings. Even in her most recent work, we see the Talented Tenth revived in some fashion and radicalism scaled down to a liberal enterprise.

In 1995, four years after the appearance of *Breaking Bread*, hooks's *Killing Rage: Ending Racism* was published.[10] Her chapter "Black Intellectuals—Choosing Sides" offers a more explicit injunction for the development of black intellectuals. Hooks's writings appear to encourage others to *organize*. However, this appearance is somewhat deceptive. First, hooks is not identified with and writes of no experiences in political organizations. Though political affiliation, or membership, or activism is not a prerequisite for political writers, if progressive proselytizers had political experience in organizing, their calls for engagés would be more grounded. Hooks's words about and perceptions of activism rather than her deeds as an activist constitute her political framework. Therefore readers trust in a knowledge that, on some levels, remains purely speculative. Equally problematic is that hooks reconfigures organizing as literary production or speech; consequently, if we uncritically accept this reconfig-

uration we must not ask why the writer on insurgency and revolution has no experiential knowledge of radical organizing in
a political group. Finally, and more importantly, what makes
me wary of accepting hooks as a model of political insurgency
are her words. She herself states that her primary objective is to
"encourage more black folks to choose intellectual work"[11]—
not to encourage people to activism. In fact, her perception
that black communities reject black intellectuals and writers is
a constant theme in her reflections.[12]

Arguing that the "heart of intellectual work is critical engagement with ideas,"[13] *Killing Rage* asserts the need for time
and privacy: "Even though an exchange of ideas can and does
take place in a communal context, there is necessarily a private
solitary dimension to intellectual work."[14] Hooks also makes a
critical distinction between academics and intellectuals, a distinction that many black intellectuals fail to observe. For
hooks, the "intellectual work of writers like Baldwin and
Hansberry tends to be obscured when discussions of black intellectual traditions focus on academics or writers who teach in
university settings. Most black academics (like their white and
nonwhite counterparts) are not intellectuals. No unitary black
intellectual tradition can be developed if black academics stub-
bornly resist acknowledging the work of writers who are also
critical thinkers or if attention is only given those thinkers who
manage to acquire recognition in the white mainstream."[15]

Hooks couples this distinction between academics and
intellectuals with a reference to the political differences
between feminist academics: "Since many women in the academy are conservative or liberal in their politics, tensions arise
between those groups and individuals like myself, who advocate revolutionary politics."[16] Linking intellectual work with
political action, hooks writes that intellectual production is "a
gesture of political activism if it challenges us to know in ways
that counter and oppose existing epistemologies (ways of
knowing) that keep us colonized, subjugated."[17] She adds:
Such "work has that potential only if the individual is committed to a progressive political vision of social change."[18] For
hooks, "many black intellectuals and/or academics are not
choosing to espouse radical or revolutionary progressive politics. A useful discussion of the role of black intellectuals would

not only critically examine why this is so, it would also articulate strategies of constructive intervention and contestation."[19] Hooks's claims for black intellectualism offer insights that shape the following reflections about other black feminist contributions.

Rearticulation Specialists

Seeking an alternative epistemology to hooks's theory, one encounters the "progressive political vision" of Collins's *Black Feminist Thought*. Although it also reinscribes hierarchy, *Black Feminist Thought* differs from *Breaking Bread* in that it identifies community struggle or caretaking as the source of theorizing in black women's "everyday reality." Bridging dichotomies between intellectual and activist, Collins elevates the engagé, privileging the community caretaker in the form of the black schoolteacher/social worker. In doing so, she inscribes an inherent transgressiveness into liberal teaching, just as hooks does into liberal academic or literary production. Like hooks, Collins attributes to the academic intellectual a superior ability, reflecting a female Talented Tenth. Du Bois's repudiated elite is an indispensable model for Collins, who writes that the "existence of a black women's standpoint does not mean that African-American women appreciate its content, see its significance, or recognize the potential that a fully articulated Afrocentric feminist standpoint has as a catalyst for social change."[20] Collins's black feminism also elevates the agency of an intellectual caste in black feminism even though her theorizing seems to carry a more democratic intent than that of bell hooks. As argued earlier, the effect is to write radicalism out of black women's political activism.

Maintaining that the marginalization of black feminism or womanism is rooted in the historical dismissal of African-American women intellectuals by European Americans and African-American male intellectuals, Collins decenters Eurocentric and masculinist thought to provide an "epistemological framework" for evaluating black feminist thought as distinct from other "arenas of intellectual inquiry." The major contributions of her encyclopedic project center on arguments for a more inclusive role for the feminist black (academic) intellectual and for identifying community organizing as central to the formation of intellectual work. Given that she privileges organizing, it is surprising how little space Collins devotes to her section on political activism and how she reconstructs teaching as political activism (similar to the ways in which hooks represents literary production as political activism).

Black Feminist Thought's brief discussion of African-American women's activism focuses on black women domestics, grade-school teachers, and college educators. Collins writes of teachers in a tradition tied to community leadership in which "Black women used their classrooms and status as educators for African-American community development." Evelyn Higginbotham has noted the contradictory or mixed politics of this form of female Talented Tenth endeavors in black community development. Collins's uncomplicated portrait of black women teachers allows her to write that "Teaching becomes an arena for political activism wherever it occurs."[21] The question is, what type of political activism? Various forms—conservative, liberal assimilationist, and radical—occur in teaching. Rather than confront the competing ideologies of black women teachers, Collins highlights teaching as an inherently progressive site for activism.

When she notes that "increased access to other managerial and professional careers and the suburbanization of the Black middle class" has diminished teaching as "an arena of Black Women's political activism,"[22] she does not explore her own presentation of teaching as just another "managerial career"; if it is, then what type of political arena does it constitute for Collins? True, indoctrination and socialization occur in the classroom. But all political activism (by black women) is not inherently progressive. Since African-American politics encompass conservative and liberal ideologies, classroom teaching is also an arena for promoting antiradicalism.

Failing to note ideological differences, validating black women's teaching, Collins urges the importance of this educational role for women, writing that "Angela Davis counsels middle-class Black women to build on the Black women's activist tradition."[23] Her awareness of black class conflicts surfaces as she quotes Davis: "Black women scholars and professionals cannot afford to ignore the straits of our sisters who are acquainted with the immediacy of oppression in a way many of us are not. The process of empowerment cannot be simplistically defined in accordance with our own particular class interests. We must learn to lift as we climb."[24] Employing a radical's argument for privileged black women to align themselves with poorer black women still does not radicalize professional teaching.

The problem is not so much tied to the limits of black women's ideological commitments as to the nature of institutional teaching itself. Consider that historically, progressives were forced from their teaching jobs because of their political commitments. Before the gains wrought by civil rights demonstrations gave them the option of voluntarily leaving teaching careers for more lucrative careers, black women were fired for antiracist activism. In fact, there is a long history of such punitive treatment towards progressive black teachers. Ida B. Wells-Barnett describes in her memoir how she was forced out of teaching and into journalism due to her editorials denouncing the racism of the school board and the sexual impropriety and economic malfeasance of white school board members buying sexual favors from young (incompetent) black female teachers. Antiprogressivism and sexism forced Anna Julia Cooper out of the Dunbar High School's principalship. The daughter of a schoolteacher, Ella Baker refused a teaching career because of the punitive power local white school boards had over progressive educators; after graduating from Shaw University, she left the South to organize with laborers and union activists in New York City. Jo Ann Robinson and Septima Clark were dismissed from their teaching positions because of their antiracist activism decades later in the South as they worked with civil rights groups. Angela Davis was targeted by California Governor Ronald Reagan and fired from her teaching position at UCLA for her membership in the Communist Party USA.

Black women expressed radical commitments in spite of, not because of, their teaching positions. Most institutional educators, black women included, likely avoid activism that jeopardizes their teaching careers. This suggests that teaching, in academia or elsewhere, may be a deradicalizing political site, irrespective of Collins's claims for its intrinsic progressivism.

The claims Collins's makes for teachers, who obviously have contributed and continue to contribute to progressive politics, are part of her attempts to bridge a conceptual schism between intellectualism and activism concerning black women. *Black Feminist Thought* maintains that the "struggle for a self-defined Afrocentric feminist consciousness occurs through a merger of thought and action" that rejects either/or dichotomous thinking. For Collins, "deep divisions among theorists and activists" are generally fabricated; she argues that by "espousing a both/and orientation that views thought and action as part of the same process, possibilities for new relationships between thought and action emerge." Black women then "embrace a both/and conceptual orientation" as an outgrowth of their experiences living "as black, female and often poor." In such an existential matrix, "Very different kinds of 'thought' and 'theories' emerge when abstract thought is joined with concrete action."[25] Collins argues that the "dialectic of oppression and activism, the tension between the suppression of Black women's ideas and our intellectual activism in the face of that suppression, comprises the politics of Black feminist thought."[26] As a sociologist, her work provides greater detail regarding the effects of poverty, labor exploitation, and the absence of enforced civil and social rights, and the presence of dehumanizing cultural images in African-American women's lives. She offers an important critique of how black social and political thought is limited by reformist ideologies and masculinist bias; yet providing no analysis of black feminist reformism, her text exorcises conservatism and radicalism in black feminism in order to promote a respectable liberalism.

Collins remains vague about how black feminist academics manage to escape recreating the style and methodology of academic elites "probing" the lives of women in ways that distort or appropriate the thought of nonelite black females. She maintains that black women's positions as "outsiders within" fosters the reclamation process of black feminist intellectuals. Yet their positions within or in assimilation into a caste of professionalized thinkers, as well as opportunities or desires to transform themselves from outsiders into tenuous insiders, can hinder this reclamation process. The contributions of black feminist theorists to antiracist, antisexist and community-centered theories are considerable. Still without a self-referential critique of elites, the progressivism falls short of structural rethinking. This deficiency is evident in *Black Feminist Thought*'s promotion of exclusionary hierarchies concerning knowledge production.

Using Peter Berger and Thomas Luckman's *Social Construction of Reality: A Treatise on the Sociology of Knowledge*,[27] Collins argues for a two-level or tiered reality in intellectual life: Everyday reality articulated in African-American women's standpoints and theoretical reflections on that reality made through the interventions of specialists or experts "who rearticulate Black women's standpoints." This interdependency between black women's standpoints and black feminist thought permits academic intellectuals to provide the "theoretical interpretations of Black women's reality by those who live it."[28] Her distinctions grant the academic, here one engaged in community dialogue, a superior status given her role in rearticulating the understandings of nonelite African-American women enmeshed in "everyday reality." Collins appears antielitist when she writes, "Rather than raising consciousness, Black feminist thought affirms and rearticulates a consciousness that already exists."[29] However, only the experts or specialists, by virtue of their academic training, do theory in her book. The problem with rearticulation specialists is that if we assert that African Americans speak of their lives only on a descriptive personalized level (unless they write in the language of academic theory), then theory is categorically denied nonelites who are not assimilating into academic modes. If "everyday language" is incompetent to communicate black feminist thought's liberation message, nonelite communities as well as community caretakers are captive to academics. In addition, if specialists rearticulate not so much for black women, which Collins emphasizes, but for academic audiences, they choose a style approved by academic intellectuals, one inaccessible to nonelites, one that recolonizes the materiality of peoples lives. Since not only merit but also ideological compatibility or conformity determine inclusion in academic canons, liberal or mainstream black feminist writings that are more marketable in academe than radical or revolutionary black feminist works may constitute the dominant discourse for rearticulation.

Subordinating the intellectualism and radicalism of non-elite, community-based black women to black women specialists, Collins fails to differentiate between political ideologies or explore how black women academic specialists might rearticulate African-American women's everyday reality to conform to prevailing paradigms or market black feminism. The willingness to critique academic specialists' promissory and progressive claims to theory, as well as their literary interventions (or in some cases inventions) in the lives of nonelite women suggests more radical responses to the hierarchies and erasures of academic intellectualism. Departing from the normative, academic paradigm, which hooks adopts and Collins adapts, Elsa Barkley Brown and Bernice Johnson Reagon offer more far-reaching critiques.

"Scholar-Mothers" and "Two-World Straddlers"

Elsa Barkley Brown rejects validating specialists in black women's theorizing in "Mothers of Mind," which appeared in the black women's journal *SAGE*.[30] Brown discusses the questions that students and scholars raise regarding the value of black women's "personal accounts of their lives." Using her mother's instruction, she offers answers: "My mother has taught me the arrogance of such a question and she regularly combats any signs of my succumbing to the Eurocentric tendency to assume that those of us who have trained to analyze people's lives are better able to understand them than the people whose lives they actually are."[31] Rejecting Collins's rearticulation specialists, she notes that she has developed "great respect for people's abilities to understand their own lives": "I have learned to listen, not just to what they tell me about the particulars of their lives, but also to the ways in which they define them for themselves."[32]

Without mentioning Zora Neale Hurston's political conservatism, Brown cites Hurston as a model of black female intellectualism that circumvents academic Eurocentrism. Hurston, she writes, while not the first black woman social scientist to do so, acknowledged "the need to break out of the traditions in which she was trained" given the "influence of her community on her ability to develop works more clearly reflective of the true experiences of Africanamerican people."[33] Brown also references Joyce Ladner's *Tomorrow's Tomorrow: The Black Woman*[34] which is contextualized by civil rights activism. Brown uses Ladner's scholarship to argue that we must bridge the span between academic training for objective standards and community-focused work that addresses and redresses the conditions of impoverished, urban African-American girls. Having highlighted other intellectuals, Brown situates her own experiences as a scholar within nonelite black intellectual traditions. Following a tradition of black intellectuals "who understand the limitations of the paradigms and underlying assumptions that pervade Western educational institutions and bookshelves," she advocates that scholars "draw upon our own communities—and for Africanamerican women especially, the women in our communities—to help us understand and depict the lives of Africanamerican people in a way that they /we would recognize as reality."[35] For her own part and contribution, Brown writes that she seeks to "build upon the experience of my scholar/mothers in recognizing the difference between the two views and noting the important role that my community, especially the women in it, has played in my development."[36] According to Brown, the most critical instruction in her development as a scholar came from her mother, who taught her "how to ask the right questions," and how to understand and form theoretical concepts and frameworks. Her mother's community work and memory of the activities of local people mark her as historian or social scientist, in Brown's estimation.

Rather than infer intellectual deficiencies or a uniform hostility on the part of nonelite African Americans, Brown addresses the complex, contradictory stances of black communities to academic life. Her narrative on her mother's intellectualism illustrates the ambiguous and conflicting messages in black communities toward academic intellectualism. Brown's mother earned a graduate degree in mathematics in the 1930s; unable to find employment teaching because of racial barriers and job discrimination, she worked as a domestic. While she cautioned her daughter not to become too impractical or "over-ly" intellectualized, she also collected money from among the extended family for Brown's graduate studies and lived with her daughter and grandchildren, taking care of the household chores. Brown's mother sent dual messages; intending both the survival of the individual scholar and the well-being of black community, she provided directives toward community care as well as insights into black culture, politics, and history. Brown herself viewed these ties to community as a source of creative tension between caretaking and independence, community and individual. This tension, writes Brown, can lead to a balance or synthesis: "Afrocentric scholarship requires understanding on a concrete level that 'I am because We are; and because We are, therefore I am.' There can be no I unless there are We."[37] The essay closes with Brown's reflection: "With my mother's understandings to guide me, I am slowly becoming a historian in spite of my academic training."[38]

Bernice Johnson Reagon also emphasizes the development of intellectual and moral instruction that takes place in a community extraneous to that of academic communities. Neither Brown nor Reagon offer explicit definitions of community in their essays. Brown reasserts the training of the black intellectual within the African-American community. Reagon constructs community caretakers as intellectuals who apprentice in black communities; here, training is also a central concept. Yet Reagon's "'Nobody Knows the Trouble I See;' or, 'By and By I'm Gonna Lay Down My Heavy Load'"—which appears in a special issue of the *Journal of American History* devoted to discussions of Martin Luther King Jr.'s plagiarism in his Boston University dissertation—makes nonacademic community the final arbiter of standards for black intellectuals.[39] Reagon's phrase, "There Are Those of Us Who Straddle," refers to the challenges and balancing acts of intellectuals raised in communities of subordinate, oppressed people, who are later trained in the dominant culture. King illustrates such an intellectual for Reagon.

Walking between two worlds is neither inherently traumatic nor isolating, maintains Reagon, who notes that crises and slippages are ever present. The greatest danger, Reagon writes, is that some who have acquired technical or academic training never return to a nonelite community. Disappearances result because individuals learn the lessons of professionalization too well or because they are traumatized by "trying to master two systems at variance with each other."[40] Reagon's alternative to succumbing to either tendency is the intellectual life of the straddler. Those who straddle are born into the community and sent out to work in the larger society as caretakers of that community, according to Reagon, whose concept of straddling is a dynamic grappling with two diverging foundational entities.

The intellectual who bridges academia and community activism is not rootless; straddling entails a stance. The straddler's acquired stability is forged between competing value systems, power relationships, and structures of dominance. Neither system is sacred. Rather, each offers tools. Defining the objective of straddling as mastery of both systems, Reagon writes that the goal is to be flexible without becoming "two-faced." The two-faced act one way in order to be recognized, rewarded, or simply not punished in a dominant, "white world"; and act in other ways to be "authentic" or acceptable in a marginalized "black world" of nonelite communities. To be consistent, to avoid a performing blackness in either world, entails circulating in both and reworking the knowledge provided in each. Since none of the rules is sacred in (or of) either world, Reagon's test is how effectively the rules function to support and serve the community.

Describing King as a great, effective straddler—one at home in two worlds who manipulated the material tools of different sites in order to advance democracy and justice—Reagon seems to suggest that to better judge King from where he stood, we need to stand there ourselves. For Reagon, "a true master is one who creates an offering with such power and originality that a new direction is established within the genre."[41] Obviously, in this context, the genre goes beyond academic or literary production. Having the ken of two worlds develops the authoritative voice unrestricted by academic codes (including those that deny the validity of nonelite community standpoints). "'Nobody Knows the Trouble I See;' or, 'By and By I'm Gonna Lay Down My Heavy Load'" notes that Martin Luther King Jr. "spoke with one voice sounding the ethos of the Movement in all the places under the sun, and he was heard and understood."[42] Those who study "the work of this kind of life" should be aware, writes Reagon, that if they review "evidence generated in only one place, it can only result in a distortion."[43]

Referring to "original sound" as signature, Reagon maintains that King signed his work. Those who articulate in their own voice, with their personal style or signature, are highly respected within African-American culture, according to Reagon. In contradistinction to conventional academic standards are the standards of marginalized communities: "In some fields of Western academic culture, originality is expected to be drawn from one's data, or one's analysis of data, or some combination of both. Sound and style are not key priorities."[44] If many African Americans live in a society where style and voice, not data analysis, are seen as signatures then these two cultures contradict and clash over different value standards. Reagon is explicit that the final arbiter is not academic intellectualism: "African-American sound is primary evidence. The question of where your offering comes from, what orchards you have harvested to put together the contribution you make, is a test for the audience."[45] Those, writes Reagon, "who sit under the sound of your voice who must know our culture—its ways and its text—well enough that we can tell whether you can stand before us and sing again."[46] The key audience here are communities. Judgment by community—which was rescinded by hooks, mitigated by Collins, and highlighted by Brown—contextualizes Reagon's black feminist theorizing on responses to academic intellectualism.

For Reagon, agency and intellectualism reside in nonacademic communities: One's parents and community elders send this intellectual forth with the charge to development. Reagon surpasses academics hooks, Collins, and Brown in her validations of community. Like the others, she holds advanced graduate degrees; however, this author, teacher, Smithsonian director, and founder of Sweet Honey in the Rock theorizes with the least restraint from academic norms. Reagon maintains that not only does the community train, it gives the call. Her views are not widely shared among academics. Those who embrace academic-intellectual elitism or argue that Reagon's arbiter or judge, the black community, is merely an invention, are unlikely to privilege black communities in this fashion. Yet the formulations of "'Nobody Knows the Trouble I See'; or, 'By and By I'm Gonna Lay Down My Heavy Load'" are not merely rhetorical. The essay particularizes its argument to the public intellectual, specifically the activist in the Southern civil rights movement in the 1950s and 1960s who challenged the social constraints and state violence directed against blacks.

The black intellectual is called into an apprenticeship in service that legitimizes her or his "song"; the primary audience of black intellectuals, as nonacademics, dictates responsibilities greater than those of academic life. Since the audience is the final arbiter for Reagon's black intellectual, the two- (or multiple-) world straddler is the creation or product of African-American communities. In Reagon's theorizing, the most competent judges are not seated in academe, although the degree to which she believes straddlers are able to democratize academic intellectualism and black elitism is unclear.

Reagon's argument for King as a two-world straddler mirrors her discussion of Fannie Lou Hamer as a "cultural carrier." Reagon, who worked with Hamer, describes her as a cultural worker who inspired people to counter dehumanizing political and emotional practices.[47] As a model or conduit for the development of others, Hamer, writes Reagon, expressed thanks for the opportunity to become more like herself, that is, to "raise" her own self in struggle.[48] Reagon notes that Hamer "took up space" and "moved by the sound of her voice and the power of her living."[49] Cultural carriers, according to Reagon, first carry spirit, take up enough space, without apology, to speak freely and honestly; and take great risks to change ourselves, the environment, and oppression that conditions our bodies. Continuance is only guaranteed by self-determination, by self-care. She describes how, in responding to whites' fears, blacks eventually fear themselves, seeking invisibility by "blending in." Trying not to be "too black" or "too loud" they consequently fail to take as much space as they need to stay alive and free.[50] Which, observes Reagon, is considerable space. Taking space for change involves great vulnerability and political risk. Describing how Hamer risked unemployment, beatings, and her life for social justice, Reagon notes that seizing space for social change is risky; yet, in her arguments, because

Hamer's legacy as a cultural carrier merges the secular with the sacred, the political with the spiritual, with liberatory intent, the risks are seen as justified.

The Constraints of Caretaking

The use of black women as maternal helpmates for a community perpetually in crisis, as "superwomen" not generally accorded equal status as intellectuals, haunts antiracist democratic movements. Black feminist writings pointedly delineate the repressiveness of such constructions. Alongside the works of hooks (or Wallace), we find the critiques of the icon of the black female caretaker offered by womanist theologian Delores Williams.

For Williams, survival or resistance require caretaking/mothering. She argues that Alice Walker's concept of "womanist" manifests in mothers relating to their children, and in black women such as Harriet Tubman who are not biological mothers yet nevertheless nurture great numbers of black people in the liberation struggle.[51] Williams flags the pitfalls of black women's nurturing for black communities in her discussion of women's roles in the churches, contending gender justice and equity in the black community, as well as an equitable division of labor are essential in community development.[52] She notes that the roles of black women as community caretakers dispel or reinforce the stereotypes of black mothers as vampire or mammy; however, even in the black church the seemingly powerful position of "mother of the church" reproduces black women's subservience. "Like the ante-bellum mammy, mother of the church exerts considerable authority in the church family," writes Williams, who observes that often the influential mother of the church fails to "challenge the power and authority of the patriarchal head of the church, usually a male preacher." When such women function as "a healer of relationships within the congregation" and are given considerable influence because of their ability to communicate Christian values, the black church with its own enormous influence in black communities "empowers" them as community caretakers.[53]

Black feminists understandably reject the mothering model of caretaking critiqued by Williams. However, mothering and nurturing occur in radical fashion; for instance, the "movement mommas" of the civil rights movement did not necessarily restrict themselves to a leadership role delineated by the church or any other black institution. The issue of gender parity in theory and intellectual life remains central; it also remains contextualized by the larger struggle over elite or democratic notions of intellectual ability.

Hooks, Collins, Brown, and Reagon attempt to bridge the divide between academic elite worlds and nonelite black communities. Central to these feminist writings on intellectualism is a progressive politics shaped by community concerns and the uneasy relationships of black academic intellectuals to nonelite peoples and social justice. With elitism amid their progressivism, or progressivism amid their elitism, black feminist community caretakers range from the philosopher queen through social worker to radical activist. Amid its diverse political ideologies, black feminist thought (in its diversity) offers a distinct ethical project in terms of agency. Its social justice project is more responsible and humane than the visions of exclusionary, conservative academic projects that deny or thrive on sexual/class/racial divisions. It is as well less inclined to the disingenuousness of newer canons that mask or reproduce racism and antifeminism in their intellectual transcendence of the materiality of race and gender.

Hooks, Collins, Brown, and Reagon each present transgressive theories for academic intellectualism. Since the transgressive is not synonymous with the transformative, their political differences toward radicalism in black feminist theory remain critical points to debate. The politics of black feminisms likely reflect their designated audiences—where one stands when theorizing determines who benefits from the theories. The positions of caretakers or activists who are neither captivated by nor held captive to oppressed or oppressive sites provides a productive stance or perhaps a straddler's stance for liberating theories with an alternative, democratic vision that forgoes academic elitism.

Educators may both imitate the bias of elite institutions and/or radicalize oppressive structures.[54] In their educational sites and debates, black feminists or womanists posit standards for judging the work of intellectuals as connected to a besieged community. The extent to which black women understand themselves to be preoccupied or consumed by caretaking and nurturing roles for black communities influences our discussions of community responsibilities as admirable political relationships or entrapment. The limits of caretaking are circumscribed by its designation as a female attribute or function. There are other limits, though, that are best explored in contemporary constructions of the black intellectual, generally understood as male and heroic, an elite removed in some ways from the daily chores of community building.

Charlene Mitchell prior to arrest at Angela Davis's trial, San Jose, California, January 1972.

8

Elite Educators and
the Heroic Intellectual

There is never any question of being either rejected or welcomed by the people.
What they ask is simply that all resources should be pooled.

—Frantz Fanon
The Wretched of the Earth

In the wake of the civil rights movement, social justice activism altered the composition of university classrooms and departments, creating African-American, ethnic, and women's studies programs. Many of these programs engaged in off-campus organizing to support community groups. Their continued existence increased the numbers of black, Latino-Chicano, Native-American, Asian, and women faculty. However, the radical, democratic nature of such programs has dissipated in the postmovement era of corporate "restructuring."[1]

Herman Gray notes that for black academics and others, the downsizing of universities and increased competition for jobs accelerated the commodification of (black) scholars-performers. (The considerable publicity for the ethnic stars at elite schools, observes Peniel Joseph, "popularizes the fiction that race and gender equity within a virulently racist and sexist academy have finally been attained."[2]) Along with the academic star system, the "black star" as popular or elite intellectual began to rise in the collegiate arena. Its rise was accompanied by the promotion of anti-affirmative-action laws to restrict the access of poor and working-class people of color to universities.

California's "Proposition 187" and its anti-affirmative-action "civil rights" initiatives were battles waged for control over the university's mission and to restrict the extent of its ethnic diversity.[3]

On one hand we have an educated elite and elite educators with access to academe (and its resources) and the students privileged to enter. On the other hand we have nonelites who, since the 1970s, have faced growing barriers to their access to the university as the traditional training site for the Talented Tenth, and a source of economic as well as social mobility. Generally, it is the university-educated as consumers who purchase the products of academics or elite educators; elites who respond to the educated consumer's demands for information and entertainment gain popularity and profit. Educated elites may as well become regulated by production that meets the consumer's curiosity for fetishized blackness. A diverse group, educated consumers still tend to share an attraction for black intellectualism as entertainment and an aversion for nonentertaining knowledge produced by nonelites that indicts both elites and consumers as complicitous in, or indifferent to, the reproduction of inequality.

Within this context, reconfiguring the black leader as intellectual-academic filters responses to social crises through an academic lens. Framed in a historically privileged, insular, and bourgeois site, this lens is not noted for its (support of) antiracist radicalism and for campaigns for economic justice. In fact, in corporate educational enclaves, the presence of poor, working-class people and African Americans is diminishing while corporate CEOs are increasingly the preferred candidates for university presidencies. What, then, frames the relationships between elite educators or intellectuals and nonelites, such as other academic employees—the workers in the cafeteria, maintenance plants, and secretarial pools?

When one renders black intellectualism synonymous with black academics, the intelligentsia increasingly distances from past and present material, democratic struggles for social justice. Given the poverty, crime, and social denigration many blacks face, as they are caught between being commodified, ignored, or scapegoated by the dominant culture, one would think that analyses and strategies aimed at combating repressive state practices/social inequalities would preoccupy the most prominent contemporary black intellectuals. But do they? Perhaps, the representation of radicalism as an intellectual endeavor situated within the rhetoric of academic transgressives and hybrids makes radicalism seem especially rootless and insubstantial.

Many academics struggle against injustice and inequality. But if this select caste sees itself as privileged, authoritative experts on racial-sexual politics and culture, or democratic praxis, it promotes a self-serving elitism that obscures nonelite agency. Thinking and writing about activists (which is apparently different from working with them) can produce progressive perspectives. However, both educators who study activists and those who ignore them may be influenced by a spectator's view of politics, and such a ken can limit a scholar's ability to comprehend the complexities of risk-taking resistance to oppression.

Where contemporary academic intellectuals supplant militant, antiracist politics with ritualized race discourse, they define the black intellectual as the purveyor of resistance rhetoric. Such academics may reconstruct the black hero or heroine as the radical rhetorician, and in their constructions of black political engagement defuse and disperse traditional meanings of resistance.

Cornel West's black postmodern intellectual and Jerry Gaio Watts's black heroic intellectual reflect the contemporary debates on the chasm between activists-intellectuals, academic intellectuals, and radicalism. Black intellectuals such as Derrick Bell and Lewis Gordon, and the Indian intellectual Aijaz Ahmad, offer other interpretations of progressivism and political courage that more closely reflect radical politics. Placing these antiracist, elite educators on a continuum of academic progressives, we can see that the center is held by West. To his right stands Watts, and to the left of both are Bell, Ahmad, and Gordon. The terms "center," "right," and "left" are imprecise, yet they remain useful to our discussion below.

The Public Intellectual as Pragmatic Politician

West emphasizes the importance of participating in political activist struggles as well as criticizing elites. He addressed a 1991 meeting of socialist activists-intellectuals on this point.

"Local activists must become more and more at the center of how we think about the condition for the possibility of social motion and social movement," he said.[4] "Critiques of leaders in the limelight must be relentless," West asserted, "because moments of weakness generate highlighting of leaders who are unconnected, or less and less connected, to those anonymous, invisible local activists who carry the ball courageously and heroically between moments of social motion."[5]

Yet West's own literary work, which critiques the black intellectual as inherently progressive, reveals contradictory and ambivalent stances toward the activists he promotes as models. Despite his 1991 exhortation to socialist activists, West's 1993 *Keeping Faith* chapter "The Dilemma of the Black Intellectual" (which is a reprint of his 1991 essay in *Breaking Bread*) fails to cite political activism as an "organic" black intellectual tradition.[6] Preoccupied with the production of "a great literate intellectual," he discounts autobiographies and memoirs to cite only one exemplary, living black thinker-writer—Toni Morrison.

West criticizes African Americans' suspicion of educated elites as a "truncated perception of intellectual activity." He writes that the declining quality of black intellectualism stems from both the African-American community's lack of institutional support for intellectuals as well as (elite) black intellectuals' failures to remain organically linked to the community. West cites a list of charges made by nonelite blacks toward privileged intellectuals. African-American communities' distrust of black intellectuals, he writes, stems from the arrogance and elitism of university blacks, their distance from African-American culture, institutions, and communities, their increasing marriages to nonblacks, and their "preoccupation with Euro-American intellectual products." For West, black communities see these activities as symptomatic of internalized hatred and a flight from the subordinate status that blackness holds in a white world. The "minimal immediate impact" of most black intellectuals, he adds, fuels "common perceptions of the impotence, even uselessness, of black intellectuals." According to West, the black community "lauds those black intellectuals who excel as *political activists* and *cultural artists*."[7] He theorizes that because of their limited perceptions, nonelite blacks fail to see the life of the mind as "possessing intrinsic virtues nor harboring emancipatory possibilities"; rather, they seek only "short-term political gain and social status." In *Breaking Bread* (1991), *Race Matters* (1993), and *Keeping Faith* (1993), West argues against the antipathy of the African-American community for "the life of the mind" or mental work severed from community action. Yet, black communities also understand the life of the mind as furthering long-term goals in racial uplift and social justice.

West's analysis makes important contributions toward understanding a form of American intellectualism.[8] However, a number of points should be kept in mind. First, political ineffectualness may be determined by the ideological politics of professional intellectuals rather than the activity of intellectual production itself. That is, most elite intellectuals may have a limited impact on transforming oppressive conditions that nonelites endure not because they are intellectuals, but because they are elites, and, as elites, they shy away from radical confrontations for substantive political change. That nonelites may value most those intellectuals who contribute to justice and beauty in their lives does not necessarily mean that they reject "the life of the mind." It is logical, but not anti-intellectual, that oppressed people prioritize the productions of intellectuals they find useful and enlightening, and that they make value judgments relevant to their estimation of intellectuals' ability to deliver even a brief respite from oppressive conditions.

West can narrowly define the life of the mind, and so theorize about black rejection of same, because he limits the primary sources of black intellectualism. There are two for West. Black Christian preaching and African-American music are the two indigenous traditions of Afro-American intellectual life, according to West, because institutions existed for their development within black communities. Arguing that today no black institution comparable to the black church (from which both traditions emerged) exists to produce "great" black intellectuals, he writes: "The major priority of Black intellectuals should be the creation or reactivation of institutional networks that promote high-quality critical habits primarily for the purpose of Black insurgency."[9] West's insurgency calls for new infrastructures to enhance the acquisition and production of knowledge by black intellectuals. Development within organizations and structures is indispensable for most mature thinkers. However, other sites for knowledge production, and political and moral development, exist. Liberation praxis is arguably a third indigenous African-American intellectual tradition that produced significant intellectuals. West's emphasis on conventional structures (and the Protestant work ethic rather than the political protest tradition) does not demonstrate how radical resistance for a democratic society is a site for knowledge.

Departing from the institutions of the black church for raising black intellectuals, West promotes elite academe, despite his contentions that activists should be at the center of progressive intellectualism. Intellectuals choose and validate their knowledge production sites. Academics are taught that activism is a form of nonintellectualism that detracts from scholarship and academic prestige (and therefore job security and wages). Organizing, particularly community-based organizing, is not a very popular choice for academics. Although prominent academic intellectuals, such as Harvard's West, inform us that today's premier black intellectual is an employee of an elite institution, it is also true that the newly designated site for black intellectual fecundity has proved inhospitable to democratic struggle. The elite university is a site where, West himself admits, for the black intellectual, "the linchpin of the bourgeois model is academic legitimation and placement."[10] The radical visions of engagés who confront the state, militarism, and the profiteering of transnational capitalism are rarely found in this institution for black intellectualism—an institutional site with a mission that markedly differs from the educational training sites of the original Talented Tenth in black colleges and universities.

West's rhetoric criticizes the Talented Tenth while revitalizing elites through his valorization of academe as the most important intellectual site. He rejects the concept of a Talented Tenth, but his black intellectual is at heart the academic intellectual, the college-educated elite with publications. If the best and the brightest of intellectuals are understood to teach in prestigious white universities and publish with those presses, then they are segregated to some degree from struggles in black communities for economic equity and political independence. For West, this segregation and alienation are inevitable: "Becoming a black intellectual is an act of self-imposed marginality" in "the black community."[11] This is held to be true in part because, he writes, the black community reflects the anti-intellectualism of the broader American society.

Academic credentials are indispensable to the idea of the radical intellectual at least as rhetorician. Constructing a typology of American intellectualism, West lists four models of black intellectual activity: the bourgeois model of the humanist; the Marxist model of the revolutionary; the Foucauldian model of the postmodern skeptic; and the insurgency model of the critical organic catalyst. Although he identifies the last as the most progressively viable tradition, West sends mixed messages. He acknowledges the bourgeois model as limited, but then proceeds to describe it as "inescapable for most black intellectuals" in the same ways in which he considers self-imposed marginality "inescapable." The inability to escape marginality is tied to West's locus of knowledge production: "Most of the important and illuminating discourses in the country take place in white bourgeois academic institutions and ... the more significant intellectuals teach in such places."[12] Given the hierarchies in institutional settings, it appears that the most important discourses only take place in bourgeois, affluent, primarily white academic institutions because "the more significant" bourgeois intellectuals teach there. Which is logical given its tautological elitism. (West obviously would not wish to foreclose the opportunity of exploring the lives and work of radical intellectuals of various ethnicities who work in nonbourgeois and nonwhite institutions.)

Of his four models—bourgeois humanist, postmodern skeptic, revolutionary Marxist, organic insurgent—the Marxist model is the only one to earn West's opprobrium. He refers to it as "a knee-jerk reaction" by black intellectuals "to the severe limitations of the bourgeois model (and capitalist society)."[13] Du Bois, a longtime Marxist with a brief membership in the Communist Party USA, is an unlikely candidate for a "knee-jerk reaction," as are C. L. R. James, Claudia Jones, and other black Marxists or communists. West observes that "the Marxist privileging of black intellectuals often reeks of condescension that confines black prophetic roles to spokespersons and organizers."[14] Yet, he makes no similar claims about the condescension of bourgeois, white academe, which often relegates black intellectuals to markers of colored authenticity and representation in black performance. Preoccupation with black literary production rather than with black literate intellectuals leads West to list James, Du Bois, Oliver Cox, and Harold Cruse as the only candidates for the title of major black Marxist theoreticians. West's construction of black intellectuals as dupes of Marxism is not novel. With rhetoric that hints at anticommunism, he writes that "the Marxist model yields black intellectual self-satisfaction which often inhibits growth." Other intellectuals disagree. In contradistinction to West, Ahmad argues that the explanatory power of this system of thought rests with the claim that Marxist concepts "pose sufficient systemic coherence and are sufficiently grounded in the historical process itself to be able to generate new concepts through self-criticism and through realignment with new events and knowledges that arise within the historical process itself."[15]

Forgoing any analysis of black Marxists (or even a text such as Cedric Robinson's *Black Marxism*) in his essays on black intellectualism, West reductively depicts Marxism to argue that black intellectuals' encounters with Marxism (communism or socialism) result in "either dogmatic submission to and upward mobility within sectarian party or preparty formations or marginal placement in the bourgeois academy equipped with cantankerous Marxist rhetoric."[16] Seemingly, bourgeois and postmodern black academics, who do not have a similar reputation for being ill-tempered and naive, are less constricted and controlled in bourgeois organizations and institutions than their Marxist counterparts are in radical organizations and institutions. Unfamiliarity with the political traditions of black radicalism that extend beyond the literature of prominent black leftists works to infantilize black Marxists and communists. West's claim that Marxism is the "purgatory" of "our postmodern times" through which black intellectuals "must pass" in order to develop as sophisticated thinkers echoes his earlier arguments in *Prophesy Deliverance*.[17]

(We could make the same assessment of bourgeois and post-modernist thought.) Yet, "The Dilemma of the Black Intellectual" contradictorily recommends Marxian philosophy as a temporary but necessary learning phase and pronounces Marxism a "debilitating" model that caters to the "cathartic needs" of blacks while working to "stifle the further development of black critical consciousness."[18] The only intellectual type that West labels as *revolutionary* is the only model to receive his vituperative analysis. If West's evaluation is built on his personal experiences with Marxist thinkers, then his reflections on his own marginalization (similar to the testimonial offered by his *Breaking Bread* co-author bell hooks) would strengthen his criticisms. However, West does not particularize his statements to his own experiences. Rather, he generalizes to all black intellectual engagement with Marxism. His only evidence is the paltry "great literature" among black Marxists. Yet there is also a paltry amount of "great" or even good literature by those who identify as black postmodernists, which is presumably West's own cadre of intellectuals that supplants the Marxists. By using caricature to dismiss the radical-left tradition of black intellectualism West reassures employees of bourgeois academe of their privileged status as radical rhetoricans. However, black radical intellectualism is much more nuanced and creative than its caricatures.

Dispensing with the black Marxists, West turns to what he seems to suggest is a more invigorating and potentially radical form of black intellectualism: The Foucauldian model, which "promotes a leftist form of postmodern skepticism."[19] Privileging "revolt" over "restoration, reformation, and revolution," these intellectuals interrogate "power-laden discourses." West observes that the Foucauldian model "suits the critical, skeptical, and historical concerns of progressive black intellectuals" while supplying "a sophisticated excuse for ideological and social distance from insurgent black movements for liberation."[20] This type, with its distance from activism and material struggles, gives way to the last model, a hybrid or synthesis of the preceding three. Preferable to the bourgeois academic, black Marxist, or Foucauldian skeptic in the development of black intellectualism is the insurgency model.

According to West, the insurgency model is based on the bourgeois model but emphasizes human will and heroism without constructing them as individualistic and elitist. Making an important counterargument to elite and romantic constructions (found in the writings of hooks and Watts), *Keeping Faith* proposes an alternative to "the solitary hero, embattled exile and isolated genius—the intellectual as star, celebrity, commodity." West's preferred leader based on the insurgency model privileges collective intellectual work for communal struggle. Consequently, the insurgent, writes West, both rejects bourgeois "naivete about the role of society and history" and "ingeniously incorporates the structural, class and democratic concerns of the Marxist model ... [recognizing Marxian] naivete about culture." The insurgency model attains from the Foucauldian model "the preoccupation with world skepticism, the historical constitution of 'regimes of truth,' and the multifarious operations of 'power/knowledge' while recognizing the postmodern skeptics' "naivete about social conflict, struggle and insurgency."[21] West does not explore how this hybrid (embodied in a reflexive, left, bourgeois academic cognizant of activists) might further black academics' distance from black radicalism. For instance, an insurgent intellectual such as West examines historical and contemporary African-American intellectual traditions without referencing Wells-Barnett, Frederick Douglass, black trade unions, and (with one reference to) black feminism. As a response to social crises and an improvement over previous models, this hybrid fourth model carries an untrustworthy promissory note. Its insurgency seems conspicuously devoid of political risk taking and engagement while shaped by a radical agency with specificity. From this insurgency, the heroic intellectual as isolated individualist emerges to interpret political phenomena and emancipatory projects, for both elites and nonelites who, rightly so, view this intellectual's interpretations with some indifference or suspicion.

The Black Literary Hero

Seeking to elevate the political stature of the black writer, Watts's *Heroism and the Black Intellectual: Ralph Ellison, Politics, and Afro-American Intellectual Life* constructs a "heroic black intellectualism" that is even more aggressive than West in its claims for isolated black intellectuals as heroic, political individuals—yet is equally devoid of political risk.[22] Challenging criticisms of black literary figures during the civil rights movement, Watts offers a brief discussion of the movement's failures. The movement declined by 1967 because of policy successes (such as the 1964 Civil Rights and the 1965 Voting Rights Acts) as well as government failures to redress black poverty, according to Watts. As a consequence of the 1960s urban rebellions, the "image of the black civil rights activist as a victim of 'un-American' southern racist brutality was replaced by the image of the match-and-brick-wielding, anti-American, black militant violator of law and order," writes Watts, who observes that whereas the former image "had generated guilt in a significant portion of the white American populace . . . [this] latter image would generate white fear and resentment."[23] Watts also notes that black unrest in the late 1960s created a political climate in which "Vice President Hubert Humphrey's racial liberalism was replaced by Spiro T. Agnew's spiteful venom."[24] Watts seemingly attributes white disaffection for antiracist struggles primarily to the failings and violence of African-American protest. Although shifts in alliances with, representations of, and responses toward blacks occurred, criticial information is missing from this narrative. First, it fails to discuss the use of repressive violence by a racist citizenry and state to derail civil rights activism. Second, it does not acknowledge that the image of black protestor as troublemaker and criminal existed before urban unrest and the 1965 burning of Watts. The criminalization of black protests and protestors was a dominant image in the South during the 1950s and 1960s desegregation struggles, despite the fact that these sit-ins and demonstrations were famous for their nonviolent civil disobedience under the leadership of James Lawson and Martin Luther King Jr. (King's 1963 "Letter from a Birmingham Jail" addresses this criminalization of peaceful civil disobedience and protest.) Also, white liberal support for black protestors did not diminish merely because of urban rebellions. Liberalism retreated from the increasingly radical, nonviolent stances taken by movement leaders and activists. For instance, both white and black liberals defected from the pacifist radicalism embodied in King's stance against poverty and for the rights of all poor people; liberals also distanced from opposition to the war in Vietnam and to imperialism in U.S. foreign policy. There were obvious limitations to black, grass-roots radicalism. Yet Watts offers a skewed, partial portrait of the intensity of struggle and the violent repression that greeted it. His limited portrait of political protest will shape his interpretation of heroism.

Of the historic association of black intellectuals to political activism, Watts cites Du Bois as an example of "a model of highbrow political engagement"; Ida Wells-Barnett and Monroe Trotter as "intellectuals in the guise of militant journalists"; and Charles Houston. (Bell also writes of this Harvard Law graduate who, as the dean of Howard University Law School, mentored "a cadre of black lawyers in those techniques and strategies that would one day confront and overturn *Plessy v. Ferguson.*"[25]) He as well mentions psychologists Mamie and Kenneth Clark and feminist Episcopal priest Pauli Murray. Watts cites diverse examples of black female and activist intellectuals to argue that nonactivist black intellectuals, "in the guise of thinkers, ideologues, and conveyers of knowledge," have also made critical contributions to African-American liberation politics. Using as an example the historian Carter G. Woodson, Watts contends that the scholar-recluses conducting "serious antiracist research" were "inadvertently engaged."[26] He discredits criticisms of their form of distant engagement, particularly those offered in Harold Cruse's *The Crisis of the Negro Intellectual,* which argues against such reclusion, as a form of nonengagement and self-protection, for activists in the midst of a mass movement. To counter Cruse, Watts highlights Ralph Ellison as an ideal model of black intellectualism. Ellison is Watts's heroic intellectual. Watts writes that Ellison "refused to accept the popular claim that the only viable and ethnically legitimate black intellectual style is a politically engaged one."[27] (Geoffrey Jacques argues that in downplaying Ellison's participation in the Congress for Cultural Freedom in the 1950s and his leadership among liberals in the Kennedy era, Watts may be using Ellison as a strawman in his advocacy for the disengaged black intellectual as exemplary intellectual.) According to Watts, Ellison's stance of engaged distance "was perhaps more difficult for him to defend than his refusal to adopt black nationalism."[28] The historical context within which Ellison wrote was that of a social movement, and the repression against those waging it. Unsurprisingly in this context, black intellectuals faced intensified demands for their physical participation in movements in which other blacks risked violent reprisals and imprisonment.

Watts, though, opposes any criterion for evaluating the black intellectual outside of his or her own intellectual or artistic standards. Much of his displeasure at what he sees as attempts by African Americans to police others, such as gifted African Americans, is directed against black nationalism and Cruse. For Watts, "many of the black intellectuals who embraced black nationalism had little authentic commitment to black nationalism as an oppositional form of politics ... they appropriated nationalism because they thought that it was a rhetoric and ideology that could generate substantive benefits from the academy and/or the state."[29] This criticism, which is reminiscent of Kilson's observations (noted in chapter 6), undoubtedly also holds for black integrationists who appropriated antiracist rhetoric to advance their individual careers. Watts's construction of a monolithic nationalism conflates capitalists and socialists, conservative opportunists and radical visionaries. He consequently misses the complexity of an ideology and movement that cannot be reduced to Kilson's dismissals of opportunism or West's reified Marxism. (Amid his erasure of the specificity of black radicalism, Watts offers an incisive critique of some forms of Afrocentrism: "The widely practiced attempt to predicate black American pride on a knowledge of the great kings and kingdoms in African history ... assumes that the greatness of a people lies in their ability to conquer and rule others, which after all simply validates the greatness of a Western world that dominated the black world. Instead of proudly proclaiming that we too have tyrants, black intellectuals might want to help delegitimize empires as the basis of human pride."[30])

Offering a reified black nationalism as black activism to juxtapose with the disengaged literary artist, Watts says little or nothing about class politics. He also forgoes a critical reading on the Talented Tenth: College-educated blacks were viewed primarily as a managerial elite by white liberals such as the American Baptist Home Missionary Society who financed their education, professional careers, and integrationist politics. How does this creative, isolated individual escape a similar dependency with her or his institutional or individual patrons?

Crises transcend questions of authenticity or the alleged absence of politics. In a power-laden society and culture, although forms of intellectualism are politicized, they do not politicize equally, with the same intensity or the same ideological intent. Watts deemphasizes the prioritizing of radical agency in response to injustice. He argues against what he describes as two polarized, antagonistic themes in black intellectualism—the hyperpoliticized and the depoliticized—yet fails to mention or critique the hyperintellectual or literary careerist who models for his heroic individual. For Watts, Harold Cruse reflects the hyperpoliticized discourse of those "who tend to think that all Afro-American artistic and intellectual activity is reducible to political intentions."[31] (*Heroism and the Black Intellectual* references Amiri Baraka's "dogmatic Marxist-Leninism" to show that the hyperpoliticized is not restricted to black nationalism.) Depoliticized discourse stems from "those students of Afro-American intellectual life who either have taken politics out of their interpretations of black intellectual activity or have reduced the field of artistic political activity to textual practices."[32]

Like West, Watts sends mixed messages about progressive activism and black intellectualism. On one level he writes that it is important to study the "roles that intellectuals traditionally play" in relationship to power and status as reflected in their professions of choice.[33] However, he also writes that "traditional Afro-American intellectuals, like all traditional intellectuals, have as one of their priorities, if not their highest priority, the reproduction of themselves as intellectuals."[34] Echoing West's observations but without his critique of the limitations of bourgeois black intellectuals, Watts argues that traditional Afro-American intellectuals are those most compatible to "all traditional intellectuals." Watts's ideal model is based on Euro-American sociology's "seminal scholars" as white male writers. People engaged in a struggle against subordination, and the intellectuals they raise, are not "traditional" in this sense, and certainly not in comparison to elites from the dominant society. Like West, Watts argues that the black community provides neither the material support nor evinces interest in supporting "traditional intellectual and artistic activities." To illustrate his argument, he cites the dilemma of black opera singers who are anomalies in both African-American and European-American culture. The traditional, for Watts, is the European (American) bourgeois intellectual and artist. Watts stresses that given the similarities between white bourgeois intellectuals and black intellectuals, if black intellectuals disabuse themselves of the notion of accountability and knowledge production tied to community resistance, they might then attain the status of heroic intellectualism. But Watts embraces a standard for measuring heroism that reinforces notions of black intellectual and artistic inferiority by using essentially criteria based on a mixture of racial uplift ideology and romanticized notions of elite, high culture steeped in competitive struggles for recognition and validation as an exceptional individual.

Heroism, then, for this black intellectual is achievable only through individualism. Rejecting the criticism that political disengagement is a bourgeois "luxury that intellectual members of subjugated groups can ill afford,"[35] he maintains that this stance privileges the needs of the oppressed over the "creative ambitions of the individual intellectual." Such criticisms of bourgeois apathy and narcissism, writes Watts, function to dismiss "black artistic ambitions as inherently privativistic unless they are placed in the service of a greater goal." Watts uses Ellison to insist that "one's private artistic creations inherently advance the status of the entire group, not to mention the nation at large or even humanity."[36] But what if (or when) the private individual as ambitious artist is misguided or guided by self-serving interests? What informs and corrects this black creativity? Logically, it would benefit from collective insight or assistance, given its fixture in a commodities market structured by the ambitious writer and the buying power of those able to reify and purchase black creativity. A dialogue with community, understood as larger than its politics, enables the artist to have a sounding board, to see if nonelite blacks find her or his works representative and politically and spiritually beneficial rather than dehumanizing or amateurish or simply ignorant. Such an exchange or dialogue would conceivably assist in the development of isolated intellectuals. But perhaps the point that Watts attempts to make is that such intellectuals should not be judged, at least not by nonelite, "anti-intellectual" blacks.

Watts's heroic black intellectuals have no need for mass communities or criticisms from nonelites. He does not introduce the possibility of privatism or egoism among black intellectuals. Only black nationalists qualify as racial opportunists and self-promoters in his analysis. The goal of self-service or advancement is portrayed as a more artistic and heroic objective than community service for collective advancement; in fact, although he criticizes the binary opposition of activism and intellectual individual, Watts reasserts the antagonism, this time with the ambitious artist as victor. This is predictable, given that this construction of the black political leader is embedded in elitism: "Certainly black Americans stand to benefit from the active political engagement of their intellectual strata . . . however, there is little reason to assume that a fiction writer and essayist like Ellison would have held any of the keys to black advancement had he chosen to become more involved in activist black politics."[37] One can counter Watt's argument with another locus of knowledge production: Certainly the "intellectual strata" stand to benefit (and have benefited) from the active political engagement of black Americans. However, there is little reason to believe that black activists would have held any of the keys to radicalizing black intellectual elites even if those intellectuals attempted to become less alienated from activism.

For Watts, the "serious black artist must be nothing less than heroic through 'heroic individualism.'" This raises a number of questions for black intellectuals: Why is this concept of heroism tied to individualistic success—an existential Horatio Alger story for escaping black "social marginality and victim status" in white society? Why is it self-referential rather than community-referential? Why bourgeois rather than radical? Why is it determined by social acclaim in the literary or academic marketplace of elites rather than by an oppressed people's recognition of and remembrances for intellectuals' contributions?

What Watts sees as Ellison's belief that "the ambitious black artist must be a heroic individualist" says more about the politics of individualism and ambition than the politics of resisting genocide. Perhaps resistance is not his point. "As long as the black community remains oppressed, traditional black intellectuals and artists may have their ethnic legitimacy brought into question," writes Watts, "Such assaults can be generated within or outside the black community. Sometimes they can be quite debilitating."[38] Personal attacks about not being "black enough" or being "white-identified" are discouraging for critical thinkers. But some elites seem defensively preoccupied about being criticized by nonelite blacks who may charge them with indifference and alienation from black struggles. Watts does not consider that rather than ethnicity, it may be political and moral commitments that are called into question in the challenges that nonelite blacks and others issue at elite intellectuals. Oppressed people always retain the right to criticize. Their criticisms may be particularly pointed when aimed at intellectuals who see themselves as unfairly bound by service to black communities or the matrix of communal antiracist struggles that inhibit the flowering of their individual intellects and artistic creativity.

For example, we could criticize Watts for not explaining how, in his construction of the heroic intellectual, those swept up in the euphoria of ambition and individualism retain their artistic abilities, while "those who were swept up in the euphoria of political engagement relinquished their creative abilities as artists." Given that his heroic intellectual is accountable only to himself, Watts probably feels no need to explain. The demands that progressive intellectuals, in their accountability, return material and spiritual resources to oppressed people would fall on deaf ears under this construction of black heroes.

Raising the Threshold of Political Courage

In contrast to Watt's analysis of heroism, Bell's *Confronting Authority: Reflections of an Ardent Protester* contends that the civil rights movement and antiwar protests demonstrate the efficacy of mass uprisings in which "individual participants in those movements perform heroic acts, often at tremendous personal cost."[39] Concerning the "academic who is satisfied with things as they are, or who views social evils only as subjects for study and debate," Bell offers a critique that radically departs from those of West and Watts. As a human rights activist, Bell initially worked in black communities and as a civil rights litigator; in his later activism as a law professor he jeopardized his academic employment. Bell describes academics who acknowledge their function as "social critics" rather than "social reformers" to be theorists with integrity. He maintains: "Academics who claim that simply by writing about the need for change, they are fighting to make that change set a standard for judging themselves which they will not and cannot meet."[40] For Bell, mere academic activity "will neither move those in power nor create the groundswell that will force those in power to move."[41] He argues that "effective intellectual effort requires active involvement. It is inconceivable that Dr. King could have so powerfully conveyed his frustrations and defended his struggle in his 'Letter from a Birmingham Jail' had he not composed that letter in prison—literally on the field of battle."[42] On the battlefield, we find the most difficult and productive sites of knowledge production and the most unsettling lessons for accountability.

Elite intellectuals' dependence upon status and privilege calls to mind instances where contemporary black academics benefit from militant, antiracist/sexist struggles and agitation protests that they generally did and do not wage. For example, in 1992 at the University of Massachusetts–Amherst, a multiethnic/racial coalition of hundreds of students took over the University Administration Building as a demonstration of outrage to the acquittal of Los Angeles police who beat Rodney King; the acquittal had led to increased student critiques of racism on campus and of the low representation of faculty and students of color. The coalition was led by a smaller collective of approximately twelve student leaders, who were also multiethnic, had equal representation of women and men, and included openly gay and lesbian student leaders. In their planning meetings, the students drafted a reform petition to the university chancellor and barricaded themselves in the building late into the night until their demands were met. When the chancellor came to see the students, he was greeted by the students chanting: "Hire ten faculty of color, five women and five men, and No Clarence Thomases!" Because the students were virtually locked out of the hiring process, they were left with little say over the inclusion of radical, or at least liberal, progressive, perspectives among the incoming tenure-track faculty. Since those hired in various university departments were not generally informed that student protests had led to the appropriations of funds for their employment, incoming faculty were unlikely to be disposed toward feeling accountable to radical agency, particularly on the part of students with no institutional power.

The same year that students occupied UMASS's Whitmore Administration Building, Bell took a leave of absence as a tenured professor in Harvard's School of Law because of Harvard's refusal to hire a black woman or a "woman of color" on a tenured/tenure-track position and its insistence that none of the applicants were qualified for the job. Bell's *Confronting Authority* offers an account of radical agency in academe, in which elites are obscured from, or obscure, the protest traditions from which they benefit. Bell acknowledges that in his protests before leaving campus on unpaid leave—Harvard basically fired him after the two-year grace period for research leaves—there was "a patriarchal element" in his "protective feelings" concerning Harvard's black women students.[43] Yet he writes that he was surprised that his agitation for Harvard's Law School to recruit a woman of color as a tenured/tenure-track professor generated criticism from African-American women legal scholars and professors. His critics, according to Bell, were not irate that his protest had designated him as spokesperson for black women law faculty; the women denounced what they viewed as the implications of his agitation. The "black women law teachers who criticized my protest," Bell writes, "want deeply to believe that they are hired and promoted based on their ability."[44] *Confronting Authority* points out that the source of discontent and disappointment among some black women law colleagues was that Bell's ardent protest "made it more difficult for them to believe what many blacks understandably want to believe: that we are selected and advanced based on our ability."[45] Contending that law academics are employed in white institutions—"whatever our qualifications and potential," Bell cautions that because of social and campus political protests for the inclusion of women and people of color, as beneficiaries of these struggles, "we should never forget, we hold tenured professorships at major, white law schools, when men like Charles Houston and William Hastie never did."[46] Black academic elites as a group, whatever their abilities as individuals, attain privileges denied most blacks because of antiracist organizing and protests and the threat of unrest from a black mass. The American Baptist Home Missionary Society proselytized this understanding while promoting university training for the Talented Tenth.

Other intellectuals expand upon Bell's references to the conservative roles of elite educators. Ahmad and Gordon respectively explore the deradicalizing aspects of postcolonial and postmodern studies in academe. For Ahmad, romantic constructions around academic "migrating intellectuals" mask their elitism and distance from progressive political actions with notions of "hybridity" and transgressive travel. Ahmad writes that within cultural theory that emphasizes literature and deconstructive writing, the term *postcoloniality* engenders certain maneuvers that inhibit the memory of earlier debates on postcolonialism in politics and theory; these debates focused not on literary production but on the class constructs and social projects of emerging states and regimes that "arose in Asia and Africa decolonisations."[47] Ahmad criticizes the "postmodern kind of erasure" of the history and origin of the term postcoloniality. Obscuring the origin of this term in the political, material phenomena of postcolonial struggles also effaces a concept of history, social, political and cultural formations that exist(ed) independently of European colonialism. Colonialism via European expansion, writes Ahmad, becomes reduced in postcoloniality to the axis of history and thought, leaving us with only three periods of time and space: The precolonial, colonial, and postcolonial. Post-colonialism's "periodising history" thereby ensures that colonialism becomes the structuring principle of historical narratives so that "all that came before it becomes a prehistory of colonialism" as the millennium's diverse social and production practices are gathered under the rubric "precolonial."[48]

Gordon echoes Ahmad's concerns in "Uses and Abuses of Blackness: Postmodernism, Conservatism, Ideology," where he discusses postmodernist erasures of political praxis and national history.[49] The "Uses and Abuses of Blackness" in postmodernism essay raises questions about the compatibility of postmodern and black intellectual elites with conservative politics. In his presentation of this essay at an elite West Coast graduate program, Gordon noted that postmodern and academic discourse have become increasingly inaccessible during the rise of right-wing politics and resurgent racism. In a counterrevolutionary era of punitive policies against the poor and people of color, postmodernism's postrevolutionary rhetoric fails to address the specificity of antiblack racism and oppression. In effect, Gordon argued, it tended to express greater concern for black people as texts rather than as black people whose lives were in struggle. This focus on politics as rhetoric obscures political reality: "The political dimension of the political is rendered invisible by virtue of being regarded as purely performative—or, as in more Foucauldian/Nietzschean articulations of this drama, purely manifestations of will to power. *What* one performs is rendered immaterial. Whatever 'is' is simply a performance."[50] This leveling-out process encouraged a political nihilism that crystalized in the 1980s with the political-correctness charge used against the "articulation of interests" of the disempowered by "leveling out the perception of power into an equal-opportunity-affair of 'relative truths.'" The "epistemological core is a consciousness of limits skepticism and judgment skepticism," argues Gordon: "Judging judgment becomes the order of the day, and denial of any politically legitimate position beyond the denial of defending such a position is its consequence."[51] So, where "judgments are judged untenable," elites "can dominate and judge without being judged."[52]

Although the charge has become popular among conservatives and reactionaries, progressives also deploy the political-correctness club. In fact, the phrase originated among the left as a dismissive against those considered to be too zealous in their advocacy of social justice for marginalized groups. The left apparently polices its radicals, which was the point of

Gordon's presentation. However, his analysis, like Bell's confrontational politics and Ahmad's critique of postcoloniality, received a less than cordial greeting from academic elites.

The Heroic Intellectual

In contrast to elite educators, privileged by maleness, advanced degrees, and university affiliations (even those stigmatized for their radicalism or Marxism), other models of heroic intellectualism exist.

In 1995, at the Schomburg sixty-fifth birthday celebration commemorating Charlene Mitchell's fifty years of national, political leadership, Lennox Hinds, cochair and general counsel for the National Alliance Against Racist and Political Repression, praised the activism of Mitchell with Marx's observation, "Philosophers have only interpreted the world in various ways. The point, however, is to change it."[53]

Mitchell is an activist intellectual without degrees, book contracts, or university appointment. Yet she is also an educated leader who has worked for decades in progressive movements against poverty, racism, sexism, and repression, seemingly with no egoistic sense of personal heroism. Since activists also exist as intellectuals, how are we to assess their forms of intellectualism in relationship to the forms popularized by our elites?

For Hinds, Mitchell "has never forgotten what she learned from her parents' roots, that the vast majority of the nation's and the world's people are workers" who never have had access to wealth. "Charlene's wealth," he notes, "is that she has never paused."[54] Mitchell is a founding member, a national cochair, and the national coordinator of the Committees of Correspondence (CoC) which was formed in 1992 when she left the Communist Party USA As a key leader in the Committees of Correspondence, an antiracist and democratic-socialist organization of 2,000 members, she works largely with intellectual leftists such as teachers, librarians, journalists, and trade unionists. Mirroring a black intellectualism foreign to the writings of West and Watts, Mitchell's long history of political organizing and intellectual leadership offers an interesting juxtaposition with the models of insurgent intellectual literary hero. Failing to deal with the specificity of nonelite black Marxist leadership, we miss the point that the vast majority of the most significant twentieth-century black radicals were not published authors, although they were intellectuals. For example, Mitchell's model of intellectual activism reveals deep-seated, courageous commitments for social justice rather than a reflex, nonreflective reaction to social inequities and labor exploitation under capitalism.

Both women and youths have provided important models of black heroism, intellectualism, and leadership, models unfamiliar to most academic discourse and nonacademic discourse that privileges adult males. Mitchell's life serves as a catalyst for reflections on social justice and heroic intellectualism. Her early life suggests that we rethink the scant attention paid to the political thought and agency of youth. During her early teens, she read literature such as Charles Dickens's novel *Tale of Two Cities*, works on the French Revolution, and Marx and Engels's *Communist Manifesto*. Texts on class inequalities, economic exploitation, and poverty influenced her early thinking (much as later generations of youths would reflect on race, class, and agency by reading E. Franklin Frazier's *The Black Bourgeoisie*). In the 1940s, Mitchell joined American Youth for Democracy, organized by tenants in the Cabrini housing in Chicago where she lived. In 1945, at the age of fifteen, she worked with the organization to desegregate a Chicago bowling alley that, following common practice at the time, refused to admit blacks on weekends. After seeking and winning legal remedies—a judge ordered the bowling alley to stop its discriminatory practices—Cabrini youths resorted to other strategies when the bowling alley disobeyed the court ruling: They staged a successful sit-in. Later that year, a Chicago movie theater, again following common practice, restricted black patrons to the balcony and allowed only whites to sit in the orchestra. The Cabrini youths, with Mitchell as a leader, mobilized a show of multiracial unity and broad-based commitments to social justice by organizing theater patrons. While white demonstrators staged a sit-in in the balcony, black demonstrators occupied seats in the orchestra. After two days of sit-ins the Chicago theater provided open seating. Mitchell joined the Communist Party USA in 1946. Though World War II had ended, corporations accruing substantial profits continued to freeze workers' wages. When the Southern Illinois coal miners struck that winter, the teen and her youth group supported them with the difficult task of convincing community people who relied on coal to heat their homes not to blame the miners for the strike. Within one month of organizing, these communities, after debating the relationships of mine owners to mine workers, began donating food and funds to support strikers. Mitchell's engagement as a teenager was reflected in varying degrees of risk and efficacy by teenagers and youths throughout the United States who struggled with racist and economic disenfranchisement. Constructions of black intellectualism and heroism can obscure perceptions of the historical and contemporary agency and political thought of young people.

Many people seem unaware of the financial, emotional, and political resources necessary for intellectuals and activists to withstand censorship and repression from federal and local governments attempting to curtail and control American radicalism. For instance, black intellectuals were adversely affected during the McCarthy era in the early 1950s when the Smith Act and the Walter-McCarran Act legalized the arrest and intimidation of members of progressive labor and civic organizations as well as members of the Communist Party USA. Under McCarthyism, Mitchell, married and with a small child, was forced underground for three years with her family; she continued organizing in different parts of the country with no known address. FBI agents who harassed Mitchell's mother, Naomi Alexander, in attempts to get information on her whereabouts, misinformed Alexander that her daughter had been killed in an automobile accident. Demanding that the FBI leave, and stop interrogating her, Mitchell's mother defiantly countered, "If Charlene is dead, you killed her." By 1955, when political prisoners from this era were being released, Mitchell's family had moved to Los Angeles where they began organizing in the black community. She was elected an executive member of L.A.'s NAACP youth council and held this position until 1957 (the group later disbanded, reportedly because the NAACP discouraged its involvement in demonstrations). Two years later, as the administrative secretary for the Communist

Party of Southern California, Mitchell was called before the House Committee on Un-American Activities. Mitchell, barely thirty years old, issued a public statement that she was proud to be a communist, and defying Congress, refused to cooperate with the House Committee.

We need to factor such confrontations into our debates on political courage and public service. Whatever our ideological stances, American intellectuals in good faith must admit that the participation of black thinkers in the ranks and leadership of radical organizations criminalized by the U.S. government cannot be reduced to the whimsy of disillusioned Americans. By rethinking our constructs of intellectualism and heroism shaped by educational elites, we recover the political praxis of radical intellectualism. What we know of Mitchell's activist intellectualism is but a fraction of the knowledge yet to be recovered in the popularized debates on black intellectualism. For example, in addition to her other engagements, Mitchell, in 1967, became a founding chair of the Che-Lumumba Club of the Communist Party of Southern California, and with other members organized against police brutality by building a coalition, the Community Alert Patrol, to monitor police activity in black neighborhoods. In 1968, she ran for president of the United States on the Communist Party ticket, becoming the first African-American woman to be nominated and to run for that office. Also that year, she traveled extensively throughout the United States to promote the Poor People's March and Campaign. In 1969, as the FBI COINTELPRO targeted the Black Panther Party, she convened the Emergency Conference to End Repression Against the Black Panther Party. In 1970, Mitchell coordinated the Committee to End Genocide, which presented to the United Nations a petition signed by tens of thousands, indicting systematic antiblack racism in the United States. That same year she became executive secretary of the largest political prisoner campaign in the United States, the National United Committee to Free Angela Davis and All Political Prisoners. For two years the committee built the political environment that allowed Davis, who had been on the FBI's "most wanted" list, an open trial and eventual exoneration of all charges. The National Alliance Against Racist and Political Repression, organized in 1973, grew out of that campaign;

Mitchell initially served as its founding executive director. She has also remained active in international politics, reflecting Du Bois's vision of the new Talented Tenth as internationalists.[55]

Like Ella Baker and countless other black leaders, Mitchell has produced no autobiography. However, like Baker and other black intellectuals, she has written newspaper articles, essays, political speeches and treatises, organizational position papers and governing guidelines, as well as analyses of political crises that have shaped political movements. Although such texts are not as privileged as those by elite educators, Mitchell, like Baker and others, has educated and continues to educate a political body of progressives. Their roles as nonelite educators embody the "insurgency" and "heroism" too often treated in a romantic or speculative fashion.

Progressive Intellectuals

Progressive black intellectuals may be judged not by what we say but by what we do about injustice. The most reliable marker for our political commitments and courage remains risk-taking engagements with nonelites. Engaging the specificity of radicalism, we can orient ourselves by political phenomena and an epistemology in which experience via political activism is indispensable. Our experiences lead to reflections, judgments, and finally actions that produce further experiences that lead to more critiques that end to begin with more thoughtful deeds. Perhaps, for a few like Charlene Mitchell, their wealth will be that they never pause in refining and expanding progressive praxis. More realistically for most, our wealth will be that, having paused to take stock of our intellectual strengths and liabilities, our radical commitments and pretensions, we move again toward democratic community.

Neither forgoing communal acts with nonelites nor reducing introspection to the purely self-referential, contemporary intellectuals active in struggles are singularly in a postion to refrain from reading people's lives and needs as the text of a "phantom constituency."[56] Black intellectuals such as Mitchell clearly suggest that other political readings exist. Those who contextualize obscurantist academic or master narratives within their larger ideological frameworks see that schooling in political engagement may prove to be elite educators' strongest tie to radical theory that addresses social crises and state repression. And, having been so schooled, some better mark a path or clearing toward an intellectualism of heroic proportions.

Photo courtesy of Martha Stewart

Black Intellectuals in the Age of Crack forum participants: bell hooks, Henry Louis Gates Jr., Cornel West, Glen Loury, Eugene Rivers, Margaret Burnham, and Anthony Appiah, Harvard University, Cambridge, Massachusetts, 1992.

Conclusion
Radicalism and Black Intellectual Life

On November 30, 1992, at Harvard University's John F. Kennedy School of Government, prominent African-American educators gathered for a forum titled "Black Intellectuals in the Age of Crack" to discuss the responsibilities of black intellectuals to black communities in crisis.[1] Aside from Rev. Eugene Rivers, all the panelists were well-known academics: bell hooks (Oberlin), Henry Louis Gates Jr. (Harvard), Cornel West (Princeton), Glen Loury (Boston University), Margaret Burnham (M.I.T.), and Anthony Appiah (Harvard) as the moderator. Burnham, a lawyer, was the only parttime academic and the only activist with experience in political movements. Distinguishing between the academic and the intellectual, panelists debated the leadership roles of black intellectuals in dealing with the afflictions of black Americans. Rivers argued that black intellectuals needed to move beyond ideological posturing and rhetoric to build infrastructures for black communities. West maintained that a market-driven civilization and the "gangsterization of America," particularly black America, undermine our attempts to live humanely. Hooks emphasized the importance of affluent black intellectuals leading by the example of their lives (and consumption patterns) rather than by their speeches about transforming capitalism and class hierarchy. For Gates, black intellectuals needed to produce "new organizational structures" and to "stop feeling guilty about being chosen by God or community to be an intellectual." Loury, surmising that survivor guilt affects only the alienated, maintained that through class elitism and housing integration "we have segregated ourselves, then turn around and lecture the people we left." Burnham, a former SNCC activist and a leader in the "Free Angela Davis Campaign," said that when black intellectuals engage in struggle, they have a heightened sense of community, one largely absent within academe, which influences the relationships of black intellectuals to black communities.

Black elite academics noted that the ethos of the academy and that of black community are contradictory. What was not as readily addressed was whether or not creating the necessary space for black elite intellectuals to do their work could in good faith take place outside of creating the necessary space and employment for nonelite blacks, laborers, and workers to obtain and maintain economic self-suffiency in nonexploitative jobs. Highlighting a schism between elites and nonelites, an audience member who identified herself as a mother and counselor asserted that nonelite African Americans fear that black intellectuals are "intellectualizing them to death." After this stated distrust for university elites, following the trajectory of the panel discussion, invoking the old Talented Tenth and the panacea of university training for black mass equality, she then asked: "If intellectualism makes blacks middle-class, and nurturing makes blacks intellectuals, then how do we nurture the urban poor so that they can survive the academic arena?"

Paradoxically, panelists and audience members debated the leadership of black elites while identifying themselves as radicals in order to espouse commitments independent of governing elites and assimilation politics. Few offered developed strategies reflecting radicalism. Still, the continued references to radicalism as an exemplary form of reliable or effective black leadership invite reflections on radicalizing black intellectuals.

Radicalizing Black Intellectuals

In its 1857 Dred Scott decision, the U.S. Supreme Court blurred the distinction between Northern free and Southern enslaved blacks, furthering the divide between citizens and human chattel. The intent of U.S. policies crystallized for many African Americans, who were subsequently radicalized by the Dred Scott decision. Feeling the futility or obscene irony of appealing to the federal government, nonelite and elite African Americans met the Supreme Court decision with mass disobedience, armed resistance, emigration to Canada or Mexico, and repatriation to Africa.

Vincent Harding describes how, in the aftermath of Dred Scott, African-American leaders had great difficulty in seeing that individual racists and slaveholders were not the only obstacles to black freedom. The "hallmark of antebellum black radicalism," writes Harding, was not "the call to armed insurrection";[2] rather, radicalism was embodied in "a careful, sober capacity to see the entire American government, and the institutions and population which it represented, as the basic foe of any serious black struggle, whatever its form might take. It was America, not simply slaveholders, which needed to be transformed, and above all the government and its institutions."[3] Harding notes that African Americans often lost that insight because the "consequences were most often too frightening to face consciously for any sustained period of time."[4] Agitating for change, black "men and women recognized the temporary, episodic need for such resistance to the government, but even then the long-range implications were not fully articulated save in moments of extreme rage and under great provocation."[5]

Postmodern black intellectuals see little possibility of a return to the court's 1857 disavowal of African-American human rights. Like most American intellectuals, they reason that constitutional law can redress the rights violations that constitutional law, and social neglect, inflict. In confronting dehumanizing state policies, these intellectuals will unlikely stray outside the liberal or conservative frameworks shaped by legal strategies and federal court appeals. What, then, constitutes the hallmark of postmodern black radicalism?

Today, identity claims to radicalism are made irrespective of any "careful, sober capacity" to analyze the state, its institutions and populace. Sometimes claims are issued because of the intellectual's distance from confrontations with state repression. As subversive lifestyles and speech pose as surrogates for political activism, disconnected from political organizing, they tend to function as performance, and in performance reinscribe subordinates as entertainers, spectacles, or objects of discourse.

Speech acts or rhetoric as political acts, though political, are not inherently radical. Speech acts hardly function as a form of political (as opposed to rhetorical) radicalism when severed from the struggles of nonelite communities. To explore this "activism's" relationship to political organizing, we must ask and answer a number of questions. How do we distinguish between the experiential acts in political organizing that create the subject matter for the radical rhetorician and the literature or speech that is commodified as black revolutionary performance? How does mere teaching or writing about radicalism within a corporate institution qualify one as a "radical"? How does the literary or academic radicalism of elites supersede or mitigate the radical acts of nonelites that create the subject matter for their work? Without the rhetorician, radicalism continues, but can the rhetorician make meaningful claims to radicalism without the agency of the activist?

Noting the differences between the theorizing of intellectuals engaged and those removed from community organizing, we see that progressive intellectuals who restrict their political interventions to speech acts may claim the title of radical activist; however, the radical rhetorician is not necessarily the engagé. Redefining radical activism as the literary production of nonactivists is apt to be a disingenuous political act. If intellectuals need only declare themselves as militant rather than be recognized by or organize with activists, then politics as a phenomena is supplanted by the individualism of the political egoist. The extremes to which progressives take the American ideology, or cult, of individualism are noted by Manning Marable, who writes: "Among many white and black American intellectuals, there exists a profound bias towards individualism as opposed to collective action."[6]

Like Marable, David Bromwich—who argues that it is difficult to know what *radicals* would be, given their scarcity—notes the problematizing of American radicalism filtered through individualism. For Bromwich, "words are acts that change our lives";[7] yet he also writes that since Emerson, U.S. literary radicalism's social reform rarely collaborated "with the short-term plans of reformers."[8] According to Bromwich, cultural radicalism is more prevalent than political radicalism because Americans are inclined towards the avant-garde or radical individualism;[9] although, American cultural individualism produces a bewilderment that is "paid for by the eclecticism, the impatient or capricious energy, and above all the discontinuity of our radicalism in politics."[10]

The privileging of free agents and free enterprise radicalism overshadows the organized efforts of nonelite community thinkers and activists. Contemporary black intellectuals' constructions of resistance as rhetoric or artistic expression problematize political agency. These constructions signal a break with the notions of race leadership tied to the Talented Tenth's pragmatic function. Since such radicalism rarely leaves the campus or lecture hall, it often transpires within the enclaves of academe or publishing. It therefore constitutes a flight from traditional forms of politics in which relevance was gauged by the intellectual's intervention in collective struggle with others to contravene community crises.

Fanon's Native Intellectual

Following the exhortation of the older African-American woman, the Harlem intellectual who assisted me in Liberation Books, I study Fanon for insights into the crisis of black intellectualism. The resurgent interest in Fanon during this time of heightened racism and repression, manifesting in punitive policies towards the poor and incarcerated, has spurred some intellectuals to grapple with the challenges of his revolutionary theory. Fanon's dissection of the polarized existences of colonizing master and colonized servant illuminate the injustices of our time: The exacerbation of extreme wealth and poverty, racial castes, and sexual abuse, the criminalization of subaltern groups.

In *The Wretched of the Earth,* Fanon distinguishes between the "civil servant" or state intellectual and the "native intellectual" or revolutionary thinker. Reminding intellectuals that radical liberation theory serves those lacking sufficient land

and bread, Fanon presents us the native intellectual, a thinker committed to justice, to serve as a mirror for our reflections. In placing the mirror squarely before us, he warns not only of intellectual concealment; he also advises against an intellectualism that distances from justice struggles in order to offer truncated concepts of repression and liberation. The people, Fanon writes, "take their stand from the start on the broad and inclusive positions of bread and the land: How can we obtain the land, and bread to eat? And this obstinate point of view of the masses, which may seem shrunken and limited, is in the end the most worthwhile and the most efficient mode of procedure."[11]

Fanon's native intellectual is disciplined by the daily revolutionary struggle for independence, freedom, bread and land. Perhaps the affinity that progressives, blacks, or Third World peoples feel toward Fanon is that he neither argued for sophisticated critiques as a surrogate for activism nor romanticized black or mass culture as inherently revolutionary. Instead, Fanon set high standards reflecting the even higher stakes for the native intellectual engaged in social change. Measuring the usefulness of theory and the efficacy of intellectuals by their ability to deliver, he writes with conviction: "Truth is that which hurries on the break-up of the colonialist regime."[12] For such declarations for liberation theory, Fanon has been criticized and dismissed, sometimes, as Lewis Gordon notes, without serious consideration for his political thought by intellectuals who write "as though there is nothing to be liberated from but liberation discourse itself."[13] What is unique to this revolutionary theorist is that he advocates the decolonization of not only language and imagination but the materiality upon which language and the mind reflect.

Fanon's native intellectual strategically responds to human oppression as if the life of the mind experienced political ethics and revolutionary politics as more than tropes. Viewing the political agency of intellectuals through the framework of Fanon's "revolutionary intent," we invariably find ourselves connected to those most vulnerable to exploitation and oppression. Since the prey of police, military, prisons, state executions, and wars are foremost in Fanon's reflections, he sees the relevancy of engaged intellectuals as being tied to their proximity to political struggle. Fanon writes that the Algerian revolution benefited Algerian intellectuals by allowing them to encounter "the extreme, ineffable poverty of the people" as well as "to watch the awakening of the people's intelligence and the onward progress of their consciousness."[14] In the United States the civil rights and poor people's movements of the late 1950s and 1960s, and the American Indian Movement of the early 1970s, similarly enabled critical thinking and democratic politics among U.S. intellectuals by placing them in contact with America's colonized. Here, the struggles of the people—red, brown, black, yellow, white, in reservations, barrios, ghettos, sweatshops, labor camps, and penal institutions—will provide new meanings for understanding the significance of Fanon and his native intellectual for the next century.

In reconsidering our relationship to the Fanonian legacy, we can reassess our ties with radical intellectuals incarcerated for their revolutionary intent. In the United States, Mumia Abu-Jamal, Geronimo Pratt, Susan Rosenberg, Marilyn Buck, Leonard Peltier, and Carmen Valentin all followed the "obstinate view of the masses" for bread and land as well as the Fanonian dictum that "the minimum demands of the colonized" and a successful revolutionary struggle mandate "a whole social structure being changed from the bottom up."[15]

Questions aside from bread and land—for instance, political and cultural independence, spiritual renewal, sexual, ethnic, and religious freedom—preoccupy us as well. But physical sustenance or survival remains the sine qua non that only property-tied elites may take for granted. In radical or reactionary movements, the debates and battles around the allocation of resources and the right to resources is never peripheral. Non-elites gauge the relevance of elite intellectuals by their responses to bread and land or the lack thereof. In our work for these as well as social and political freedoms, for lives with dignity and spirit, our life stories shall reflect, democratize, and radicalize an agency that transcends the limitations of the Talented Tenth.

Postscript: Black Intellectual Life Stories

As a signature of black intellectual commitments, the African-American autobiography or life story reflects a communal ethic. Toni Morrison argues that the black autobiography is a classic to U.S. black literature, because it allows a writer as both representative and singular to say: "'My single solitary and individual life is like the lives of the tribe; it differs in these specific ways, but it is a balanced life because it is both solitary and representative.'"[16] Morrison says the conventional American autobiography, influenced by literary narcissism, "tends to be 'how I got over—look at me—alone—let me show you how I did it.'"[17] Consequently, it is "inimical," she writes, "to some of the characteristics of Black artistic expression and influence."[18] But contemporary African-American autobiographers do not uniformly share the communal ethic of Morrison's black classics. Black autobiographies written within the context of political movements, from abolitionist and antilynching to political-economic enfranchisement, better reflect Morrison's classic black autobiography infused with communal ethic. However, some contemporary autobiographies reference black liberation movements only to display the narcissistic tendencies Morrison attributes to American autobiography.[19]

Assata Shakur's poem, "Current Events," published in her autobiography, satirizes the relationship of politics to fashion. Being "sixties black," Shakur observes can be the source of both disdain and romanticism:

> i understand that i am
> slightly out of fashion.
>
> The in-crowd wants no part of me.
>
> Someone said that i am too sixties
> Black.
> Someone else told me i had failed to mellow.[20]

Being "in style" is a political marker. African-American autobiographies represent a diverse range of politics and ideologies—from Shakur's *Assata: An Autobiography* to Henry Louis Gates Jr.'s *Colored People*. If style, popularity, and marketability are shaped by ideological compatibility with the dominant norm, then radical black intellectuals may always prove unfashionable and therefore remain largely obscure.

Stylish or not, our debated and debatable understandings of political ethics, radicalism, and democratic, communal relations reflect our life stories.[21] In these life stories, in the best of the tradition, intellectuals balance the solitary and representative, the individual and communal, finding community liberation indispensable to but not synonymous with personal freedom. Maintaining our equilibrium, we can highlight the failings of black communities without reducing the tribe to tribalism, and, in this precarious rootedness, rising above elites, challenge dehumanizing policies for a democratic society.

Notes

Preface

1. James Baldwin, *No Name in the Street* (New York: Dial Press, 1972) 196.
2. *Ibid.*, 196.
3. *Ibid.*, 10.

Introduction

1. Toni Morrison, "The Marketing of Power: Racism and Fascism," *The Nation*, 29 May 1995, excerpts from a speech delivered at Howard University, 2 March 1995.
2. *The Journal of Blacks in Higher Education* (1994): 43.
3. For Morrison, African-American intellectuals who grapple with social crises and mentor future generations of black intellectuals are engaged in work that goes beyond the parochial or self-interested, given that our battles as a racialized, oppressed sector mirror the "flash points" of national crises. See: interview with Toni Morrison, Albert Raboteau, et al., "African American Intellectual Life at Princeton: A Conversation" *Princeton Today* (Summer 1993): 8–9.
4. Ibid., 8.
5. See: Toni Morrison, *Playing in the Dark: Whiteness and the Literary Imagination* (New York: Vintage Books, 1992) ; David Theo Goldberg, *Racist Culture: Philosophy and the Politics of Meaning* (Cambridge, MA: Blackwell Publishers, 1993); Lewis R. Gordon, *Bad Faith and Antiblack Racism* (New Jersey: Humanities Press International, 1995).
6. In October 1994, the *New York Times* printed Malcolm W. Browne's "What Is Intelligence, and Who Has It?," a favorable book review of Richard J. Herrnstein's and Charles Murray's *The Bell Curve* (New York: the Free Press); J. Philippe Rushton's *Race, Evolution, and Behavior* (New Brunswick: Transaction Publishers), and Seymour W. Itzkoff's *The Decline of Intelligence in America* (Westport: Praeger). Considered reliable sources for high-brow intellectuals, the *New York Times* and the respective book publishers legitimized and marketed the new eugenics. For more critical reviews, see Adam

Miller, "Professors of Hate," *Rolling Stone* 20 October, 1994; and John Sedgwick, "The Mentality Bunker," *GQ*, November 1994.

7. See: Harold Cruse, *The Crisis of the Negro Intellectual: A Historical Analysis of the Failure of Black Leadership* (New York: William Morrow and Company, 1984); Cedric Robinson, *Black Marxism: The Making of the Black Radical Tradition* (London: Zed Books, 1983).

8. See: Michael Bérubé, "Public Academy," *The New Yorker*, 9 January 1995: 73; Robert S. Boynton, "The New Intellectuals," *The Atlantic Monthly*, March 1995: 53 ; Leon Wieseltier, "All and Nothing At All, the Unreal World of Cornel West," *The New Republic*, 6 March 1995: 31; Adolph Reed "What Are The Drums Saying Booker? - The Current Crisis of the Black Intellectual," *The Village Voice* 11 April 1995: 31.

9. Michelle Wallace, "For Whom the Bell Tolls: Why America Can't Deal with Black Feminist Intellectuals" *Voice Literary Supplement* November 1–7, 1995.

10. Manning Marable, "Black Intellectuals in Conflict," *New Politics* vol. 5 no. 3 (Summer 1995): 35.

11. Peniel Joseph, "The Post Civil Rights Era," *New Politics* Vol. 5, no.4 (1996): 52.

12. *Ibid.*, 53

Chapter 1

1. C. L. R. James, *American Civilization* (Oxford: Blackwell, 1993) 265.

2. *Ibid.*, 276.

3. *Ibid.*

4. *Ibid.*

5. *Ibid.*

6. *Ibid.*

7. Evelyn Brooks Higginbotham, *Righteous Discontent: The Women's Movement in the Black Baptist Church, 1880–1920* (Cambridge, MA: Harvard University Press, 1993) 25.

8. *Ibid.*, 27.

9. *Ibid.*, 44. According to Higginbotham, "the educated ministry and laity established access to correct doctrine through literacy and rational discoure. They upheld the legitimacy of their leadership and authority in theological interpretation through preaching, teaching, and writing."(44)

10. Henry Louis Gates Jr. and Cornel West, *The Future of the Race* (New York: Alfred A. Knopf, 1996).

11. W. E. B. Du Bois, "The Talented Tenth Memorial Address," (1948) in *Writings by W. E. B. Du Bois in Periodicals Edited by Others*, Volume Four: 1945–1961, ed. Herbert Aptheker (Millwood, NY: Kraus-Thomson, 1982) 78.

12. W. E. B. Du Bois, "The Talented Tenth," (1903) in *Writings by W. E. B. Du Bois in Non-Periodical Literature Edited by Others*, ed. Herbert Aptheker (Millwood, NY: Kraus-Thomson, 1982) 75.

13. Thomas Holt, "The Political Uses of Alienation: W. E. B. Du Bois on Politics, Race, and Culture, 1903–1940," *American Quarterly* 42, no. 2 (1990): 316.

14. Du Bois, "The Talented Tenth," 17.

15. *Ibid.*, 20.

16. W. E. B. Du Bois. *Dusk of Dawn: An Essay Toward an Autobiography of a Race* (1940; New York: Shocker, 1968) 70.

In this passage, Du Bois differentiates himself from his ideological opponent Booker T. Washington, writing: "Mr. Washington, on the other hand, believed that the Negro as an efficient worker could gain wealth and that eventually through his ownership of capital he would be able to achieve a recognized place in American culture and could then educate his children as he might wish and develop his possibilities" (Du Bois, 70).

17. David Levering Lewis, *W. E. B. Du Bois: Biography of a Race, 1868-1919* (New York: Henry Holt Company, 1993) 286.

18. Du Bois, *Dusk of Dawn*, viii.

19. Ibid., 217. A turning point in Du Bois's thought on agency is *Black Reconstruction* (1935), where the masses step to center stage in race leadership.

20. *Ibid.*

21. *Ibid.*

22. *Ibid.*, 70.

23. Du Bois, "The Talented Tenth: Memorial Address," 79.

24. *Ibid.*, 80.

25. *Ibid.*

26. *Ibid.*, 83.

27. *Ibid.*

28. *Ibid.*

29. W. E. B. Du Bois, *In Battle for Peace, the Story of My 83rd Birthday* (New York: Masses and Mainstream, 1953) 76.

30. *Ibid.*, 76-77.

31. Ernest Allen argues that the alienation, the two-souls-in-one dilemma, which Du Bois ascribes to all African Americans, in fact pertains most specifically to the black middle class or black elites.

32. David Du Bois, "Understanding the Legacy of W. E. B. Du Bois," *Emerge* October 1993: 65.

33. Kevin K. Gaines, *Uplifting the Race: Black Leadership, Politics, and Culture in the Twentieth Century* (Chapel Hill: University of North Carolina Press, 1996) xiv.

34. W. E. B. Du Bois, *The Philadelphia Negro* ([1899] New York: Schocken Books, 1967).

35. Henry Louis Gates Jr. and Cornel West, *The Future of the Race* (New York: Knopf, 1996) vii.

36. Ibid., xv.

37. *Ibid.*

38. Gaines, 17.

39. *Ibid.*

40. Angela Davis, *Angela Davis: An Autobiography* ([1974] New York: International Publishers, 1988) viii–ix.

41. *Ibid.*, 110.

42. *Ibid.*

43. *Ibid.*

44. *Ibid.*, 111

45. Francis Beale founded SNCC's Third World Women's Alliance in 1969. In the 1970s the organization became the Alliance Against Women's Oppression. It disbanded as an organization in 1989.

46. Francis M. Beale, "W. E. B. Du Bois and Black History Month," *CROSS-ROADS* 28 February 1993.

Chapter 2

1. W. E. B. Du Bois, "The Damnation of Women," (1920) in *Darkwater: Voices from Within the Veil* (New York: Schocken Books, 1969) 181.

2. Bettina Aptheker, "On 'The Damnation of Women': W. E. B. Du Bois and a Theory of Woman's Emancipation," *Woman's Legacy: Essays on Race, Sex, and Class in American History* (Amherst: University of Massachusetts Press, 1982) 78.

3. *Ibid.*

4. *Ibid.*, 77–88.

5. Carolyn J. Hardnett, "The Unbroken Du Bois Circle: The Women Behind the Noted Historian," *Emerge* October 1993: 66.

6. Lewis, 328.

7. Du Bois, "The Damnation of Women," 172.

8. *Ibid.*, 164.

9. Lewis, 451.

10. *Ibid.*, 449–450.

11. According to Lewis, after Du Bois's mother, Jessie Fauset and Mary Church Terrell figure peripherally in his political autobiographies.

12. Patricia Morton, "The All-Mother Vision of W. E. B. Du Bois," *Disfigured Images: the Historical Assault on Afro-American Women* (New York: Praeger, 1991) 65.

13. *Ibid.*, 57.

14. *Ibid.*, 64.

15. *Ibid.*

16. *Ibid.*

17. *Ibid.*, 61.

18. Nagueyalti Warren, "Deconstructing, Reconstructing, and Focusing our Literary Image," in *Spirit, Space and Survival: African American Women in (White) Academe*, eds. Joy James and Ruth Farmer (New York: Routledge, 1993) 111. Warren uses Catherine Stark's definition of "archetype."

19. *Ibid.*

20. Du Bois, "The Burden of Black Women," 291.

21. Du Bois, "The Damnation of Women," 173.

22. For a discussion of Cooper's dismissal, see: Mary Helen Washington's Introduction to *A Voice From the South* by Anna Julia Cooper (New York: Oxford University Press, 1988), and Kevin Gaines's "The Woman and Labor Questions in Racial Uplift Ideology: Anna Julia Cooper's Voices from the South," *Uplifting the Race: Black Leadership, Politics and Culture in the Twentieth Century* (Chapel Hill: University of North Carolina Press, 1996).

23. See: Washington, Introduction to Cooper, *A Voice From the South*, and

Leona C. Gabel, *From Slavery to the Sorbonne and Beyond: The Life and Writings of Anna J. Cooper* (Northampton, Mass: Smith College Studies in History, 1982) Vol. XLIS.

24. See: Washington, Introduction to *A Voice From the South.*

25. Paula Giddings, "The Last Taboo," in *Race-ing Justice, En-gendering Power: Essays on Anita Hill, Clarence Thomas, and the Construction of Social Reality,* ed. Toni Morrison (New York: Pantheon Books, 1992) 447.

26. Cooper, 31.

27. *Ibid.,* 30–31.

28. Du Bois, "The Damnation of Women," 173. Washington also points this out in her introduction to Cooper's work.

29. Cooper, 31.

30. Washington, xxviii.

31. *Ibid.,* xlvii.

32. Du Bois, *Dusk of Dawn,* 29–30.

33. Du Bois would later sit with a shotgun on the front steps of his home during the Atlanta race riots by white mobs.

34. Du Bois, *Dusk of Dawn,* 67.

35. *Ibid.*

36. *Ibid.*

37. Ida B. Wells-Barnett, *Crusade for Justice: The Autobiography of Ida B. Wells* (Chicago: University of Chicago Press, 1970) 280–281.

38. In 1889, revolutionizing journalism as an effective medium for antiracist organizing, Wells-Barnett became the first woman secretary of the Afro-American Press Association. In addition to *Southern Horrors,* numerous newspaper articles, editorials, and the posthumously published memoir *Crusade for Justice: The Autobiography of Ida B. Wells,* her written legacy includes: *A Red Record: Lynchings in the U.S., 1892, 1893, 1894* (1895) and *Mob Rule in New Orleans* (1900).

39. Lewis, 393–394.

40. Du Bois, *Dusk of Dawn,* 224.

41. Wells, *Crusade for Justice,* 326.

42. Lewis, 397.

43. Thomas C. Holt, "The Lonely Warrior: Ida B. Wells-Barnett and the Struggle for Black Leadership," in *Black Leaders of the Twentieth Century,* eds. John Hope Franklin and August Meier (Urbana: University of Illinois Press, 1982) 50.

44. Holt observes that Wells-Barnett claimed to have elevated Du Bois to national leadership in 1899 by advocating that the Afro-American Council board of directors, whose antilynching bureau she headed, appoint him as director of its business bureau. This claim is likely overstated. Du Bois seemed destined for national prominence.

45. Lewis, 413.

46. Du Bois, *Dusk of Dawn,* 252.

47. *Ibid.,* 228.

48. *Ibid.,* 265.

49. *Ibid.,* 295–296.

50. *Ibid.,* 289.

51. *Ibid.*, 289.

52. Paul Gilroy, *The Black Atlantic, Modernity and Double Consciousness* (Cambridge, MA: Harvard University Press, 1993).

53. For reviews of this work, see: *Social Identities* vol. 1. no. 1 (1995).

54. David Roediger, *The Wages of Whiteness: Race and the Making of the American Working Class* (New York: Verso, 1991).

55. Manning Marable, *How Capitalism Underdeveloped Black America* (Boston: South End Press, 1983) 70.

56. Ibid., 100.

57. Assata Shakur, *Assata: An Autobiography* (London: Zed Press, 1987) 223.

Chapter 3

1. Between 1889 and 1940, 3,800 black men and women were lynched in Southern border states, according to John D'Emilio and Estelle Freedman, *Intimate Matters* (New York: Harper and Row, 1988) 216. Lynch victims were often unjustly accused of crimes such as theft or the destruction of property and assault; however, African Americans were also lynched for talking back to whites, being in the wrong place at the wrong time, economic competition with whites, and exercising their political rights, such as the right to vote.

2. See: Angela Davis, "Rape, Racism and the Myth of the Black Rapist," *Women, Race, and Class* (New York: Vintage, 1983).

3. Gerder Lerner writes that generally a sexual assault against a black woman rather than against a white woman "set a lynching in motion." For instance, in 1918 in Mississippi, two African-American brothers visited a white dentist who had raped two African-American teen-age girls, impregnating one; a few days later, when the dentist was found murdered, a white mob responded by lynching all four youths. In Oklahoma, whites hung Marie Scott, whose brother killed the white man who raped her. See: *Black Women in White America* ed. Gerda Lerner (New York: Vintage, 1973).

4. Reportedly the figures are five percent for black male sexual assaults against white females and eight percent for white male sexual assaults against black females.

5. See: Alice Walker "Advancing Luna- And Ida B Wells," *You Can't Keep a Good Woman Down* (New York: Harcourt Brace Jovanovich, 1981). Because Walker offers her fiction as political commentary, rather than fantasy, the issue of historical accuracy in representation remains as relevant for her short story as it does for Smith's scholarship.

6. Valerie Smith, "Split Affinities," in *Conflicts in Feminism* eds. Marianne Hirsh and Evelyn Fox Keller (New York: Routledge, 1990).

7. For black women, 1892 became a watershed year: The greatest number of lynchings were reported then. Among the 241 victims were 160 African Americans (five of whom were women or girls); several of the victims were friends of the young Ida B. Wells. When Negro Club women convened their largest gathering to that date for a testimonial for Wells in Brooklyn later that year, they raised $500 to publish Wells's pamphlet, *Southern Horrors*, and financed a speaking tour for her to launch antilynching campaigns in the United States and England.

8. Martha Hodes cites charges against black males for sexual violence during this time period in her essay, "The Sexualization of Reconstruction Politics," in *American Sexual Politics*, eds. John C. Fout and Maura Shaw Tantillo (Chicago: University of Chicago Press, 1990).

9. Ida B. Wells, *A Red Record* (Chicago: Donohue and Henneberry, 1895) 13.

10. *Ibid.*

11. Angela Davis, "Rape, Racism and the Capitalist Setting," *The Black Scholar* (April 1978).

12. Wells, *Crusade for Justice*, 137.

13. *Ibid.*

14. *Ibid.*

15. Wells, *A Red Record*, 11.

16. *Ibid.*

17. *Ibid.*

18. See: Loretta Ross, "Rape and Third World Women" *Aegis* (Summer, 1983).

19. Mary Church Terrell, National Association of Colored Women, 1904. Quoted in Lerner, 205.

20. "One study of sentencing found that black men convicted of raping white women received prison terms three to five times longer than those handed down in any other rape cases. Yet, at the same time that black-on-white rape evoked the most horror and outrage, it was by far the least common form of violent sexual assault. An investigation of rape cases in Philadelphia in the late 1950's found that only three percent of them involved attacks on white women by black men" (D'Emilio, 297).

21. Joanne M. Braxton, *Black Women Writing Autobiography: A Tradition Within a Tradition* (Philadelphia: Temple University Press, 1989) 122.

22. *Ibid.*

23. *Ibid.,* 137–138.

24. Walker, 92

25. *Ibid.*

26. *Ibid.,* 93–94

27. *Ibid.,* 94.

28. *Ibid.*

29. *Ibid.,* 93.

30. *Ibid.,* 98.

31. *Ibid.,* 103.

32. *Ibid.*

33. *Ibid.*

34. *Ibid.,* 104.

35. For a critique of Central Park Case representations, see Joy James, "Coalition Cross Fire: Antiviolence Organizing and Interracial Rape," *Resisting State Violence: Radicalism, Gender, and Race* in *U.S. Culture* (Minneapolis: University of Minnesota Press, 1996).

36. Smith, 275.

37. *Ibid.*

38. Walker, 90.

39. Smith, 281.

40. *Ibid.*

41. Walker, 97 quoted in Smith, 282. Smith writes: "In an oddly and doubly counter-feminist move that recalls Wells's own discrediting of the testimony of white victims, the narrator wants to believe that Luna made up the rape; only Luna's failure to report the crime—her silence—convinces her that the white woman has spoken the truth" (Smith, 281–82).

42. Walker, 97.

43. *Ibid.*

44. Smith, 273.

45. *Ibid.*, 273–274.

46. *Ibid.*, 274.

47. *Ibid.*, 272.

48. The possibility of "border-crossing" identity receives little attention in this work which misses an oppurtunity to closely scrutinize Wells-Barnett's writings.

49. Smith offers insights that could be further developed. For example, she writes that although black women are extremely vulnerable to rape, their "invisibility as victims" within the [antirape] movement and their perception that the movement was indifferent to the racist use of the rape charge mitigated black women's support for this movement (Smith, 276). This passage suggests a monolithic, white-led antirape movement; but in fact, African-American women independently organized and educated against rape and sexual violence. Challenging the stereotype of African-American women as sexually promiscuous and indifferent to sexual violence, Wells-Barnett worked in Chicago's Negro Women's Club movement to assist black women fleeing sexual exploitation and violence in the South only to become sexual prey in the North. Through the Negro Women's Club movement, Wells-Barnett and other African-American women later established halfway houses or safe houses for black women migrating North to escape sexual and labor exploitation in the South. The antirape movements in their plurality have historically been led by women of various ethnicities and classes.

   "Split Affinities" repeats Davis's argument from the late 1970s to assert that "the relative invisibility" of black female rape victims "reflects the differential value of women's bodies in capitalist societies" (275–76). Where "rape is constructed as a crime against the property of privileged white men," writes Smith, "crimes against less valuable women—women of color, working-class women, and lesbians, for example—mean less or mean differently than those against white women from the middle and upper classes" (276). This argument could be expanded by noting that not only do some women's bodies have "greater value" than others under patriarchal, white-supremacy capitalism, some women's bodies have "greater value" than the bodies of some men. Noting the differential value of men's bodies is equally important; for such considerations point to the differing weight of prosecution and punishment. Credibility in prosecution is based upon the identity of the accused as well as the accuser.

Chapter 4

1. Bostonian free blacks undermined the militant abolitionist work of Maria Stewart (1803–1869), because she violated conventional gender roles. The first U.S. female to publicly lecture on politics and the first published black woman political writer, Stewart called for black women to develop their highest intellectual abilities. After pro-slavers assassinated David Walker, her associate and co-publisher of the *Liberator,* Stewart increasingly displayed a radical militancy and religiosity that incensed racists and alarmed conservative free blacks. Assuming that the fate that claimed Walker awaited her, Stewart wrote: "Many will suffer for pleading the cause of oppressed Africa, and I shall glory in being one of her martyrs.... [God] is able to take me to himself, as he did the most noble, fearless, and undaunted David Walker." Unlike Walker, she lived to face another form of martyr-

dom. Pro-slavery whites cursed her incendiary abolitionism; but Bostonian free blacks censured Stewart for violating bourgeois gender sensibilities and claiming divine revelations (both estranged her from the male-dominated church and its Paulist scriptures). In her last public speech until the close of the Civil War, "Farewell Address to Her Friends in the City of Boston, Delivered September 21, 1833," Stewart castigates her own community of black elites: "I find it is no use for me as an individual to try to make myself useful among my color in this city. . . . my respected friends, let us no longer talk of prejudice, till prejudice becomes extinct at home. Let us no longer talk of opposition, till we cease to oppose our own." Stewart disappeared from public as a political speaker for over three decades. Two hundred years after her "Farewell Address," black elites continue to silence black female leaders for their bold public stances. See: Maria Stewart, "Religion and the Pure Principles of Morality, The Sure Foundation on Which We Must Build" (1831), in Marilyn Richardson, ed. *The Political Speeches of Maria Stewart* (Bloomington: Indiana University Press, 1987) 70–71.

2. At the January 1995 installation of Dexter King as director of the Martin Luther King Jr. Center for Peace and Nonviolence in Atlanta (a position he inherited from his mother, Coretta Scott King), the younger King closed his speech by calling for a new wave of civil rights activism. Evoking the names of historic black civil rights leaders such as Adam Clayton Powell, Malcolm X, Martin Luther King Jr., his address, aired on National Public Radio, mentioned no women.

3. Marginalization due to radicalism is common for militant women. Perhaps because of her militancy, military strategist and Civil War veteran Harriet Tubman garners less popularity than Sojourner Truth, who has become a feminist icon in ancestor reverence. Tubman and Truth, as ancestral kin, provide models of agency upon which to reflect and consider the spirit of current times and struggles. Their political traditions are at times eagerly studied and embraced, at other times just as enthusiastically discredited. What creates ambivalence is both the stereotype of the radical woman as uncivilized and the militancy with which she asserts her humanity and the risks she takes in doing so. This aversion to militant women is not limited to historical black figures: On a 1995 National Public Radio interview, a white trade unionist recalled that after being shot by antiunion agitators while organizing at Tennessee's Highlander Folk Center in the 1930s, nurses at the local hospital disdainfully treated her, offended not only by her union activism but that she was so "unladylike" as to get herself shot.

4. Quoted by a SNCC activist, Center for Constitutional Rights Reception, New York City, 8 December 1987.

5. Charles Payne, "Ella Baker and Models of Social Change," *SIGNS* (Summer 1989) 898–899.

6. Antonio Gramsci, *Prison Notebooks* (New York: Columbia University Press, 1992).

7. See: Ella Baker, interview by John Britton, Civil Rights History Documentation Project, Moorland-Spingarn Library, Howard University, 19 June 1968, 77; and, Joy James, "The Political Praxis of Ella Josephine Baker," (master's thesis, Union Theological Seminary).

8. James, "The Political Praxis," 4; Baker, Interview, 77.

9. See: Jack Bloom, *Race and Class in the Civil Rights Movement* (Bloomington: Indiana University Press, 1987); Taylor Branch, *Parting the Waters: America in the King Years, 1954–63* (New York: Simon and Schuster, 1988); John Brown Childs, *Leadership, Conflict, and Cooperation in Afro-American Social*

Thought (Philadelphia: Temple University Press, 1989); David Garrow, *Bearing the Cross: Martin Luther King and the Southern Christian Leadership Conference* (New York: William Morrow Company, 1986).

10. Childs, 161, FN #18.

11. *Ibid.*, 134.

12. Kathlene Cleaver, "Sex, Lies, and Videotapes," paper presented at the University of California–Berkeley, April 1995.

13. Malcolm X, *The Autobiography of Malcolm X* (New York: Grove Press, 1965).

14. George Jackson, *Blood in My Eye* (New York: Random House, 1972).

15. See: Frederick Douglass, *Narrative of the Life of Frederick Douglass* ([1845] New York: Signet, 1968); Harriet Jacobs, *Incidents in the Life of a Slave Girl: Written By Herself*, eds. L. Maria Child and Jean Fagan Yellin (Cambridge, MA: Harvard University Press, 1987).

16. Michelle Wallace, *Black Macho and the Myth of the Superwoman*. (New York: Dial, 1979); See Introduction, note 9.

17. According to Morgan, her circle of political friends featured: "white men imitating black men's style, white women imitating white men's imitation." She adds parenthetically: "No one wants to imitate the black women, who are at the bottom of the heap, trying to imitate the black men and meanwhile keeping it all together." Morgan knows best her own political history and associations. However, accepting this generalized description of black and white activists leaves us with an image of antiracist radicalism as performance. With a generalizing portrait of women as uniformly both the imitators of black males and as black super-women, Morgan places African-American women on a pedestal to pity them. She misses the opportunity to discuss black women's oppression by black males alongside the specificity and diversity of black female agency, and African-American women's political intelligence and impact upon civil rights. See: Robin Morgan, *The Demon Lover: On the Sexuality of Terrorism* (New York: W. W. Norton, 1989) 225.

18. See: Anne Moody, *Coming of Age in Mississippi* (New York: Dell, 1968); Bernice Johnson Reagon, "My Black Mothers and Sisters Or On Beginning a Cultural Autobiography" *Feminist Studies* no. 1 (Spring 1982); Angela Davis, *Angela Davis: An Autobiography*; Assata Shakur, *Assata*. All four women grew up in the South during the 1940s and eventually became active in radical civil rights organizations. Now an author-lecturer, Anne Moody was born in 1938 in Mississippi and organized with the NAACP and SNCC there, and at one time was at the top of a KKK assassination list because of her SNCC activism. Bernice Johnson Reagon is a Smithsonian director and founder of Sweet Honey in the Rock, born in October 1942 in Georgia. Reagon was an SNCC activist as well as a member of the Freedom Singers, 1962–1963. Angela Davis, a University of California professor, was born in 1944 in Alabama, was active in SNCC, the Soledad Brothers Defense Committee, and the Communist Party. Underground in the 1970s and later on trial, she became one of the most well-known political prisoners in the radical movements of oppressed people. Assata Shakur, born in 1947 in New York City and a former member of the Black Panther Party, was forced underground in 1971 after being targeted by the FBI COINTEL-PRO. Arrested in May 1973 after a shootout on the New Jersey Turnpike during which her companion and state troopers died, Shakur stood nine trials from 1973 to 77, ending in three acquittals, one hung jury, three dismissals, one mistrial, and in 1977, a conviction, by an all white-jury. The conviction was tied to possession of weapons (none of which proved to have been handled by her) and attempted murder of a state trooper who

sustained a minor injury and admitted during cross-examination to having lied under oath; in retraction he admitted that he had never seen Shakur with a gun, and that in fact she had not shot him. Nevertheless, Shakur was sentenced to life plus 26-33 years; she escaped from prison in November 1979 and is now in exile in Cuba. See: Lennox Hinds, Foreword to *Assata*.

19. Moody, 129.

20. *Ibid.*, 261.

21. *Ibid.*, 268.

22. Davis, 129.

23. *Ibid.*, 130–131.

24. *Ibid.*

25. Shakur, 242.

26. *Ibid.*

27. Patricia Hill Collins, *Black Feminist Thought* (Boston: Unwin Hyman, 1990).

28. *Ibid.*, 140.

29. *Ibid.*, 15.

30. *Ibid.*, 15–16.

31. Ibid., 151–152. Black churches responded to civil rights militancy with ambivalence. Some black women and men had to go around or confront church pastors' reticence toward joining the movement.

32. *Fundi: the Story of Ella Baker* was screened in the late 1980s at an antiracism organizing conference at the University of Michigan's Ella Baker-Nelson Mandela Center. Historian Barbara Ransby, a founder of the center and conference organizer, has researched and published on the life of Ella Baker.

Chapter 5

1. Hannah Arendt, *On Violence* (New York: Harcourt, Brace and World, 1969).

2. Arendt's reporting on Eichmann's Nazi war crimes trial in Israel (which shaped her concept of the banality of evil) and her life-long support for her former consort, lover, and teacher, the German philosopher and Nazi Martin Heidegger, are better known controversies than her stance against civil rights activism.

3. See: Ward Churchill and Jim Vander Wall, *Agents of Repression: The FBI's War Against AIM and the Black Panther Party* (Boston: South End Press, 1989).

4. The FBI memo cites the late Malcolm X as "the martyr of the movement today," with Martin Luther King Jr., Stokely Carmichael, and Elijah Muhammad as aspirers to the title of "messiah." It dismisses Muhammad as too old and describes King as a potential threat if he should "abandon his supposed 'obedience' to 'white, liberal doctrines' (nonviolence) and embrace black nationalism." See: Clayborne Carson, commentary, *Malcolm X: The FBI File*, ed. David Gallen (New York: Carroll and Graf, 1991) 17.

5. Joanne Grant, *Black Protest: History, Documents and Analyses 1619 to Present* (New York: Ballantine, 1968) 513.

6. Two cases illustrate the government's investment in anti-civil rights violence. FBI informant Gary Thomas Rowe was instrumental in the arrest of an Alabama Klansman in the murders of white civil rights activist Viola Liuzzo and Leroy Moton, the black organizer accompanying her. Liuzzo, who had been driving civil rights protestors in her car throughout the day,

was shot during her return home. Rowe was in the car when the shots were fired at Liuzzo. Described as "a Klansman's Klansman," he was known for his affinity for violence, for leading beatings of Freedom Riders, and for storing explosives. As he eventually became an embarrassment for the government, the Justice Department had to shield Rowe against charges that he might have carried out bombings in Birmingham or even himself conducted the fatal shootings of Liuzzo and Morton.

Several years later in Chicago, another government agent, William O'Neal, became minister of defense for the Chicago Black Panther Party. O'Neal drew a diagram for the 1969 predawn raid in which Fred Hampton and Mark Clark were killed by Chicago police. Since the police did not immediately seal off the premises, local black activists took citizens on a tour of the building to view the bullet holes and the blood-soaked mattress where Hampton died. Even blacks who did not consider themselves activists or radicals were outraged and politicized by the assassinations. The FBI was implicated in the deaths, and the government settled a $1.8 million civil suit with the families of Hampton and other victims.

7. William Patterson, ed. *We Charge Genocide: The Crime of Government Against the Negro People, A Petition to the United Nations* (New York: Civil Rights Congress, 1951).

8. "The Brutal Reason Why Racial Integration of American Colleges, Universities, and Secondary Schools Was Not the Principal Concern of Black Intellectuals in the Pre-World War II Period," *The Journal of Blacks in Higher Education* 6 (Winter 1994/1995).

9. *Ibid.*, 74.

10. Reagan's laying wreaths in Germany's Bitburg cemetery, which housed the graves of SS stormtroopers, underscored Nazi "victimization." In its racialist plea, the rallying call to restore American pride or greatness entails the exculpation of racial and sexual dominant groups. It also requires the validation of white, heterosexual male privilege in a society that has great difficulty in distinguishing white, straight male pride from racist, homophobic patriarchy, and its national interests from foreign intervention and dominance.

11. At the televised national memorial for the Oklahoma bombing victims, a black woman standing before a huge, unfurled U.S. flag, sang "God Bless America." This finale for a nation in mourning gave the audience permission to express strong emotion. Embracing under the banner of national unity, those who had been sitting somberly for the service rose to their feet and cheered and wept.

12. Just as "lynching" and the black image have been used by conservatives and reactionaries to signal their victimization, black antiracist and resistance rhetoric has also been appropriated. Using revolutionary rhetoric to mask counterrevolutionary acts, in 1985, Wilson Goode, Philadelphia's black mayor, proclaimed that "by any means necessary" the city would prevail in its confrontation with MOVE, the back-to-nature black fringe organization. Malcolm X's slogan was also used a decade later, in the aftermath of the Oklahoma City bombing, by white militia extremists to justify their violent assaults against government employees and agencies. Rightwing militias did not advocate violent retaliation against the government for the 1985 bombing and incineration of black MOVE victims, although the 1993 Branch Davidian inferno, with its mostly white casualties, became a militia rallying call. National sentiment reflected that of the militia. There was little widespread support or sympathy among moderates for the MOVE victims but national anger at the Waco deaths.

In a National Public Radio interview following the Oklahoma City bombing, extremists stated that they had three options: the election box, the soap box, and the bullet, evoking Malcolm X's famous speech, "The Ballot or the Bullet," thirty years prior for black freedom. Klan and neo-Nazi activists organize with the chant of "White Power!" Some eighty years after Du Bois, Wells-Barnett, and others worked to plan the National Association for the Advancement of Colored People, neo-Nazi and former Klan leader David Duke helped to found the National Association for the Advancement of White People. Likewise, the "Black Power!" chant has been picked up and distorted by people of diverse ideologies. (Most trace the slogan to Lowndes County Black Panther election party and Stokely Carmichael's chants captured in the *Eyes on the Prize* documentary; Manning Marable's *BLACKWATER: Historical Studies in Race, Class Consciousness, and Revolution* [Dayton, OH: Black Praxis Press, 1981] cites its first appearance in 1957 in Richard Wright's *Black Power*.) Ironically, white supremacists pattern their demands for "White Power!" after the Black Panther 1970s slogan of "Black Power," failing to note that the Panthers's complete, nonracialist refrain also demanded "Brown Power to Brown People," "Red Power to Red People," and "White Power to White People"—in effect, "power to the people" rather than domination by the police or state. Selective references to the Black Panthers, to glorify or revile the party or individual activists, generally fail to mention Huey Newton's support of gay and lesbian rights in the Panther paper, the party's anti-imperialism or its coalitions with radical whites, such as Peace and Freedom Party activists and the Gray Panthers. According to Maggie Kuhn, a 1968 founder of the Gray Panthers, the Black Panthers and Gray Panthers initially had strong collaborative interactions based on their mutual opposition to the Vietnam War.

13. National media reported in January 1996 a federal investigation of the "good ole boy roundup," a gathering of law-enforcement personnel in the woods of Tennessee marked by racist slurs and banners, as well as heavy alcohol consumption. The report cites that only a few federal agents regularly attended the annual events, which were organized by a retired agent of the Federal Bureau of Alcohol, Tobacco, and Firearms around 1970.

14. *KlanWatch*, the publication of the Southern Poverty Law Center, documents the continuance of Klan lynchings and the roles of other racist groups in racial terror. For instance, a cadre of white supremacist soldiers stationed at Fort Bragg, North Carolina, murdered a black couple in winter 1995.

15. The Thirteenth Amendment, added in 1865 to the U.S. Constitution, explicitly exempts prisoners from protection from slavery or involuntary servitude. Article XIII reads: "NEITHER SLAVERY NOR INVOLUNTARY SERVITUDE, except as a punishment of crime whereof the party shall have been duly convicted, shall exist within the United States, or any place subject to their jurisdiction."

16. Derrick Z. Jackson, "The Wrong Face on Crime," *Boston Globe*, 19 August 1994, 19.

17. Thomas Edsall reports that from 1980 to 1990, as documented by the U.S. House Ways and Means Committee's March 26, 1990, Tax Progressivity and Income Distribution report, the pretax income for the U.S. population in the poorest first decile fell from $5,128 to $4,695, while rising in the fifth decile among the lower-middle or working class from $32,674 to $33,760. The tenth decile saw its income rise 37.1 percent, from $105, 611 to $144,832. The wealthiest five percent saw their pretax income increase from $142,133 to $206,162, while the incomes of the ultrarich mushroomed, from $312,816 to $548,969, a gain of 75.5 percent. When

incomes are averaged, everyone gained 15.5 percent in their income during the 1980s. See: Thomas Edsall and Mary Edsall, *Chain Reaction* (New York: W. W. Norton, 1991) 119–220.

18. Jason DeParle, "Census Report Sees Incomes in Decline and More Poverty," *New York Times*, 7 October 1994, A1.

19. Concerning death sentences in interracial rape cases, D'Emilio and Freedman write that "between 1930 and 1964, ninety percent of the men executed in the United States for rape were black" (D'Emilio, 297).

20. Mumia Abu-Jamal, *Live from Death Row* (New York: Addison Wesley, 1995).

21. In a 1995 conference at a university in the Midwest, a women's studies scholar presented a paper on Fanon's concept of revolutionary violence discussed in *The Wretched of the Earth* as reversals in which the colonized appropriate the tactics of their oppressors. Fanon's position was criticized by the feminist professor who, quoting Lorde's adage, suggested that black women's music such as Salt-N-Pepa (and their rap video "Shoop") and TLC serve as more appropriate examples of reversals in which women take on the objectifying, violating male gaze to use it against men. This assertion that black women engage in resistance to colonization through sexual aggression, however, replays the stereotype of lascivious black females and fails to examine how "revolutionary violence," sexualized and produced as a market commodity, constitutes resistance. Sexualized in political resistance, African-American political agency remains the synonym for black pathology—sexual violation and violence. Centering sexual aggression in (black) women's bodies as revolutionary violence to enable women to victimize men problematicizes black resistance to state violence. Noting the over-sexualization of black males linked with violence, Stanley Crouch in a January 1995 NPR interview satirized gangsta rap as "*Birth of a Nation* with a backbeat."

22. Henry Louis Gates Jr. interview with Terry Gross, *Fresh Air*, National Public Radio, 1994.

Chapter 6

1. Paul Robeson, *Here I Stand* (Boston: Beacon Press, 1971).

2. Geoffrey Jacques explores Robeson's life in his unpublished paper "Fragments Like Speech: African American Intellectuals in the 1960s."

3. Robeson, 96.

4. *Ibid.*

5. *Ibid.*, 98.

6. *Ibid.*

7. *Ibid.*, 102.

8. *Ibid.*, 105.

9. *Emerge* reports that a record number of African Americans, twenty-four, ran as Republicans for the House with two elected from predominantly white districts in the 1994 elections.

10. Robeson, 99.

11. *Ibid.*

12. Marable, *BLACKWATER*, 93.

13. Martin Kilson, "The New Black Intellectuals," (1969) in *Legacy of Dissent: Forty Years of Writing from* Dissent *Magazine* ed. Nicolaus Mills (New York: Simon and Schuster, 1994).

14. Kilson, 255.

15. *Ibid.*
16. *Ibid.*, 255–256.
17. Malcolm X's thought had a pervasive, widespread impact on identity and racial pride.

    On a 1987 trip to Puerto Rico and the Dominican Republic with a delegation from Union Theological Seminary, I found that many people, including Haitians living in the Dominican Republic, denied the existence of racism on the islands and disclaimed any identity as "blacks," this despite the racial stratification and classification on each island. Haitians were segregated into bateys or work camps in the Dominican Republic, while in neighboring Puerto Rico, the poorest were usually the dark-skinned. In meetings with educators, union organizers, religious leaders, and elected officials, the only person we met who addressed the concentration of poverty among those with darker skin and the idealized beauty image and lineage tied to European or Indian (Taino), but not African, blood was a white man. At a meeting in his offices, this upper-class, blond, blue-eyed socialist senator, the most European person met in our travels, stated that he was never proud of being a "black man" until his student days at Harvard in the 1960s when he heard Malcolm X speak at the university.
18. Carson, 25.
19. After leaving the Nation of Islam, his interaction with Southern civil rights organizers, particularly those in SNCC, shaped his political thought and influenced activists. James Cone notes that Malcolm refered to Hamer, the SNCC leader and Mississippi Freedom Democratic Party congressional candidate, as an important black leader. See: James Cone, *Martin and Malcolm* (New York: Orbis, 1990) 279.
20 Malcolm X petitioned the United Nations in the 1960s to end U.S. violations of African-American human rights. The U.N. organizing connected with his travels abroad: On July 17, 1964, attending the African Summit Conference in Cairo as representative of OAAU, he distributed a press release on OAAU letterhead on behalf of twenty-two million Afro-Americans in the United States and appealed to delegates from thirty-four African nations to lobby the U.N. to stop U.S. oppression of African Americans. While in Kenya that fall, he met with SNCC's John Lewis and Donald Harris on October 18. See: Carson's *Macolm X.*
21. See: Rosemari Mealy, *Fidel and Malcolm X* (Melbourne, Australia: Ocean Press, 1993).
22. *Ibid.*
23. See: E. Frances White, "Africa on My Mind: Gender, Counter Discourse and African American Nationalism," *Journal of Women's History* 2 (Spring 1990); and Barbara Ransby and Tracye Matthews, "Black Popular Culture and the Transcendence of Patriarchal Illusions," *Race and Class* 35: no 1 (1993).
24. Native American Paula Gunn Allen writes that "your mother is not only that woman whose womb formed and released you," rather the term *mother* refers "to an entire generation of women whose psychic, and consequently 'physichape' made the psychic existence of the following generation possible." For Allen, "Failure to know your mother" or "your position and its attendant traditions ... in the scheme of things, is failure to remember ... your right relationship to earth and society. It is the same as being lost" (Paula Gunn Allen, *The Sacred Hoop: Rcovering the Feminine in Native American Tradition* [Boston: Beacon Press, 1988]).
25. Discomfort with black women who use violence to resist oppression appears in Toni Morrison's *Beloved*, where the "unnatural mother" appears

with vengeance. *Beloved* is based on the factual story of the enslaved mother Margaret Garner who, as Morrison recounts, "kills her children rather than allow them to die in slavery." This defiance raises the question of this mother's stability. For Morrison, the brutality of enslavement certifies Garner's sanity. Yet, in *Beloved*, for her crime whites imprison the Garner figure, whom they have already animalized; after her release, the black community, revolted by her deadly, militant mothering, ostracizes her. In a BBC interview, stating that she desired to write about self-suicide by examining the life of Garner, Morrison reviews the self-destruction of not one mother but of black communities that judged Garner's act as void of, rather than overwhelmed by, love during brutal captivity.

26. Shakur's poem "To My Momma" recounts her relationship with her mother, whom she describes as someone "who has swallowed the amerikan dream / and choked on it." Learning about both pain and resistance from her parent, Shakur writes "My roots run deep / I have been nourished well." Conventional respectability is not the cornerstone of this form of mothering, Shakur counsels her mother: "You must not feel guilty / for what / has been done to us. / Only the strong go crazy. / The weak just go along" (Shakur 193–194). Having spent a good part of her childhood in the South with her grandparents, Shakur recalls that while all of her family worked to impart a "sense of personal dignity," her grandmother and grandfather "were really fanatic about it" (19).

27. Referring to such mothering by her parents, Davis recalls growing up in a neighborhood in Birmingham, Alabama called "Dynamite Hill," so named because of the frequency of terrorist bombings against African Americans moving into the previously all-white neighborhood. Of the familial mothering to cope with the racist violence of her childhood, Davis writes that the "more steeped in violence our environment became, the more determined my father and mother were that I, the first-born, learn that the battle of white against Black was not written into the nature of things." Speaking of her mother's belief that "love had been ordained by God" and that whites' hatred of blacks "was neither natural nor eternal," Davis notes how her mother worked with blacks and whites, including communists, to free the Scottsboro Boys. Sallye Davis struggled so that her daughter could see the potential of white people and rather than "think of the guns hidden in drawers or the weeping black woman who had come screaming to our door for help . . . [focus on] a future world of harmony and equality." Writes Davis, "I didn't know what she was talking about" (Davis, 79–80).

28. Reagon, "My Black Mothers and Sisters," 81–82.

29. *Ibid.*, 82.

30. *Ibid.*

31. Cone, 279.

32. Reagon, "My Black Mothers and Sisters," 81.

33. Shakur, 267.

34. *Ibid.*

35. Reagon, "My Black Mothers and Sisters," 83.

36. The varied definitions and criticisms of black feminism suggest the commonalities and differences among black women. Collins defines black feminism as "a process of self-conscious struggle that empowers women and men to actualize a humanist vision" and to "develop a theory that is emancipatory and reflective" for black women's struggles (Collins, 32). Alice Walker contrasts black feminism with white or Eurocentric feminism, coining the term *womanist*. For Walker, womanist renders the adjective

"black" superfluous for women of African descent. She likens this construction to white women's use of the term *feminist* without using the preface "white." Hooks expands upon Collins's humanist vision and Walker's cultural critique to define feminism as "a commitment to eradicating the ideology of domination that permeates western culture on various levels—sex, race, and class . . . . and a commitment to reorganizing society so that the self-development of people can take precedence over imperialism, economic expansion, and material desires" (bell hooks, *Ain't I a Woman* [Boston: South End Press, 1983]). Among black feminists, the writings of Julianne Malveaux, Regina Arnold, Leith Mullings, Bonnie Thornton Dill, and Angela Gilliam make important contributions to an integrative analysis which addresses class politics.

37. At the October 16, 1995, "Million Man March," Louis Farrakhan urged the one million black men in attendance to join a political organization, and a spiritual community within a mosque, temple, or church. He also issued a call to register eight million African-American "brothers and sister" to vote not by the color but the agenda of the candidate ("We are no longer going to vote for somebody just because they're black . . . we tried that"); to "adopt" (visit and assist) one inmate as a friend for life; and to remember the political prisoners and the twenty-five thousand black children in need of adoption. In his closing pledge, Farrakhan stated "I ('say your name') will not abuse or harm other people, engage in sexual abuse of children or women, domestic battery, or call women by the 'b' word." Critiques of the Farrakhan speech and other assessments of the march appear in *The Black Scholar* vol. 25, no. 4 (Fall 1995)

38. Author's personal papers.

39. "African American Women in Defense of Ourselves" (paid advertisement), *New York Times* 17 November 1991, 53.

40. "African American Women in Defense of Ourselves," in *The Black Scholar* vol. 22, no. 1 & 2 (Winter 1991–Spring 1992).

41. Author's personal papers.

42. Gay, lesbian, and bisexual blacks were activists in the civil rights and black liberation movements, and some identified as black nationalists. In gay and lesbian critical race theory, writers challenge bourgeois sexual sensibilities and black sexual conservatism. Intellectuals marginalized by their sexual preference include Bayard Rustin, James Baldwin, Audre Lorde, Marlon Riggs, and Essex Hemphill. Writings such as Lorde's "Sister to Sister: Black Women Organizing Across Sexualities," Hemphill's criticism of Afracentric writer Francis Cress Wellsing in "If Freud Were a Neurotic Colored Woman" or Riggs's "Black Macho Revisted: Reflections of a SNAP! Queen," analyze homophobia in black intellectualism and culture. Black homophobia and obsessions with "Negro faggotry" represent "the desperate need for a convenient Other *within* the community, yet not truly *of* the community, an Other to which blame for the chronic identity crises afflicting the black male psyche can be readily displaced," writes Riggs, who argues that the black family tree's iconography reveals "a line of descent from Sambo to the SNAP! Queen, and in parallel lineage, from the Brute Negro to the AIDS-infected Black Homo-Con-Rapist" Where black eros or sexuality is the rage while black people are not, the black as Other is blamed for the identity crisis troubling white America. African-American homophobia, classism, and misogyny inflict this crisis on other blacks. (Marlon Riggs, "Black Macho Revisited: Reflections of a Snap! Queen," in *Brother to Brother: New Writings by Black Gay Men*, ed. Joe Beam, et al. [Boston: Alyson, 1991] 254–55).

43. Kristal Brent Zook, "A Manifesto of Sorts for a Black Feminist Movement," *New York Times Magazine,* 12 November 1995.

44. Henry Louis Gates Jr., "Thirteen Ways of Looking at a Black Man," *The New Yorker* 23 October 1995.

Chapter 7

1. bell hooks and Cornel West, *Breaking Bread* (Boston: South End Press, 1991).

2. Terry Eagleton, "Criticism, Ideology, and Fiction" in *The Significance of Theory.* (Cambridge, MA: Blackwell, 1990).

3. hooks, *Breaking Bread,* 152.

4. *Ibid.,* 156.

5. *Ibid.,* 162.

6. Toni Morrison, "Rootedness: The Ancestor as Foundation," in *Black Women Writers (1950–1980)* ed. Mari Evans (New York: Anchor Press, 1984) 344–45.

7. *Ibid.*

8. hooks, *Breaking Bread,* 148.

9. Ingrid Sischy's 1995 interview with hooks about *Killing Rage* discusses her use of "left" terminology.

   When Sischy asks hooks why she uses the term "radical" rather than "humanitarian" to describe antiracists, hooks replies: "Because you can be humanitarian and still hold prejudiced views. . . . many Christians say, 'I hate homosexuals, but I feel that I have to be tolerant and accepting because that's what my humanitarian Christian values would have me do. I hate the sin, but not the sinner.' To do away with that kind of thinking means that you have to assume a radical position." When Sischy responds: "Isn't it incredible that one would still have to regard this view as 'radical'?" hooks offers an ambiguous rejoinder:

   "Yes. And I think we have to be all the more radical today, because the tyranny of the rhetoric around political correctness has made it so hard for people to take a stand." (bell hooks, *Interview,* October 1995, 124–125).

10. In *Killing Rage,* hooks discusses how the authors of *Breaking Bread* were motivated by a desire to "affirm the primacy of intellectual work in contemporary African-American life. . . . repudiate the notion that to become a black intellectual and/or academic means that we assimilate and surrender passionate concern with ending white supremacy, [and to] encourage more black folks to choose intellectual work." bell hooks, *Killing Rage: Ending Racism* (New York: Henry Holt, 1995).

11. hooks, *Killing Rage,* 230.

12. *Killing Rage* offers insight: "Political activism may be expressed by the type of work progressive black intellectuals choose to do. To politically counter anti-intellectual and/or academic thought in black life that persists in portraying educated black folks as traitors (a representation that has concrete foundation), insurgent black critical thinkers must be accountable. That means the work we individually do, and the work of our peers, must be continually interrogated." hooks, 236.

13. hooks, *Killing Rage,* 228.

14. *Ibid.,* 229.

15. *Ibid.*

16. *Ibid.,* 231.

17. *Ibid.*, 234.

18. *Ibid.*

19. *Ibid.*, 237–238.

20. Collins, 30.

21. *Ibid.*, 150–151.

22. *Ibid.*, 160.

23. *Ibid.*

24. Davis quoted in Collins, 160.

25. *Ibid.*, 29.

26. *Ibid.*, 5–6.

27. Peter L. Berger and Thomas Luckmann, *Social Construction of Reality : A Treatise on the Sociology of Knowledge* (Garden City, New York: Anchor Books, 1967).

28. Collins, 22.

29. *Ibid.*, 31–32.

30. Elsa Barkley Brown, "Mothers of Mind," *SAGE* vol. 6, no. 1 (Summer 1989).

31. *Ibid.*, 9.

32. *Ibid.*

33. *Ibid.*, 5.

34. Joyce Ladner, *Tomorrow's Tomorrow: The Black Woman* (Garden City, NY: Doubleday, 1971).

35. Brown, 6.

36. *Ibid.*

37. *Ibid.*, 9.

38. *Ibid.*, 10.

39. Bernice Johnson Reagon, "'Nobody Knows the Trouble I See'; or, 'By and By I'm Going to Lay Down My Heavy Load,'" *Journal of American History* vol. 78, no. 1 (June 1991).

40. *Ibid.*, 113.

41. *Ibid.*, 118.

42. *Ibid.*, 117.

43. *Ibid.*

44. Italics, Reagon, 118.

45. *Ibid.*, 119.

46. *Ibid.*

47. Bernice Johnson Reagon, "Women as Culture Carriers in the Civil Rights Movement: Fannie Lou Hamer," *Women in the Civil Rights Movement: Trailblazers and Torchbearers 1941–1965* eds. Vicki Crawford, Jacqueline Anne Rouse, and Barbara Woods (Brooklyn: Carlson, 1990) 203–218.

48. *Ibid.*

49. Bernice Reagon, *The Songs are Free*, Interview with Bill Moyers, PBS, 1991.

50. *Ibid.*

51. Delores Williams, "Black Women's Surrogacy Experience and the Christian Notion of Redemption," in *After Patriarchy: Transformations of the World's Religions* eds. Paula Cooley et al. (New York: Orbis Press, 1991).

52. *Ibid.*

53. *Ibid.*

54. Black colleges and universities graduate the highest percentage of African-American students precisely because of community caretaking through faculty and staff social interaction with, and mentoring of, students. Since greater teaching loads and counseling detract from literary production, educators at historically black colleges and universities, like those at Native American colleges, community colleges, or teaching institutions, are usually devalued as scholars. Only community service seems to rank lower than teaching in elite constructions of academic intellectualism.

Chapter 8

1. Supreme Court rulings undermining academic affirmative action and the merger of Black Studies programs with Ethnic Studies reconfigures academic sites.

2. Joseph, 53.

3. Herman Gray made these observations as a respondent to paper presentations at the "Black Intellectuals and Pedagogies of Activism Panel," American Educational Research Association, San Francisco, April 1995.

4. Cornel West, "We Socialists," *CROSSROADS* 12 (July–August 1991) 4.

5. *Ibid.*

6. Cornel West, *Keeping Faith: Philosophy and Race in America* (New York: Routledge, 1993).

7. *Ibid.*, 71.

8. White Extremists have responded to West's political contributions with death threats. See: S. Monroe, "Go West: Inside Cornel West's Mind" *Emerge* September 1996.

9. West, *Breaking Bread*, 144.

10. West, *Keeping Faith*, 75.

11. *Ibid.*, 67–68.

12. *Ibid.*, 76.

13. *Ibid.*, 78.

14. *Ibid.*

15. See: Aijaz Ahmad, *In Theory: Classes, Nations, Literatures* (New York: Verso, 1994).

16. West, *Keeping Faith*, 78–79.

17. Cornel West, *Prophesy Deliverance! An Afro-American Revolutionary Christianity*, (Philadelphia: Westminster Press, 1982).

18. West, *Keeping Faith*, 79.

19. *Ibid.*, 81.

20. *Ibid.*

21. *Ibid.*, 83–84.

22. Jerry Gafio Watts, *Heroism and the Black Intellectual: Ralph Ellison, Politics and Afro-American Intellectual Life* (Chapel Hill: University of North Carolina Press, 1994).

23. *Ibid.*, 5.

24. *Ibid.*

25. *Ibid.*, 7.

26. *Ibid.*, 8.

27. *Ibid.*, 13.

28. *Ibid.*

29. *Ibid.*, 8–9.

30. *Ibid.*, 19.

31. *Ibid.*, 11.

32. *Ibid.*

33. *Ibid.*, 14.

34. *Ibid.*

35. *Ibid.*, 21.

36. *Ibid.*

37. *Ibid.*

38. *Ibid.*, 23.

39. Derrick Bell, *Confronting Authority: Reflections of An Ardent Protester* (Boston: Beacon Press, 1994) 126.

40. *Ibid.*, 106.

41. *Ibid.*

42. *Ibid.*

43. *Ibid.*, 116.

44. *Ibid.*, 118.

45. *Ibid.*, 119.

46. *Ibid.*

47. Aijaz Ahmad, "The Politics of Literary Postcoloniality" *Race and Class* 36:3 (1995): 1.

48. Ahmad asks what is gained by ignoring significant distinctions in order to "denounce an undifferentiated 'postcolonial Islamic world' in the name of . . . the newly marketed category of 'postcolonial writer'?" (Ahmad, 2).

49. Lewis Gordon,"Uses and Abuses of Blackness: Postmodernism, Conservatism, Ideology" *Her Majesties Other Children: Philosophical Sketches from a Neocolonial Age* (Landham, MD: Rowman and Littlefield, Forthcoming).

50. *Ibid.*, 135–136.

51. *Ibid.*

52. *Ibid.*

53. Charlene Mitchell, Celebration Pamphlet, author's personal papers.

54. Lennox Hinds, "Charlene Mitchell: a tireless torchbearer," birthday greetings, Schomburg Center for Research in Black Culture celebration, 1995.

55. Mitchell's international standing among socialists and progressives was evident in her participation in the 1993 fourth Foro de Sao Paulo in Havana, Cuba, where, as a guest observer, she represented the Committees of Correspondence (CoC). An annual conference of left parties and movements from Latin America, Central America, and the Caribbean, the Foro was attended by 112 member organizations that focused on the impact of World Bank and International Monetary Fund policies on (under)development in the region. Mitchell also served as an official international observer of the first free elections in South Africa in April 1994. The following April, she was an invited observer by the Ninth Congress of the South

African Communist Party and later visited Namibia as the guest of Toivo Ja Toivo, minister of mines and energy. In November 1995, again representing the CoC, she attended Japan's AKAHATA Newspaper Festival for progressive journalists and press.

56. Paul Gilroy writes that neonationalism "incorporates commentary on the special needs and desires of the relatively privileged castes within black communities, but its most consistent trademark is the persistent mystification of that group's increasingly problematic relationships with the black poor, who, after all, supply the elite with a dubious entitlement to speak on behalf of the phantom constituency of black people in general." Gilroy's problematic treatment of African Americans raises the issue of whether it is significant to note that this critique cuts both ways, against privileged castes who acknowledge or disavow the existence of black communities while using blacks as their object of study. The struggles for voting rights and against police brutality and the new eugenic movements do not suggest Gilroy's black "phantom constituency." See: Gilroy, 33.

Conclusion

1. This conference was videotaped by the American Friends Service Committee, and is available through their Cambridge, Massachusetts office.

2. Vincent Harding, *There Is a River: The Black Struggle for Freedom in America* (New York: Vintage, 1983) 200.

3. *Ibid.*

4. *Ibid.*

5. *Ibid.*

6. Marable, *Blackwater*, 114.

7. David Bromwich, "Literary Radicalism in America 1985," (1985) in *Legacy of Dissent* ed. Mills, 199.

8. *Ibid.*, 205.

9. *Ibid.*, 211.

10. *Ibid.*, 205.

11. Frantz Fanon, *The Wretched of the Earth* (New York: Grove Press, 1963) 50.

12. *Ibid.*

13. Lewis Gordon, *Fanon and The Crisis of European Man* (New York: Routledge, 1995) 146.

14. Fanon, 188.

15. *Ibid.*, 35.

16. Morrison, "Rootedness," 339.

17. *Ibid.*, 339–340.

18. *Ibid.*, 340.

19. Counter to Morrison's classic black autobiographies, Elaine Brown's *A Taste of Power* (1992) and Henry Louis Gates's *Colored People: A Memoir* (1994) suggest individual egoism, a sense of getting over and personal triumph reflecting heroic individualism. Both books were favorably reviewed in the *New York Times Book Review*. On April 30, 1995, the *New York Times* listed Gates's book under the "New & Noteworthy Paperbacks" column, reprinting the 1994 phrases of reviewer Louis D. Rubin Jr., who praised the "rich and often comic detail" to be found among "the considerable pleasures in this splendidly told memoir."

Notwithstanding its strengths for some readers, this black autobiography is shaped by self-congratulatory expressions of having made it (out of blackness). Within its pages, readers find simplistic, cartoonlike images of black people as the colored primitives that sharply contrast with the sophisticated black storyteller. Gates underutilizes collective political or social consciousness, although the black movements are in part the backdrop for his autobiographical tale.

Brown, unlike Gates, was an activist (and a leader) in a grass-roots movement—the Black Panther Party; the strong individual leader is central to her story. In "Singing & Dancing in the Slave Quarters," a February 13, 1996 *Village Voice* interview by Kristal Zook, Brown critiques current depoliticizing black commercial culture and middle-class feminism, even though her book may be optioned for a Hollywood film.

20. Shakur, 240.

21. In *Colored People*, Gates ridicules his mother, aunts, and uncles who were mourning at his grandmother's funeral, for fuming at their brother, who without informing his siblings of their mother's impending death, called an unknown white preacher, rather than the local black pastor, to administer the matriarch's last rites. Referring to family elders as "niggers," Gates "playfully" deploys the racial slur to reprove his family's tribalism and racial preferences. His contempt for a manner of blackness embodied in a family that came of age in the segregated South suggests that not only are the lives of assimilated, postmodern black elites *not* like the "lives of the tribe"—they are infinitely superior. See: Henry Louis Gates Jr., *Colored People: A Memoir* (New York: Knopf, 1994).

Index